D0908117

So I've Heard

So I've Heard

Notes from a Migratory Music Critic

Alan Rich

AMADEUS
PRESS

Published in 2006 by Amadeus Press
512 Newark Pompton Turnpike
Pompton Plains, New Jersey 07444

Book design by Snow Creative Services

Printed in the United States of America

ISBN 1-57467-133-2

Library of Congress Cataloging-in-Publication Data is available upon request.

www.amadeuspress.com

In gratitude, long overdue, to Joseph Kerman,
of the Department of Music, University of California, Berkeley,
from whom I learned to listen, to think, and to write

Contents

Writers

Opera

Music at the Turn

Personal Seductions

Foreword

Alan Rich has now been writing about music for the better part of a century. And yet, by standards that are more meaningful than the purely chronological, he remains the most youthful critic in the field, as readers of this book will quickly discover.

This marvelous volume—as profound as it is hilarious, as cheeky as it is Olympian, and as personal as any autobiography—reads like the work of a iconoclastic, hyper-brilliant twenty-five-year old who has somehow tapped into the memory and experience of an octogenarian professor emeritus. Rich came of age in the era of Stokowski, Toscanini, and Koussevitzky (of whom he writes with passion but blessedly dry eyes), but he is at least as interested in new music by John Adams, Thomas Adès, or a yet-to-be-discovered young composer with a premiere coming up next week. Moreover, although there are any number of masterly putdowns contained within these pages, there is nary a jaded sentence, and Rich's abiding emotion is one of love—for the art of music, for his loyal readers, and for the long opportunity he has had to bring the two together.

How does Rich stay so fresh? His writing is an inspiration to those of us who wonder what we can possibly say about our third Brahms Fourth of the season, let alone try to work up the heat for yet another "insight" into *Madama Butterfly*. Most professional critics grow middle-aged pretty early in the game, and especially those of us who cover classical music, where the same pieces (and sometimes, it seems, the same performances) are trotted out year after year, as we settle ever more deeply into our aisle seats.

Yet here is Rich, writing about Beethoven's Ninth Symphony, the absolute center of the standard repertory, and a work he must have heard hundreds of times:

> [It] starts as if on some distant planet: a faint throbbing that could be in any number of keys, with a theme that takes shape somewhere out in space, one note at a time.... Beethoven's first theme is its own kind of miracle. It crashes in on you, out of the mists of uncertainty, like the *Titanic's* iceberg, massive and gruff. Later, it splits apart in wondrous ways: now haunting and melancholy, now a horn solo like a distant benediction. Midway in the first movement, its fragments knock against one another and, with terrific energy, coalesce once more in a recapitulation both sardonic and triumphant. The interweave of counterpoints—close at hand, in the middle distance and afar—is staggering; time and again you have to remind yourselves that all this incredible detail is the fashioning of a mortal totally and tragically deaf. At the movement's end, Beethoven's incomparable theme pulls itself once more out of a mumbling, eerie blackness and flings itself against us, against the Gods.

Anybody who knows the symphony at all will understand what Rich is talking about: we may have sensed some of this ourselves, although we would never have expressed it so well. But what I find exhilarating is the way Rich's words stand by themselves—as lively, dramatic narrative prose, telling a story and evoking an internal landscape that would interest us even were we as deaf as Beethoven. Yet Rich is equally at home with the flashing one-liner: "Nothing much happens in [Massenet's] *Werther,* and it does so very prettily." Exactly.

Samuel Johnson used to say that the first duty of a book was to make us want to read it through; *So I've Heard* goes one better and makes us want to read again. Here are reviews, profiles, news items, and those longish meditations, designed for Sunday supplements, that are known in the trade as "thought pieces" (filled, for once, with some actual *thinking*). Rich is fearless in his individualism—there are no sacred cows—

and it is bracing not to know what he will say next. Shostakovich, Sibelius, Richard Strauss, even Brahms, are all taken to task at one point or another. Leonard Bernstein is recognized and appraised as the decidedly flawed titan that he was (with the accents on both "flawed" and "titan"), while Philip Glass's stock rises and falls, as it should.

Rich is an honest enough critic to admit that he changes his mind now and then. He apologizes straight off for calling Stravinsky's *Symphony of Psalms* "sentimental" in an early review (a review that nobody would have ever remembered had Rich not brought it up himself). "It didn't, you see, sound like the *Rite of Spring*, which was the only Stravinsky I knew," he explains—and one can almost sense his face reddening, all these years later. "Let that be a lesson to young writers granted too easy access to print at too tender an age."

But Rich learned—and learned quickly. "There cannot be a single right or wrong in criticism," he wrote in 1964.

> Once we assume the basic competence of the critic by virtue of the previous careful training—scholarly training, if you will—in the materials of the musical language, we must allow him the leeway of formulating his own reaction to the expanse of the repertory. His own precepts, his intellectual makeup, his emotions, his personality govern this reaction and shape the nature of his personal truth. He then employs it in his evaluation of the specific musical event, the performance or the music itself: not to lead his readers by the nose into blindly accepting his truths, but to stimulate them, delight them, even irritate them into formulating truths which are completely their own.

So I've Heard contains a lifetime of "truths" from Alan Rich. Pass them on.

Tim Page
August 16, 2005
Baltimore, Maryland

Preface

Almost all of these assorted outcries date from what the history guys would refer to as my "third" or "late" or "sunset" period when—at an age when most people have learned to know better if they ever will—I chucked a perfectly respectable New York existence, made my way west ostensibly for one year, and then lost my return ticket. For reasons that make no sense to me, or to anyone at all close to me, I have found the life in California—even the musical life—extraordinarily congenial. I don't surf; I'm not even sure I remember how to dog-paddle. I don't "make the scene" (or whatever the current expression might be). I do own a Jacuzzi, because it's good for my arthritis, and I do pick oranges in my backyard—but from a neighbor's tree.

For all or none of the above reasons, I love writing in California. The twenty-five years I've lived in Los Angeles have been a time of great musical growth: our Philharmonic and several other orchestras, our opera companies, our new-music scene, our activity in outlying areas like Pasadena and Long Beach, our new halls. I love saying "our"; in New York everything belongs to somebody else. Saying "our" or "my" doesn't mean that I have to love everything that happens here, as you will notice, but it breeds a sense of involvement, and that helps. Since I came to the *LA Weekly* in March 1992 there have been perhaps ten weeks when I haven't had to turn in somewhere around 1200 words to fill my allotted three-quarters of a page, and I'm constantly surprised and delighted at how little tread-mill this chore represents, compared with every other deadline job I've had. I've turned out half a dozen long cover stories practically sweat free, remembering the one cover story I did back at *Newsweek* (on J. S. Bach's 300th birthday), when getting every word past the assembled editorial inquisition was a process comparable to a root canal.

The *Weekly* is Los Angeles's alternative paper, which tells me that I'm writing for a larger percentage of my own people than when I wrote for the dailies. My own people—the readers I now envision—don't necessar-ily go to the same concerts that I do, or collect records of medieval motets or John Cage as I do, but they are aware, even interested, that those things exist. I am also likely to be interested in what interests *them* (except, of course, for the Botox and sex ads that fill the back pages of the paper and guarantee our paychecks). At the *Weekly* I am something of an anomaly; nobody else there writes about classical music, but everybody seems to trust me to know what I am writing about. That is the bonus that comes with old age—just before, that is, the onset of senility.

For that trust, I am grateful beyond words to the *Weekly*'s editor, Laurie Ochoa; to her predecessor, Sue Horton; and to *her* predecessor, Kit Rachlis, who hired me. That chain of gratitude extends further back into history, as I explain later in these pages, to *New York* magazine's Clay Felker, who in 1968 granted me the freedom to invent myself. In more recent times I have drawn sustenance from ongoing friendships with Ernest Fleischmann, managing director emeritus of the Los Angeles Philharmonic, whose visions in founding and supporting this city's musi-cal life are still too little comprehended; with my colleague and (so far) friendly competitor Mark Swed of the *Los Angeles Times*, who joins me in a concern for the future of both the community and the art we serve.

Writing for a daily or even a weekly paper carries the comforting assur-ance that one's words will—sooner or later and most likely sooner—see more important service lining trash cans or wrapping small packages. Preserving these words within more durable bindings is a somewhat more daunting prospect, to which I have only now acceded, sixty-two years after my first article saw print. For me the process has been greatly simplified, to the point actually of pleasure beyond words, by my Amadeus Press colleagues: by the ministrations of John Cerullo, who had the curious notion that such a collection might be feasible, and by the extraordinary perceptions and perseverance of Gail Siragusa and Barbara Norton, who hacked away at the verbiage until it began to make sense. For a writer in so abstruse a subject as classical music—cursed, furthermore, with passions for such arcane matters as the fourteenth-century Machaut and the Electronica of our time—to discover editorial colleagues who actually seem to know what he is writing about has been a rare and delightful happenstance.

Closer to home, Raymond Richards, who rents my front room, runs his rock band out back in the garage, adding to my musical vocabulary, my musical awareness—and, of course, the general noise level hereabouts. And Mark Wedin, a smart and talented young composer, rented my middle room for a year and, in return, helped lay a foundation for this book by plowing through Word files and reams of clippings, culling out the articles that he, as the idealized purchaser of such a book, might find worth reading. Let's find out now if he was right.

What you have before you is a random collection of journalistic adventures assembled, for the most part, over fifteen years at *LA Weekly*, with an occasional dip into even more ancient history. Every article is identified at the end as to its date of creation, but that also means that a great deal of the information is by now already out of date. On one page I am looking forward to the building of the Walt Disney Concert Hall; on another I am comfortably ensconced in my critic's seat in the hall, marveling at sight and sound. On one page I discuss an operating budget for the Philharmonic in the 1990s that today might not buy a decent dinner at the Music Center's restaurant. To try to update all of this bygone data would lead to madness. To try to arrange these musings in chronological order would have been another kind of folly. Let the randomness in their order stand in for the immense fun I have had in putting this book together, the more so for the help of my many friends.

Oh, and one more thing. In the early 1990s I wrote some pretty good software on music history, CD-ROMs on a platform called HyperCard that went obsolete shortly after the disks appeared. The series was called "So I've Heard," and ever since that fiasco I've been hoarding that title—which I love—for use in a proper occasion. I think this is it.

Introduction: The View from Fourscore

The interesting thing about when I turned eighty—June 17, 2004, if anyone cares—was how much of the old stuff still hung around. In the last few years I've resumed contact with my two best friends from Boston Latin, the two people most responsible for my involvement in classical music, Normie Wilson and Eddie Levin. From before high school I have paltry musical memories: failed piano lessons with a birdlike spinster at age six, years in bed with rheumatic fever and a tinny radio playing dance-band hits. At fourteen I modulated into a brighter key. Normie played the piano—better than Paderewski, it seemed to me at the time. He played a fancy solo from the Grieg Piano Concerto at every school assembly, so that concerto was the first recording I bought. Eddie collected records, so I heard a lot of music at his house. My mnemonic for the opening of the "Eroica" was "the worms crawl in...."

Eddie's record albums all had program notes, and I remember being fascinated by the ways you could describe music in words. My first records (the Grieg, Beethoven's Fifth, *The Nutcracker*) came on some cheapo label without program notes, so I wrote my own. Something about this accomplishment really inflated my own self-image (which needed inflation at the time, since my pre-med studies, mostly undertaken to indulge my parents' "my son the doctor" ambitions, were going nowhere). Somebody in physics lab one day showed me a book by Sir Donald Francis Tovey full of marvelous musical descriptions: a main theme in César Franck's Symphony returns "striding grandly in its white confirmation dress." From that moment on there was nothing I wanted to do more than write about music.

In Harvard's music department there was the spellbinding G. Wallace Woodworth (a.k.a. "Woody"), who could lecture on musical form so that every transition became a cliffhanger worthy of a Saturday matinee serial. A course with Woody on classical symphonies further stoked my passion. A letter to Rudolph Elie, music critic of the *Boston Herald*, taking issue with some trivial point he had raised about a Mozart symphony and awash in self-importance, got me the offer of a job as a stringer at three bucks a column. After graduation (Harvard, class of '45) it was on to New York, where stringers at the *New York Sun* advanced to the lordly sum of $7.50. There was no turning back. I have all that stuff in a box. Wild horses couldn't get me to look at it.

Even so, the contents of that box were enough to convince the University of California, Berkeley, to overlook my lousy pre-med grade-point average from Harvard and admit me as a graduate student in music. I had the idea that a solid musical education might set me apart from most music critics, even at the expense of time spent on singing correct intervals and working out sixteenth-century counterpoint. From Roger Sessions—creative and analytical mind of great power, speaking oracle-like through a dense cloud of pipe smoke—I learned to chart the exquisite logic of classical structure on huge expanses of squared paper. From the humanist musicologist Joseph Kerman—soft-spoken and immensely witty—I learned how music reaches and moves its hearers through the interplay of a work's own logic with the usage of its time. Blending these two kinds of teaching I learned how to get music into my bloodstream. One sublime but not solitary example was my discovery, in a Mozart seminar, of the G Minor String Quintet. When I decided to write this article, that one work, for reasons I have no need to fathom, clicked into place.

Thirty-three years ago, halfway between Berkeley and today, I had already found the words for that particular obsession.

Form in music is often written about and discussed, but not very well understood. It is overtaught, or badly taught, in music-appreciation classes. "Gotta know your classic forms before the final!!" I once heard an academic colleague screaming at some hapless student, thereby losing another potential music-lover from the ranks.

Form is simply the logical way in which the memory is engaged in the listening process. The composer makes certain basic statements at the onset of a piece—a melody, a key, a tone, a rhythm—and then involves us in tracing the course of events as he intensifies this material, varies it, departs from it, and (if he chooses) returns to it. Composers of Mozart's time tended to cast their music in fairly clear forms, just as many architects of the time were obsessed with making everything look like the Parthenon; that is why the period is called "classical."

Mozart towered above his contemporaries, because he thought up better musical ideas, and also because he refused to be complacent toward the artistic rules of the time. He had the vision to see the infinite variation of detail that these rules actually allowed.

Let me try to describe one event in a work particularly precious to me, the slow movement of the G Minor String Quintet (K. 516). The movement is in the key of E-flat major, and according to what we know from books (and what Mozart knew from his own sense of logic) we can expect the music to move from an initial statement in that key, through a harmonically unstable period of modulation, to a second stable area in the closely related key of B-flat major (the "dominant," your textbook will call it). Mozart doesn't exactly do that, however.

The somber, elegiac nature of his material leads him (or he leads it; it doesn't matter) to the key of B-flat minor. Now, if you take the two scales that start on the same note—B-flat major and minor—the most striking difference between them is the third note: D-natural for the major, D-flat for the minor. The passage in B-flat minor has been hushed, saddened, centered around the lower end of the range. Now something miraculous occurs: the first violin soars up to the top of its range with a lyrical, ecstatic melody that begins on a D-natural, thus setting in the strongest possible light the fact that Mozart has now, finally, shifted to the major key.

All he has done here is to expand, or bend slightly, the standard attitude of his time regarding key relationship. But he has also created, within classical convention, a sudden, startling drama. If I had to choose a favorite single note in all music, it would be that high D-natural in Mozart's Quintet. (*New York* magazine, January 25, 1971)

Schubert was another Berkeley discovery, thanks largely to Leon Kirchner, a fellow grad student and already an important composer. Leon had the magnificence of spirit to tolerate my terrible piano playing, and we shared in amazed discovery of this great composer's big four-hand piano pieces—the F Minor Fantasy, the A-flat Major Variations—that nobody seemed to know at the time. Thus inspired, I did my master's thesis on Schubert, earned a year abroad, and returned with every expectation of a career in advanced scholarship. My Ph.D. orals, wherein it was assumed, for example, that I could recite from memory such burning issues as the content of the card catalogs of major libraries, suggested the necessity of finding other paths.

Actually, I had already embarked on one. Berkeley in the 1950s was the home of KPFA, the first-ever venture in noncommercial, listener-supported broadcasting with all the maverick programming those concepts entailed. I joined the staff after I came back from Europe, resigned a few months later, then returned after one of the frequent palace revolts. Our doors were open to politicians and philosophers of all stripes, and to composers as well. I encountered new music and its composers not on the University of California campus but down the hill in KPFA's makeshift studios: Harry Partch, Lou Harrison, John Cage, Ravi Shankar. I put Pierre Boulez on the air during his first American visit, and I cherish my tape of three local composers totally undone by every one of this arrogant young Frenchman's revolutionist theories. The San Francisco Symphony was in the hands of an inadequate conductor named Enrique Jordá, whom the society dames adored and whom the newspaper critics at least tolerated. I didn't, on my sharp-tongued weekly broadcasts, and one of KPFA's major donors, J. D. Zellerbach of the toilet paper millions, threatened to withdraw his support. KPFA's founder, the visionary Lewis Hill, told him to climb a tree.

In 1960 KPFA acquired WBAI as its New York outlet, and I was sent to help run things, as St. Paul to the Romans. This provoked a clash between my California idealism and New York political hardball beyond the controlling powers of my rudimentary gamesmanship. One day I walked over to the *New York Times* and asked whether they needed another music critic. As it happened, they did. As low man in a five-man department I covered a steady stream of sad, hopeful debuts, usually at 5:30 on Saturday afternoons, when Carnegie Recital Hall could be rented on the cheap, and quite a few first-performance-on-this-planet events which their perpetrators imagined as advancing the cause of new music. Sometimes, however, they were right; my days at KPFA had softened my sympathetic ear toward the early escapades of Yoko Ono, the topless cellist Charlotte Moorman, and the outpourings of La Monte Young, whose fortnight-long recitals on a single sustained note represented the birth pangs of what would later take on the name of minimalism. I think I was fairly successful in isolating a thread of sanity in these events, even when my presence in the hall represented half the audience. At least, in those days, the two major papers in New York covered everything that took place in the city's greatest halls and opera houses.

You couldn't pretend that the cause of serious new music was getting much support from the New York press, however. Harold Schonberg, the *Times's* top critic, demanded that his one staff member with compositional talent, Eric Salzman, choose between the two hats; Eric chose composition and departed. In 1963, when the *New York Herald-Tribune* offered me the top job to replace its retiring critic, the Columbia musicologist Paul Henry Lang, the only message Lang had to offer at the changing-of-the-guard lunch was the hope I would continue his vendetta against his Ivy League composer colleagues. I'm afraid I let him down.

Things were happening in New York. Lincoln Center opened Philharmonic Hall in 1962 and its other components soon after, setting the pattern of the cultural supermarket that other cities soon followed—such as Los Angeles, with its Music Center, in 1964. Governmental subsidy for the arts, with all its enablements and its dangers, became a reality in 1965. Leonard Bernstein strode to glory on his New York Philharmonic podium and on the national media as well. He even attempted to drag his orchestra into a confrontation with the present day, programming an "avant-garde festival" of music by John Cage, Pierre Boulez, and other violators of the public tranquility. Having no real feeling for this kind of music, he turned the event into a laff riot. "If you can understand what this music is all about," he told the audience one night, "please tell me." "Mr. Bernstein used everything short of a Flit gun to wipe out the avant-garde at Philharmonic Hall last night," I wrote, in one of my first days at the *New York Herald-Tribune*.

Eventually the *Trib* succumbed, except for its Sunday magazine, with its Milton Glaser illustrations and its with-it masthead—Tom Wolfe, Gail Sheehy, Jimmy Breslin, Gloria Steinem, Clay Felker, and me—which still survives as *New York* magazine. It was at *New York*—thanks not so much to Felker's editorial guidance as to his willingness to leave me alone—that I assumed the freedom to invent the kind of first-person, personally involved writing about music that I did then and have been doing ever since.

By 1970 the skies had brightened perceptibly over the new-music scene. Pierre Boulez took over from Bernstein on the Philharmonic podium, only grudgingly welcomed in some journalistic circles but at least bearing the news that the musical establishment might have a message or two for young ears about the vitality in the contemporary creative scene. Kids in jeans showed up for meet-the-composer concerts at Alice Tully Hall and for informal Boulez "Encounters" in Greenwich Village. There was talk of minimalism, and it blended with talk of Dylan and Pérotin and Mahler and Stockhausen "happenings." In later years several hundred thousand people would swear they were at the Metropolitan Opera House on the two November nights in 1976 for the Philip Glass/Robert Wilson *Einstein on the Beach*.

Einstein on the Beach came to New York for two performances at (but not by) the Metropolitan Opera in November 1976, preceded by ecstatic reports from abroad, where the work had traveled by bus and truck since it burst upon a spellbound crowd at Avignon the previous summer. New York was ready, at least its young, with-it crowd. A concert at Columbia University the previous April had introduced Steve Reich's *Music for Eighteen Musicians* and the audience, myself included, had torn the place apart. We now awaited the next minimal masterpiece. Even so, it took me some weeks of reflection after *Einstein* to recognize the impact of the work—the interweave of dramatic and philosophic conception, the sheer arrogance of the musical design, the boundaries stretched and breached. The casualness of the first New York presentation—in which we were allowed, nay, encouraged, to walk out for a time and then return—made it difficult to concentrate. When *Einstein* was revived at the Brooklyn Academy in 1984 I sat through four performances, immobile. It was possible, I had learned, for a work to last five hours and still be fun.

Something that imposing, that massive, perhaps even that cockeyed, was needed as a bookmark, a defining moment. Everything about *Einstein* was different enough from anyone's previous experience—in opera, theater, or concert—that it demanded rethinking. The elements of the musical experience—time, memory, the mental tools that we use to find our place in, say, a Mozart quintet—were challenged and done away with during the five plotless hours of Robert Wilson's narrative indirection and Philip Glass's music. Yet we were carried forward; neither music nor drama was so strange that we felt lost, as we might in some dense Asian ritual. There was a cleansing quality about the music, and about the very indirection of its theatrical substance. that seemed to wash away the accretion of dense contrivance that had been issuing forth from composition seminars up and down the east coast. It engendered hostility among most of the critics, of course, because it left them without the graphs and diagrams that were easier to write about in the intricate structures of, say, the gang at Princeton.

After the impact of *Einstein* a public could be slowly wooed for the big works of Steve Reich and John Adams (whose *Grand Pianola Music* was lustily booed by a New York Philharmonic audience in 1983, unused to so much clean tonality in brand-new music). Philip Glass kept going too, riding high after *Einstein*'s fame, but trapped in a repetitive groove more confining than his own stylistic clichés. (He achieved a kind of immortality, however, through the satires of P. D. Q. Bach, one of which was titled *Einstein on the Fritz*.) (*California* magazine, November 1985)

In 1979 *New York* cloned itself (ill-advisedly, as it happened) as *New West*, and I was dispatched westward to function for a year as a bicoastal music critic. California's principal orchestras had distinguished new conductors: Edo de Waart in San Francisco and Carlo Maria Giulini in Los Angeles. Opera was thriving up north, and there were stirrings in Los Angeles and San Diego. I was to find a critic for classical music on the West Coast, turn over the keys to the kingdom, and return to the real world. Instead, I'm still here. The new-music scene in Southern California, above all, was lively and well run, but held in durance vile under the snide negativism of the *Los Angeles Times*'s Martin Bernheimer, who fancied himself the incarnation of Austria's Eduard Hanslick but actually merely skimmed off Hanslick's virtuosic vitriol with little of his profound aesthetic sensibility. It saddened me to attend interesting concerts here and overhear audiences parroting Bernheimerisms in the guise of musical wisdom. From such a dragon Los Angeles needed, and deserved rescue. Within three months Bernheimer and I were no longer speaking, a situation that did not forfeit me my claim to have truly lived.

I journeyed through local journalism: *New West* and its equally hapless successor *California*, KUSC, KFAC, *Newsweek* (long enough to do a cover on J. S. Bach; imagine that happening now!), the *Herald-Examiner* of fond memory. The day that paper folded I was actually on the *Times*'s payroll for approximately three hours; guess whose foot went down on that one. Never mind; when Bernheimer finally gave up on his efforts to remake Los Angeles as Vienna West and departed eastward, the *Times* hired Mark Swed, a fellow eager-beaver in matters of contemporary music and other forms of artistic adventure. The *Times* came out ahead, I came out ahead, and, if you don't mind my saying so, the two of us now give the area a lively musical outlook that not many American cities can match.

The musical power structure when I arrived in Los Angeles was uniquely strong and active, and it gave the lie to the suspicions my New York friends frequently voiced, that I was out of my mind to give up a decent power job in the East and move out to where nothing ever happens. The Philharmonic's Ernest Fleischmann had taken unto himself a lot of the music director's prerogatives, which had made Giulini happy and, before him, Zubin Mehta. It enabled Fleischmann to scour the world for young talent: Esa-Pekka Salonen and Simon Rattle on the podium and the lamented Robert Harth in the front office. It also encouraged Fleischmann to create brave new programs like the cheekily named Green Umbrella series and promote them properly. Lawrence Morton was still on hand; he had run adventurous new-music concerts, first (as Evenings on the Roof) on a connoisseur's rooftop studio in Silver Lake in 1939, up until this writing (as the Monday Evening Concerts) at the County Museum, and currently in search of a new venue. Leonard Stein, Arnold Schoenberg's right-hand assistant at one time, ran the Schoenberg Institute at the University of Southern California and organized musical events and symposia all over town until his death in 2004. A remarkable patron named Betty Freeman, who was simply in love with the creative process in the arts, wrote checks to pay composers' rent, commissioned new works, underwrote recordings of their music, and invited them to her home to talk about their music to small gatherings and have it performed by excellent local musicians.

I got involved with producing Betty's musical afternoons—ten years at her home in Beverly Hills and three more at the home of Judith Rosen, another enlightened patron, in Encino. I shook hands with over 100 composers—Boulez, Cage, Adams, Ligeti, and many promising unknowns. Has ever an eager observer of the arts enjoyed better access to an education in contemporary musical affairs?

Win a few, lose a few. Los Angeles finally gained its long-overdue professional opera company, although there was some ominous symbolism in the fact that the opening-night curtain on the company's first-ever performance, in October 1986, stuck halfway up and resisted all efforts at dislodging for several throat-tightening minutes. Ambassador Auditorium, Pasadena's ideal small concert hall, with the best sound of any, was shuttered as a casualty in the collapse of its governing board and looms unused to this day. The excellent Sequoia String Quartet fell victim to internal dissent, as did the well-attended Chamber Music Los Angeles concert series at the Japan-America. Inside and out Walt Disney Concert Hall sounds almost as good as it looks, and it gives the whole concept of music in downtown Los Angeles an enhanced stature at a time when that kind of boost is sorely needed. In Orange County the local Philharmonic Society belied the area's conservative reputation by producing such outrageous fare as Osvaldo Golijov's *St. Mark Passion* and György Ligeti's *Piece for 100 Metronomes.*

It is an open secret that music is in bad shape: orchestras folding, composers reduced to waiting on table. Criticism, oddly enough, may be in better shape, so long as people realize why it's important. I write criticism as a way of reporting on the rise and fall of the cultural health of the community. Sure, most of the events I write about are history by the time my reports get into print. What remains, I like to think, is the extent of my reaction: the fact that I got worked up about Esa-Pekka Salonen's performance of such-and-such a new work, or Mitsuko Uchida's way with a Schubert sonata, or Robert Wilson's staging of *Madama Butterfly* will make readers want to experience these people's work the next time around. A city that can support, and fill, a Walt Disney Concert Hall night after night—and can turn out in fair numbers for an all-Bartók concert at the County Museum and for Jordi Savall's viola da gamba at the Getty Center—is the city I feel like writing to, sharing my enthusiasms with. It's the kind of city whose future I would like to share, to help shape. When I run out of great performances to write about, there is always great music to be discovered and, a few years later, rediscovered. I don't think I will ever run out of new things to discover, and, therefore, to write about, in the Beethoven "Eroica." Or that Mozart quintet. Or Renée Fleming singing Schubert's "Nacht und Träume." Or...

When *New York* magazine gave me a page of my own, with the implication that I could be trusted to write about whatever interested me so long as I kept the magazine out of the courts, I succumbed to the delusion that I knew something about everything. Those early pages, which I keep as a kind of memento mori, contain some pretty embarrassing stuff from beyond my field of awareness, about Balanchine's choreography and rock 'n' roll. I got a free trip to London from RCA to hear their new star, David Bowie, and came back with a clever headline—"I've Been to London to Visit the Queen"—and no valid information at all. I had no background at all in these matters, just ego, and I made some dreadful mistakes. My worst howler, which I now retract, fifty-six years too late—was to condemn Stravinsky's *Symphony of Psalms* as "sentimental." (It didn't, you see, sound like the *Rite of Spring*, which was the only Stravinsky I knew. Let that be a lesson to young writers granted too easy access to print at too tender an age.)

If I've learned anything over the past few decades, it has been that there is nothing disgraceful in recognizing one's own limitations and operating within them. My admirable colleague, the *New Yorker*'s Alex Ross—forty-five years younger than I by his own admission—is doing now, wisely, what I tried to do, unwisely, back then. With the background and the breadth of intellect that I only imagined I possessed he has reinvented serious musical criticism and made it stick, relocating the boundaries of the territory so that he can write about Sonic Youth and Beethoven's Fifth and locate them exactly in the broader scheme of things. His long article from February 2004, a map of the territory brilliantly plotted and drawn, is on his Web site at http://www.therestisnoise.com/listen_to_this/index.html, and it's required reading. It tells me, as clearly as any evidence I've come across in a very long time, that there's hope for us after all, and for music, too. So far, in other words, so good.

[June 2004]

WORKS

The best experiences I can remember in a concert hall or opera house are the times when a particular performance serves to reveal something new, or something I might have forgotten, or something I have seen in a different light, about the music itself. Simon Rattle's performance of the "Eroica," quite early in his career when, he confessed, he hadn't yet mastered all of Beethoven's nine, sent me home to read and listen to Beethoven's score and think about it for hours thereafter. A rediscovered symphonic sketch from Schubert's deathbed, with its slow movement like a knife wound, sent me back over that troubled composer's lifetime. An editorial gimmick from the *Weekly*—what was the best (whatever) created in Los Angeles?—started me thinking about, and appreciating, Arnold Schoenberg's unappreciated life here. All told, I prefer thinking about music—"the works"—than about performers, unless the performers are also thinking about music.

Bach's "Brandenburgs": That's Entertainment

A mile-long toyshop, a self-refilling box of Godiva chocolates, an entertainment both profound and giddy: all of the above can pass as an accurate metaphor for any one of the half-dozen orchestral concertos by J. S. Bach generally but inaccurately known as the "Brandenburgs." Compound that estimate by six, and you'll come close to the impact of hearing all of these magical exercises at a single sitting—the very miracle that transpired at Royce Hall a few nights ago, handed off in the able ministrations of the Los Angeles Chamber Orchestra and its multitalented leader, Jeffrey Kahane.

Something not easily defined sets these concertos apart from the dozens of other orchestral works created at various times in Bach's career: a joyousness, an outpouring of inventive fantasy that leads to seemingly unworkable sound combinations—one whole work scored only for low strings, another built around a pairing of a shrill, piercing high trumpet and the mild-mannered burble of an alto recorder, yet another a jumble for horns and oboes all tangled in twos and threes. We tend to shy away from attributing an element of daring to Bach; he stands in the annals as the stick-in-the-mud who wrote in the accepted manner of his time, only better. Yet every one of these six concertos is some kind of step into unexplored shapes and sonorities; No. 5, for example, is the world's first-ever keyboard concerto—the ancestor at some remove, in other words, of the Rach 3 and *Rhapsody in Blue*.

We don't know the particulars of these works, beyond the information that they figure among the voluminous music Bach composed for his virtuoso orchestra in the court of Prince Leopold of Anhalt-Cöthen sometime before 1720, and that in 1721 he made a fair handwritten copy of these six works and sent it off to Cristian Ludwig, Margrave of Brandenburg, in hopes of getting a better job at that illustrious court. The margrave never acknowledged the offering; the chances are that his own band wouldn't have been up to the music's demands. Later there were legends—that the music ended up as a butcher's wrapping paper, or that the margrave's entire library was sold for twenty-four groschen—stories that belong on the shelf next to the one about George Washington's cherry tree. Bach himself held onto his original copies, and even recycled some choice passages. If you think of the first movement of No. 3 as a fascinating study in string-ensemble busyness, check out its later version in Cantata No. 174 ("Ich liebe den Höchsten"), where Bach has crammed horns and oboes in among the strings to create a texture busy to the point of explosiveness.

"Brandenburgs" come today in staggering profusion—nearly three pages of small print in Schwann—and in all sizes: full symphony orchestra, authentic baroque ensemble, even (shudder!) Max Reger's version for piano duet. The version I grew up on (because there was no other) is still listed: Adolf Busch's eloquent leadership from the concertmaster's chair, modern winds, Rudolf Serkin's piano. Jeffrey Kahane's version incorporated wise compromises, including modern flutes in Nos. 2 and 4 in a room where recorders mightn't carry. Tempos were on the brisk side, but such sublime moments as the exchange of dissonances between Margaret Batjer's violin and Allan Vogel's oboe, in the slow movement of No. 1, were granted time to raise goosebumps—as was Kahane himself, at a splendidly resonant harpsichord, in the astonishing cadenzas in No. 5. The sense, through all this rewarding evening, was of being present at the creation.

[December 1998]

Messiah: Songs of Survival

Handel's *Messiah* is the world's greatest music. It defines the humanness of mankind. It proclaims the miracle of survival, and the process by which it may be attained. It takes us through the darkest tragedy civilization has ever endured, and when we can bear it no longer it teaches us to yell a lusty "Hallelujah!" and move on. At Disney Hall last week a small choral ensemble from Canada voiced, with giggling delight, the news that "unto us a son is born." Not many minutes later the solo voice of Andreas Scholl cut through to the base of our spine with the horror as that same son was "despised and rejected."

Nothing else in the repertory can boast an endurance record comparable to that of Handel's masterpiece. From the moment of its first performance some 275 years ago the piece has never been off the charts. It exists beyond category. If it is "classical"—that is, music in which you only applaud at the end and are entitled to shush your neighbors at other times—it is by some distance the most popular. If it belongs in the "pop" world—well, I've never met a rock musician who didn't know what the "Hallelujah Chorus" was.

Whatever its niche, it has never been out of style. It continues to mean all things to all people. Today's mail brings a new disc: *Messiah Re-Mix.* I can't wait to hear it.

Messiah endured a complex set of revisions during Handel's time and more after his death, including inflation to 1000-voice monster-choral showpieces of Wagnerian proportions. On successive days in mid-December, however, I heard versions that more or less respected the proportions of Handel's original performances: chorus and orchestra of about thirty-five, which seems to be the accepted proportion nowadays. In other respects, the performances were vastly unalike.

At Disney Bernard Labadie had brought his marvelous small chorus La Chapelle de Québec, early-music specialists with a way of combining clarity with warmth and beauty of tone unlike any ensemble I've heard; they really became a fifth soloist along with the immensely gifted Scholl, and the splendid Karina Gauvin, John Tessier, and Nathan Berg. Twenty or so players from the Los Angeles Philharmonic constituted the orchestra, and it was obvious even on the first (of four) performances that Labadie had impressed a fair amount of stylistic awareness on the players. Two nights before there had been one of the Philharmonic Chamber Music Society concerts, Scholl in Handel arias and a Vivaldi cantata and string players in two works of Bach, and the stylistic discrepancies—the ill-defined phrasing in the Bach works in particular—merely restated the obvious news that excellent symphonic musicians do not, on their own, automatically convert into baroque stylists.

But the Labadie *Messiah*—egregiously misheard and misreported by the *Times*'s man Chris Pasles—was one of those legendary occasions when music you think you know front and back turns into an exhilarating discovery. The control of texture was especially remarkable; you had the sense that you could look into the entire musical structure from top to bottom and discover new sounds at every level. Tempos were brisk, joyous, and—in that harrowing sequence that limns the central tragedy and fills most of the center of the work—bone-scraping; the "Hallelujah" came as blessed and much-needed release.

[December 2004]

Haydn's Quartets: Four Play

Before there was Scrabble, there was the string quartet. The dinner dishes were cleared, and the company retired to the music room to try out the latest chamber-music delectation from the busy presses in Berlin, Vienna, or Paris. Music for four—the "divertimento a quattro," as it was first called—was the medium of choice: two violins to sing the main melodies in sweet harmonies, or to argue them in polite counterpoint; the viola to inject a soberer tone; the cello to supply a firm foundation. In or around 1760 the young provincial composer Joseph Haydn, shortly before assuming the position at the Esterházy palace that would keep him busy for most of his lifetime, knocked out a set of compositions for the summer quartet parties of the Viennese aristocrat Baron Fürnberg. They were admired and published as his Opp. 1 and 2. Over the next four decades their numbers would grow; more than any other medium in which he worked with astonishing prodigality, Haydn's sixty-eight quartets represent a compelling document: of his own growth of a composer, of the growth and enrichment of the musical language we know—not entirely accurately—as "classical," and of the taste and wisdom of a musical public that could recognize and support Haydn's unique genius.

Working your way through the twenty-one discs that contain this legacy on a treasurable new Philips release, you can't miss that sense of unfolding, in Haydn's own abilities and also in the world around him. Prince Esterházy furnished him with a superlative orchestra, affording

Haydn the chance to use its individual members as a laboratory for his own progressive ideas. Beyond that, the prince himself and his entourage became for Haydn the kind of audience today's composer would kill for: receptive to experiments and to attempts to expand the boundaries of the established musical forms of the time.

The quartets of his first decade at Esterház, published as Opp. 9, 17, and 20—with six quartets in each opus—celebrate that growth in eighteen daring forward steps. The four voices take on a distinctive personality; the cello is no longer merely the oom-pah support, but contributes its own voice. Several of the Op. 20 works end with fugues, intense and passionate, far removed from the earlier sense of "divertimento a quattro." Op. 20 No. 5, in the stark, rarely used key of F minor, ends with a fugue subject that would later turn up as the Kyrie in Mozart's Requiem.

The strength grows; so does the mix in these works of daring progressiveness and superb entertainment. Haydn himself described his Op. 33 quartets as composed in "a completely new and special way," and that can mean any number of things. These were the six quartets that Mozart claimed as inspiration for his own great set that he dedicated to Haydn; for both sublime composers, they served as a declaration of principle, the right of the genius to experiment and to get away with it. The second in Haydn's series has come to be known as "The Joke," for reasons clear to anyone who has applauded prematurely in the trick silences near the end; the third is "The Bird," for reasons set forth in the enchanting twittering at the start. Not all, however, is airy persiflage; the first in the Op. 33 series, in the passionate key of B minor, uneasily compresses a tense and personal outcry no less dramatic for its lack of words.

An even greater work among these "middle-period" quartets, although not as well-known, is Op. 54 No. 2, music in which everything goes against the formulas of the time in the creation of its own new rules. The slow movement is like nothing else in chamber music of any time: a passionate, rhapsodic solo for the first violin—a reflection, perhaps, of Haydn's own part-gypsy heritage—that floats like gusts of steam over a somber landscape. Then comes the minuet, hardly an elegant dance this time, with its crashing, dissonant outcries. And then the finale: not the expected, rollicking rondo but another slow movement, its profound melody briefly interrupted by a skittering intrusion but ending in a vision of infinite starlit heavens.

The best-known of the quartets are the six of Op. 76. They come late in Haydn's life, after the two trips to London, after the last of the symphonies. They share much of the eloquence of the orchestral works. The slow movement of No. 5 is again in one of the "difficult" keys—F-sharp major, six sharps—which in Haydn always implies a special profundity; its power to stop the breath links it, perhaps, to its counterpart in the Symphony No. 98. The slow movement of the last of Op. 76 is possibly the most amazing of all. It is, again, in a rare tonality—B major, five sharps—but its harmonic wanderings, chromatic and capricious, are so complex that Haydn withholds a key signature until the end, when the music comes to rest in a final burst of pride in its own power to surprise and delight.

The new recording crowns our own Angeles Quartet's Haydn project, which has been taking shape in a concert series at the Los Angeles County Museum of art (LACMA) over the past several years, with one personnel change along the way: second violinist Steven Miller replaces Sara Parkins in sixteen of the works. The set lists for $167, although I've seen it online for $126; because the one competition, the Naxos set by the Kodály Quartet—which also includes Haydn's quartet version of *The Seven Last Words of Christ*—lists for $133, the price differential is relatively minor. The Angeles performances are suave, beautifully thought out, and altogether creditable, although I do admire the extra intensity of the Kodály's Attila Falvay in rhapsodic passages such as the aforementioned Op. 54 No. 2. At a time when concern is rising over the future, if any, of serious classical recording, the appearance of this altogether distinguished venture comes as momentary solace.

[May 2001]

Mozart Moments

The best thing about this job—one of the best things, anyhow—is the chance it affords me to write about Mozart's *The Marriage of Figaro* as often as I like. I got to write about it last spring, when the Los Angeles Opera put on its so-so production. Now a new recording has landed on my desk. Actually, I've never needed an excuse; *Figaro* is always somewhere on my mind. It not only contains some of the most beautiful music I know; it is also the most convincing demonstration of the power of music to move the personages within a drama and, therefore, to move the personages out front witnessing that drama—either in a theater or at home in front of a video screen, or even just a couple of loudspeakers.

If I could prove this at all, the best way would be from one of the ensembles, when Mozart allows two or more characters to sing what's on their minds simultaneously, with the music setting them apart—the power of music, in other words, to conquer time. Mozart's own favorite ensemble in *Figaro*, or so he wrote somewhere, is the sextet in act 3. The old harridan Marcellina, who has been trying to get Figaro to marry her, has now discovered that he is actually her illegitimate son; this also thwarts the designs of the Count, who has been trying to get into the panties of Figaro's intended bride Susanna. Mother and son are now reunited in a series of gooey, saccharine, lovey-dovey phrases that show off Mozart's marvelous mastery of musical parody.

In walks Susanna, who's not yet in on developments; all she knows is that her darling Figaro is standing there cuddling in the arms of that dreadful Marcellina, and so, naturally, she throws a snit. What Mozart has been delivering to us as all sweetness and light, F major followed by C major, brightness and cheer, is nudged in two quick measures into an ill-tempered minor key. The harmony loses its direction utterly and modulates in sheer desperation, climaxing as Susanna hands Figaro a resounding slap on the ear. Finally Figaro gets in his explanation, joined by the rest of the company, and serenity—dramatic and harmonic—is restored.

But not quite. Most composers—of Mozart's time or into our own—might sense that the business of the scene was now over. Perhaps to balance the fact that Susanna has come late into the ensemble, she is now allotted new music of her own: a haunting, serene, flowing tune made up of the most innocent phrases which expand into a perfect arch of melody, a kind of benediction on the joyous resolution of the day's latest (but not last) crisis. I could argue for this moment as the most beautiful in the entire opera; perhaps Mozart felt that way, too. In any case, it is the kind of flourish that he alone could command, that last little light shined on his characters that lifts them out of artifice and onto a more accessible level where we can share their emotions, even their breath.

"This must be what the gods were like," writes Craig Seligman about *Così fan tutte* in the latest issue of the excellently wise *Threepenny Review*—which, by happenstance, landed on my doorstep on the eve of Opera Pacific's production of Mozart's sublimely ridiculous, tragic, operatic comedy. Only gods, indeed, could contrive the harmonies that rise like audible ambrosia as the girls in act 1 bind their departing swains to promises of once-a-day letter writing. Only a goddess could hurl divinely accurate thunderbolts across vast skyscapes in the way the heroine Fiordiligi proclaims the unassailability of her supernal womanly honor. And only a composer whose hand is flawlessly guided by forces from above could contrive an ensemble for four voices in which the first three enter one at a time with the same tune in exquisite harmony but the fourth (having partaken too freely from the flask) delightfully disrupts the shebang with a whole 'nother vocal line about his own drunken anger.

Pity the deprived soul whose spinal column cannot vibrate to the way Mozart uses clarinets and trombones in *The Magic Flute*. Shed a tear for the misguided misanthrope who fails to find the presence of God—by whatever name—in the music for Sarastro in that opera. Bemoan the unreconstructable rationalist who howls in horror as Schikaneder's plot-line twists, this way now and that way then, as villains turn noble and heroines turn treacherous.

That last point, over which scholars have spilled ink by the tankload since the opera was new, the current Los Angeles Opera production has made particularly solemn and stirring. Tamino has come to Sarastro's palace to rescue Pamina, who, he has been led to believe, has been kidnapped by Sarastro and held in durance vile. He is met at the entrance by one of Sarastro's priests, who queries him on his purpose and informs him that everything he has been led to believe is black is actually white, and that it will take some effort on his—Tamino's—part to prove worthy of that knowledge. "When can I achieve this goal?" asks the impatient Tamino. The priest—who is identified in the score as "Speaker" although he only sings—answers, and on his sublime last line, a solemn cadence in a key of A minor, the entire plot pivots: "As soon as friendship's loving hand leads you to our sacred band." That line of music is repeated twice again by an offstage chorus. Soft chords in the trombones enhance the solemnity. Within less than ninety seconds we have been confronted with a new plotline, and a new kind of music. It is a wrenching, extraordinary moment.

That A-minor cadence demands your attention. Mozart had almost never composed in that key; never in the orchestral works or quartets, only once in an early piano sonata. Feverishly at work in what turned out to be the last year of his life, he apparently reserved his foray into these dark and unfamiliar harmonic precincts for this simple yet intensely moving moment in this sublimely silly, wise comedy, with its still-argued-about mingling of the high-minded and the low.

Every one of Mozart's mature operas finds some new way to violate the practice of his time, whereby comedies should be funny and tragedies sad. The miraculous resolution at the end of *The Marriage of Figaro*, a sacred chorale in all but name, is all the more astonishing for the comic hurly-burly just before; Fiordiligi's lovelorn confusion near the end of *Così fan tutte* as she totters on the brink of infidelity, draws its tragic tone from the contrast with the ludicrous amorous entanglement that brings it on. But the circumstances of *The Magic Flute*—as an entertainment at Emanuel Schikaneder's house of folk comedy, as contrast to the grander operas unfurled before higher-paying audiences—make its contrasts of tone even more jolting. A single night's entertainment that embraces Mr. and Mrs. Papageno feathering their nest, Sarastro's invocation (fit for the mouth of God, wrote Bernard Shaw), and the heartbreak of Pamina's "Ach, ich fühl's" (Mozart's greatest aria, writes the scholarly Joseph Kerman) thus embraces a range of delectable jolts that no other single work, of Mozart's time or of ours, can readily offer.

What, then, is *The Magic Flute* about? Part of its greatness lies in its multiplicity of answers. To Kerman, whose 1988 *Opera as Drama* remains obligatory reading, the change of direction "can be explained very simply and very happily on the assumption that Mozart himself insisted on it." Whatever Mozart's original motivation in turning out a new titillation for his billiards buddy and fellow Freemason, something in his conscience pushed him to the realization that even Schikaneder's mess of a crowd-pleasing plot deserved his best shot. That aforementioned small miracle, the A-minor cadence that diverts Tamino's path toward godly goals, launches the opera itself toward multitudinous kinds of greatness. "All the diversities," writes Kerman, "of musical style, action, tone and mood are perfectly controlled to a single dramatic end."

Every character is filled out with a full set of weaknesses as well as strengths. The saintly Sarastro maintains slaves and punishes their transgressions cruelly. Papageno, the sweet innocent, tells barefaced lies but still gets to share with Pamina a high-minded, philosophical duet on the meaning of love. For all his newly acquired bravery, Tamino must lean on Pamina for guidance through the trials of fire and water.

Basically, *The Magic Flute* fits the category of maiden-in-distress-heroically-rescued opera greatly popular in its time, both comically and seriously treated. Alongside this, we must also countenance this none-too-subtle allegory on the concerns and travails of the Freemason movement, which at the time was far more of a political force than it later became. The psychoanalysts, too, have had their day with the *Flute*, explaining the interaction of Tamino and Pamina on Jungian terms as the *animus* reaching out to the *anima*. Much can be made of the fact that Tamino's at-first-sight passion for Pamina is motivated by a mere portrait—which, furthermore, ends up in the possession of Papageno when the two seekers actually reach Sarastro's palace. Musical scholars have grappled for centuries with the paradox that Schikaneder's cobbled-together, endearing mess of a plot follows upon the opera's impeccably tidy and beautifully organized overture—which, in true Mozartian fashion, was composed only at the last minute, after the rest of the work was already on the performers' music stands.

The abiding and most important genius of the work, however, is that none of this matters. As the beasts in the forest succumb to the enchantment of Tamino's magic flute, so do we all to Mozart's.

[1998–2001]

250 Candles for Wolfgang

Once again there is an Anniversary; I have barely gotten through the 179 CDs of Philips's 1991 complete Mozart edition, a splendid highlight of the recording industry as it then flourished. Now there will be another Mozart torrent, even as word arrives of serious record stores, and producers, too, going out of business. Consider the alternative: a *New Yorker* cartoon, stuck on my fridge like a memento mori, shows a desert, bleak beyond imagining. The caption: "Life without Mozart."

We grant him a special place—"I hate classical music, except for Mozart, of course"—because of his uncanny take on the human condition and the ease with which this understanding comes through in the music. The great late operas prove this the most easily, but they are not alone. Listen, for starters, to the amazing display of human emotions and reactions in the twenty or so minutes of nonstop interaction that ends the second act of Figaro. The Count, with murder on his mind, thunders forth his menacing octaves; the Countess, quite honestly terrified, dithers in shivering roulades. Then the closet door opens to reveal not the expected philandering Cherubino, but the blameless Susanna, and the stupefied Count is reduced to a monotone while the women giggle around him in triumph. The scene proceeds: more people join in and the music grows more complex, with every line presenting a separate, beautifully realized personage. And while all this is happening, Mozart is also working within the classic framework that involves our listening process with the logic of key change and key return, the design that makes it all work.

Verdi's operas are full of marvelous character depictions; Wagner's Ring drew tears, even in those patched-together performances at Long Beach last week. But it is to Mozart that I turn for the sublime equilibrium of musical shape and the power to stir the emotions through the balance of harmony and design. The operas make this power the most accessible because of the words. But it is a power ingrained in Mozart's music itself, almost from the start of his amazing if brief trajectory. One of the few honest episodes in Peter Shaffer's otherwise execrable *Amadeus* comes when Salieri overhears and eloquently describes the slow movement of the Serenade for Thirteen Winds (K. 361 in Köchel's chronological catalog of Mozart's works) and is undone by mingled awe and jealousy ("I was suddenly frightened.... It seemed to me that I had heard a voice of God!"). If ever words have served to describe the process of falling in love with a piece of music, perhaps beyond reason, let it be these.

You can undergo similar processes in the whole treasury of "word-less operas," the dozen or so piano concertos from Mozart's last years in Vienna, in which, time after time, the interplay between solo piano and orchestra becomes a serious, loving conversation on subject matter too subtle for words. Even more than the symphonies—and the violin concertos, which are works from youthful days—Mozart's mature piano concertos represent a synthesis between his operatic language and his individualistic orchestral idiom in which the woodwinds of the orchestra take on almost human characteristics.

This past weekend Jeffrey Kahane and the Los Angeles Chamber Orchestra began their series of Mozart piano concertos, which will run through three years. That first concert's last work—the G Major Concerto, K. 453—has a slow movement that is a marvel among marvels in this regard. The orchestra proposes a small fragment of a theme; the piano responds with the theme ever so slightly varied, the tone gradually deep-ens, then lightens, and after eight or nine minutes we find that, uncon-sciously, we've moved to the edge of our seats—as if to connect with every word of a profound, overheard discourse with words unspoken but clearly understood.

These marvelous works constitute by themselves a wide-ranging reper-tory of Mozartian dramatic devices. The March 12 program includes two works whose slow movements are almost too emotionally draining to coexist on a single program: the C-major K. 467 and the A-major K. 488. The first of these contributed a slow movement to a very pretty if morose Swedish film romance under the name of *Elvira Madigan*, where it kept getting clipped off in mid-phrase by a director obviously tone-deaf. The A-major has a slow movement of similarly breath-stopping beauty, a melody for one finger, stark and simple. And on May 21 there is the great E-flat Concerto, K. 482, most grandly orchestrated of the concertos, in which all kinds of strange and wonderful things happen in all three movements, including a conclusion to the slow movement that leaves you in a "what hit me?" state of mind.

Near the end of his life Mozart discovered the music of Bach from manuscripts in the libraries of Viennese collectors and from his own discoveries on journeys to Bach's churches in Leipzig. The possibilities of creating drama by ramming lines of counterpoint together in daring and novel ways impressed him deeply, and the parts of the Requiem that he actually completed can lead us to tantalizing speculation as to what his next works would have been, his mastery of contrapuntal devices even more firmly in hand. To me the last of Mozart's symphonies, the "Jupiter," is the real synthesis of his command over the rich, complex musical textures that he gleaned from his contrapuntal explorations. Even before the famous finale, the working-out in this exultant, extroverted work is uncommonly rich-textured, the wisps of string tone surrounding the themes in the slow movement, the brass punctuation in the minuet—could classical orchestration have moved further than this rich, lustrous sonority? Then comes the finale, with its five-part melding of voices, a composer triumphantly staking out his conquest over the complexity of his art.

It didn't end there, of course. Afterward came the profound sublimity of the Clarinet Concerto and the endearing sublimity of *The Magic Flute*. And it doesn't really end then, either. The next Mozart year comes in 2041; see you then.

[January 25, 2006]

The "Eroica": Heroism Beyond the Call

Music whose daring and originality leaves us spellbound; music whose sheer momentum staggers the imagination; music that stands for one of the most astonishing single forward steps in the history of the arts...that was some of what we heard from the Los Angeles Philharmonic last week, in the first program of Simon Rattle's two-week guest-conducting stint. The music I'm referring to is not, however, the turgid, derivative, agonizingly overwritten Second Symphony of Gerald Levinson, which had its world premiere that night, and not a couple of dinky little brass pieces by Sir Michael Tippett, which also had their first local hearing. No, the work in question is Beethoven's Third Symphony, the "Eroica," 190 years old and still aflame with the creative genius of its composer.

The performance under Rattle caught that flame. The tempos tended toward the rash—though not so speedy as those demanded by the deaf Beethoven when, late in life, he annotated most of his scores—but flexible enough to underline the great dramatic moments. Some of the splendid brightness in the tone came from Rattle's decision to reseat the orchestra according to nineteenth-century practice, with second fiddles down front on the right; this clarified the interplay within the string sections and brought out nice details. (Rattle has reseated the orchestra this way for Mozart performances on previous visits here, but never with so much ecstatic burbling from the Philharmonic's publicity department.) It was one of those rare, breath-stopping occasions when a score you thought you knew backward and forward seemed newly composed.

The power in Beethoven's "Eroica" Symphony has nothing to do with the lore of its origin—Beethoven's early admiration of Napoleon Bonaparte and the disillusion that led him to canceling the dedication after the charismatic French leader proclaimed himself Emperor. Bonaparte's political cataclysms were summer breezes compared to the upheaval Beethoven's symphony came to represent in the arts. Europe would recover from Napoleon's rampagings; the "Eroica" forever changed the concept of the symphony.

By 1805, when the "Eroica" had its first public performance, Beethoven had made his reputation as a purveyor of instrumental works structured along more or less orthodox patterns: two symphonies, three piano concertos, chamber music, sonatas. The "Pathétique" Piano Sonata, the sublime slow movement of the Third Piano Concerto, the wild passions in the C Minor and "Kreutzer" Violin Sonatas—these were already the intimations of a revolutionary spirit in music. Yet it would have been impossible, even from the evidence of these iconoclastic works, to predict the next turn in Beethoven's road. What the "Eroica" possessed above all was a quality of narrative, of being about something, a dramatic unfolding that went forward from first note to last and that struck an entirely new tone in abstract instrumental music.

The rubrics of classical structure, brought to an expressive apotheosis in the mature works of Mozart and Haydn, still demanded that a balance be struck, that a work beginning in tragedy—in a minor key, perhaps— must make its peace with some kind of "happy" ending. Mozart had, in his mature piano concertos, evolved a kind of writing that invested the soloist and the orchestral instruments with an almost human quality, as if they might be presenting a wordless aria. But Beethoven, lacking Mozart's matchless ability to turn his sublime, flowing melodies into a semblance of human speech, turned the very momentum of his music into wordless drama. In the "Eroica" he virtually invented the proposition of musical growth, where the very elements of his language seem to expand, often with explosive force, from one moment to the next. It was the work in which Beethoven first broke completely free of the classical constraints.

In the "Eroica" the classical ideal of balance between opposites is secondary to the ideal of constant dramatic impetus. At the start of the magnificent first movement, longer and more complex than any orchestral work that any composer worthy of the name had previously ventured, an opening theme is only hinted at, and its integrity is shattered by a harmonic intrusion within its first ten seconds. Only at the end of the movement is that intrusion resolved; Beethoven has, in those intervening sixteen minutes, swept us, along pathways storm-beset and sunlit, to that final realization.

To our ears today, that intrusion—a "wrong" C-sharp in the key of E-flat—is a small cloud on the horizon; music in our own time is full of notes that would be considered "wrong" by the rules of classical harmony. To judge the devastating effect of that note in Beethoven's own design, we need to share the obsessions of the conservative Viennese audience of Beethoven's time, an aristocracy made nervous by the revolutionary outbreaks throughout Europe and the Americas, threatened by a proletariat impatient to reap the gains that revolution had portended. Napoleon's shadow fell across all of Western Europe: not long after the "Eroica," the tyrant who had originally inspired it would be at the gates of Vienna, and Beethoven would retire to his cellar with a pillow over his head to blot out the sounds of the invaders' cannon.

Beethoven himself conducted the first public performance of the "Eroica," on April 7, 1805. "Truly this new work of Beethoven's contains some grand and daring ideas," wrote one critic, the Martin Bernheimer of his day, "but the sinfonie would be all the better—it lasts a whole hour—if Beethoven could reconcile himself to make some cuts in it and to bring into the score more light, clarity and unity.... Even after several hearings it eludes the most sustained attention, so that the unprepared connoisseur is really shocked. As a result this sinfonie was anything but enjoyed by the greater part of the audience."

Times change.

[January 1995]

Beethoven to the Power of Nine

In Japan, an estimable guidebook informs us, Beethoven's Ninth Symphony is the end-of-the-year music of choice, even ahead of "Auld Lang Syne" in public affection. "Concert performances are held everywhere," we are told, "and many amateur singers look forward to singing in these choruses. This can probably be a phenomenon peculiar to Japan."

I would hope so. Considering the implacable demands the choral writing in the fourth movement imposes upon its singers—the curdling chromatic lines for tenors at the start, the sopranos cranked up for ten throat-stretching bars of repeated high As later on—a worldwide outbreak of amateur-society Ninths around New Year's Day (or any other time) could only result in an epidemic of nosebleeds. Shed a tear, furthermore, for the agony visited upon parents of all those amateur singers shanghaied into participating in this avalanche of holiday Ninths. They sit there for something like fifty minutes of Beethoven's fist-shaking *orchestral* music before their loved ones onstage ever get to open their mouths with Beethoven's famous tune; is that any way to share the joys of the New Year's holiday? (Strange, isn't it, how many of classical music's Top 10—*Messiah*, Tchaikovsky's First Piano Concerto, *Also sprach Zarathustra*, and the Beethoven Ninth, say—derive their fame from episodes that take up only a tiny percentage of their full length.)

Yet the Ninth deserves its place in the pantheon of music's most honored icons. Its appearance on an orchestra's schedule is almost always as a special event: the start of the season—as with the Los Angeles Philharmonic next week—or as a reflection of some larger event. A year ago, having been accorded honorary sacredness for the day, it shared the Hollywood Bowl stage with the Dalai Lama in the Festival of Sacred Music. Its mighty brass served as Joshua's trumpets to help blow down the Berlin Wall, with a new text for the vocal forces in the finale concocted by a latter-day Joshua, Leonard Bernstein.

At the movies it has underscored one hero's madness (in *A Clockwork Orange*) and another's victory over terrorists (in *Die Hard*). It may be one of music's great liberating forces, but it has been an intimidating force as well. Anton Bruckner died at work on his Ninth Symphony. Gustav Mahler, music's most illustrious hypochondriac, was so terrified of embarking on his own Ninth Symphony that he tried to bamboozle the gods by giving it another name—*The Song of the Earth*. Its shadow even falls upon modern audio technology. The planners of the compact disc, so the story goes, used an eighty-minute Wilhelm Furtwängler recording of the Ninth as the optimum length for the new product. Be glad it wasn't the Benjamin Zander recording, which clocks in at fifty-eight.

Beethoven: The Man Who Freed Music...*Beethoven and the Voice of God* ...*Beethoven, Life of a Conqueror*: the bookshelves bulge with salivating adulations. Anyone familiar with Bach's *St. Matthew* or *St. John Passion*, Handel's *Messiah*, or Mozart's *Don Giovanni* might have problems arriving at the notion that music lay in some kind of bondage awaiting Beethoven's liberating hand. Even so, just the contrast between the real-life Beethoven the antisocial alcoholic and the genius Beethoven whose inner voices penetrated his deafness and produced the Ninth Symphony—and its eight predecessors (plus quartets, sonatas, etc.)—has raised a monumental accumulation of fact and fantasy that must needs resound in language larger than life: thus, "liberator," "messiah," "conqueror." Now approaching its own two-century mark, the Beethoven foofaraw remains grander and noisier than a comparable encrustation around any other figure in the arts before or since (Elvis possibly excepted). An early surviving review describes the Second Symphony as "a crass monster, a hideously writhing wounded dragon." It dates from 1804, and we might as well hail its uncredited Viennese author as the founder of a Beethoven industry that has continued uninterrupted ever since.

None of the above is meant, of course, as any kind of belittlement; even when winnowed out from the centuries of superheated music-appreciationese, the Ninth is one of those imponderable acts of daring that light up the artistic landscape all too seldom, sharing the top shelf with such other imponderables as Piero della Francesca's *Resurrection*, Shakespeare's *King Lear*, Mozart's *Don Giovanni*, and, yes, Beethoven's own "Eroica." The liberating-force notion can be argued; yet I don't know another work of art that so vigorously flings open a window of possibility for all the art that was to follow. The greatest testimony to the stature of the Beethoven Ninth resounds in the galaxy of later works, some of them masterworks and many not, whose direction was clearly affected by something or other that happened first in this work.

Start at the beginning. According to the classical ideal, exemplified in 104 different ways by that many Haydn symphonies or in 41 ways by Mozart, a proper symphonic first movement begins with a clear and memorable theme in a clearly defined key. Beethoven's Eighth Symphony hits you immediately, with the F majorness of its first grand, swinging tune. The Ninth, however, starts as if on some distant planet: a faint throbbing that could be in any number of keys, with a theme that takes shape somewhere out in space, one note at a time. Long after Beethoven, that way of starting a big piece of music, out in nowhereland, drenched in mystery, rumbling into shape only gradually, became entrenched in the language of high romanticism: most of Mahler, all of Bruckner, Wagner's *Ring*.

Beethoven's first theme is its own kind of miracle. It crashes in on you out of the mists of uncertainty, like the *Titanic*'s iceberg, massive and gruff. Later, it splits apart in wondrous ways: now halting and melancholy, now a horn solo like a distant benediction. Midway in the first movement, its fragments knock against one another and, with terrific energy, coalesce once more in a recapitulation both sardonic and triumphant. The interweave of counterpoints—close at hand, in the middle distance, and afar—is staggering; time and again you have to remind yourselves that all this incredible detail is the fashioning of a mortal totally and tragically deaf. At the movement's end Beethoven's incomparable theme pulls itself once more out of a mumbling, eerie blackness and flings itself against us, against the gods.

This is the greatness of the Ninth. During its creation Beethoven toyed with another kind of last movement, a purely orchestral tragedy that later became the finale of the A Minor String Quartet. The epic, tragic challenges of the first movement, he must have eventually realized, and their continuation in the demon-dances of the second movement and the fragile serenities of the third, demanded another kind of resolution. While the chorus continues to cool its heels onstage, another fierce battle rages in the orchestra as, among themselves, the players review, discuss, and reject everything they have performed in the last fifty or so minutes. It's a strange drama; confronted with, and having rejected, the fragmented reminders of the symphony's terrific opening, the demonic scherzo, and the seraphic slow movement, the orchestra falls in instead behind the simple, folkish D-major tune that, to many admirers, is *the* Beethoven Ninth, the way the "Tonight We Love" tune is *the* Tchaikovsky Concerto.

"Enough of this," the solo baritone proclaims (in Beethoven's own words), and everybody joins in a final twenty minutes of joyous, declarative, tonsil-wrecking working out of the sweet little tune, with high-flying, fatuous words by Schiller. By itself this final movement, the most famous part of the Beethoven Ninth, the part all the folks have been waiting for, is an overcomposed, clumsy essay in variation technique whose most delicious moment happens when the music stops—the colossal fart from the contrabassoon out of darkness, just before the tenor solo, after the chorus has yelled itself hoarse in the first of several climactic anticlimaxes.

If this finale has any claim to greatness, it has been ordained by what came before. In those first three movements, longer by themselves than any of Beethoven's other complete symphonies, a challenge has been thrown down: to what must then happen to bring this one work safely home, and to the directions music might take in its future. Both ways, the challenge has been handsomely met.

[September 2000]

Schubert: Finished and Unfinished

However often my ears are blessed by Schubert's Ninth Symphony, I am stirred every time by new things discovered and an uncontrollable urge to write about them. Never mind my ancient (but still readable) college thesis on Schubert's instrumental forms; never mind my faded "I Love Schubert" bumper sticker, bought long ago at the Hollywood Bowl gift shop and often drawing conspiratorial honks in traffic. Life with this one astonishing symphony is, in itself, exhilarating and self-renewing.

Most great artworks emerge from traceable sources, and produce recognizable progeny. This work, begun in 1825—Schubert's twenty-eighth year, a relatively happy time for him but only three years before his wretched death—has no such discernible bloodlines. Its outer movements struggle mightily to inflict classical structural principles upon unruly, turbulent romantic tunes; those shapes, furthermore, are colored with sounds no composer (not even Beethoven) had devised: heartrending countermelodies from the trombones in the first movement, along with some extraordinary contrapuntal clashes that give the lie to all the old bromides about Schubert's limitations, and giggling triplets from strings and winds in the last. It's possible that Brahms, who helped edit the first complete publication of Schubert's music, picked up something from the wonderfully smeary woodwind harmonies in the scherzo, but none of

Brahms's ripoffs of Schubert have anything like the naive purity of the original.

The slow movement is the crown of the work and of its power to astonish: a procession, melancholy but not funereal, interrupted from time to time with consoling, ethereal contrasting episodes, but churning forward to a point of despair—a wrenching dissonance, a silence, and then an effortful recommencement. Perhaps Schubert's hand was guided by a chain of events similar to those in the slow movement of the "Eroica"; he was never above lifting an idea or two from the Beethoven he idolized but never met. But the ceremony in Beethoven's symphony is vast and official; Schubert's is the cry of a tormented individual. There would never be another symphonic moment with its nerves so cruelly exposed—not until Mahler, eight decades later.

We'll never know what stirred Schubert to create this one work that stands so far apart from all the other miracles from his pen. Three years before he had begun another kind of romantic symphony and then set it aside with two harrowingly beautiful movements completed and a third barely sketched. He surely knew the chances so innovative a work would have in Vienna's frivolous musical society—where even Beethoven, with all his aristocratic backers, had to fight the rising popularity of Italian opera. The fate of the C Major Symphony proved Schubert right. Sure, he had had the courage this time to complete the work. But then it sat, gathering dust, until Felix Mendelssohn gave it a truncated performance more than a decade after Schubert's death.

The symphony runs long—"heavenly lengths," said Robert Schumann. Norrington's performance, which observed all repeats except at the reprise of the scherzo, ran for over an hour of wonderful, relaxed luxuriance. Other recordings I own (Wilhelm Furtwängler, George Szell, John Eliot Gardiner) bring in the work, without repeats, in about forty-seven minutes and sound rushed and trivial. Schubert's own time among us was tragically short, but he gave the best of it to his music, and we should do no less.

And Music at the Close

The man stands atop a mountain crag, looking out toward a cloud-shrouded landscape with other undefined shapes beyond. It's doubtful that Caspar David Friedrich had heard a note of Franz Schubert's music when he painted his *Voyager Contemplating a Sea of Clouds*, but his imagery is poignantly appropriate. I have copies of the painting as cover art for several of my Schubert CDs; the most telling appearance is on the disc of the work (on the Ricercar label) that scholars now know as the Tenth Symphony.

The numbering of Schubert symphonies has always driven catalogu-ers up the wall. There's no problem with the first six: youthful, exuberant works composed in the shadow of the classical masters. Then, however, the problems begin. If we count only the works Schubert himself completed, the "Great C Major" would be No. 7, and the familiar "Unfinished" would tag along as a sort of appendix. If we count the works which Schubert left in something close to performable (or, at least, rescuable) shape, No. 7 would be the four-movement work in E major that Schubert left in full but mostly unorchestrated outline; the "Unfinished" clocks in as No. 8 and the C Major as No. 9. And then there is the torso of a D-major symphony that Schubert worked on in his last few weeks, with enough filled in to link the dying, tortured, thirty-one-year-old genius to the lonely voyager in the Friedrich painting.

The manuscript turned up in a bundle of other Schubert sketches in 1978 and has been published in facsimile. Modern musicologists, among them UCLA's Robert Winter, have established the date of these pages from the manufacturer's watermarks in the paper. One of the blank staves, fur-thermore, contains some of Schubert's working-out of composition exer-cises; we know that he was taking counterpoint lessons in October 1828, mere weeks before his death. There have been a number of recent attempts to "finish" the score: the British scholar Brian Newbould, who has also produced a creditable completion of No. 7, has done the same for No. 10, although there are "holes" in the first movement that would demand a journey inside Schubert's own head to fill in properly. Neville Marriner has recorded the work as part of a Schubert box on Philips—all ten symphonies, plus a few miscellaneous sketches that Newbould has fleshed out, plus a plausible completion of the "Unfinished" that screams for reissue in this anniversary year or any other. The Ricercar disc of No. 10, conducted by Pierre Bartholomée, is still available; it includes Newbould's completion of an earlier sketch, a scherzo remarkably prophetic of the one in No. 9. A new disc on Koch International contains a fascinating and, on its own, quite moving joining of hands: *Rendering*, which works large chunks from Schubert's manuscript, including the ravishing second theme from the first movement, into an orchestral context fashioned by Luciano Berio with skill and a respect for Schubert's original thoughts that borders on awe. The new release of this work, by Christoph Eschenbach and the Houston Symphony, eloquently states its case.

It is the slow movement of Schubert's deathbed symphony that most forcefully links the composer's unfathomable visions to the romantic archetype in the Friedrich painting; it is the one movement (of the three) that can be fully reconstituted from the sketch. The B-minor landscape here is wintry; the wanderer from the end of *Die Winterreise* seems to return, stumbling through the snow, falling on ice, pursuing (or being pursued by) a phantom, a solo oboe off in the grey distances, singing its sad, elusive tune. A warm breeze sometimes blows through, a contrasting passage in the far-off key of F-sharp major, but its beauty is more painful than comforting. Visions of this kind of agonizing, tormented beauty came often to Schubert in his last year: in the adagio of the String Quintet, or the incandescent turn from bleak minor to angelic major in the slow movement of the B-flat Piano Sonata. The slow movement from this deathbed symphony astounds us; we are transported to the extreme reaches of Caspar Friedrich's vision, above all to the Gustav Mahler of the *Wayfarer* songs half a century later. (I like the way a *New York Times* critic recently described this music: not so much Schubert's foreshadowing Mahler as his "looking ahead toward Mahler remembering Schubert.")

We can never assess the force that drove Schubert in his last year—the year of the Schwanengesang songs, the Mass in E-flat, the three last piano sonatas, the String Quintet, the harrowing beauty of the F Minor Fantasy for Piano Duet—and also of that endearing, giggling trifle "The Shepherd on the Rock," which turned out to be his last completed work. Whatever the motivation, it came from an inner compulsion to create; he had long abandoned hope that posterity would discover or care about his music.

The long string of unfinished work from throughout his adult life survives to tantalize the imagination: not only the two movements of the B Minor Symphony from 1822, six years before his death, which is one of the world's authentic treasures, but another work from about the same time, in E major (Symphony No. 7), whose fully orchestrated slow introduction postulates a new romantic orchestral sound that would later ripen in the hands of Brahms. The surviving two movements of a C-major piano sonata are full of new adventure; the closing measures of the slow movement, with the harmony darting this way and that, are like nothing anyone in music had tried before. Yet Schubert laid these works aside incomplete. Had he run out of inspiration? The evidence from the completed works tells us otherwise. Had he run out of manuscript paper? Possibly; it was an expensive commodity in Vienna in the 1820s.

More likely, it was Schubert's own recognition of what he had produced that forced him to table these projects. No orchestra in uptight, conservative Vienna in 1822 could be expected to spend valuable rehearsal time on music as modern as that B Minor Symphony, with its innovative scoring for winds and its (horrors!) three trombones, all by a composer virtually unknown in high-society circles—not with all that crowd-pleasing easy-to-play Rossini around. Schubert knew this, and laid his most challenging scores aside to knock out a few piano waltzes and earn some lunch money. (Is that situation any different today—in Vienna or in Los Angeles? Funny you should ask.)

Isolation from the major performing organizations may, in fact, have had an up-side—if not for Schubert, at least for posterity. It made him the first composer in history to enjoy the luxury of creating music beyond the technique or understanding of the musical establishment of his time. Many of the works we regard today as his masterpieces didn't receive their first performances for fifty or more years after his death. Call it unjust neglect; it's just as likely, however, that the world needed that much time to catch up with him, to discover for itself the visions he had seen from that mountaintop.

[Several dates, 1986–99]

Berlioz: Thunder in Paris, Echoed Worldwide

No two works of Hector Berlioz are in any way alike; nothing from his pen resembles anyone else's music, of his time or of times to come. Mention of his music brings on images of diabolical incantations, the rattling of dry bones, and opium-induced nightmares; how, then, to explain the deep, soft musical discourse of his oratorio *L'enfance du Christ*, given so exquisitely by Esa-Pekka Salonen and the Philharmonic forces here the week before Christmas? Even to his French compatriots—in his time and in ours as well—Berlioz has always been the most unclassifiable of composers. His fame was secure in Germany, England, even Russia, long before Parisian audiences learned to sit still during his music. In Paris in 1952 I attended a series of lectures on the history of French music by the formidable teacher Nadia Boulanger, mother superior to generations of composers of all nationalities. From her eloquent evangelism I gleaned notable insights into the music of Rameau, Fauré, Debussy, Ravel, Stravinsky (!), and Milhaud; not once, however, did the name of Berlioz pass her lips.

Turn the clock back to Paris in the 1820s. (Berlioz's *Memoirs*, collected and edited by David Cairns, sets the stage eloquently.) At age twenty-four, driven by passions he had not yet learned to control or even to name, Berlioz shares in the mass astonishment of Parisians as—thunderclap after thunderclap—the city experiences its first full Shakespearian immersion with a British company ensconced for a season at the Odéon; the publication of its first French translation of *Faust*; and its first hearings of the Beethoven symphonies, led by the ardent if undertalented François-Antoine Habeneck. At all events, one familiar sight is the fiery young Berlioz, screaming out imprecations to performers, his head topped by an unruly reddish-brown thatch against which the finest barbering had been of no avail. Berlioz gains the friendship of the even younger Franz Liszt; the two sit up night after night discussing Shakespeare, Goethe, and Beethoven. Berlioz swoons under the spell of the visiting Ophelia, the Irish enchantress Harriet Smithson, and works it off by composing the *Symphonie fantastique*, which earns him his first notice by the finicky Parisian public.

This year marks the bicentennial of Berlioz's birth. The rest of the Philharmonic's observance doesn't take place until early 2004, since the orchestra has all that fancy new programming to usher it into its new abode in the last weeks of 2003. Major celebrations are scheduled all over, however; the Met has a new production of *Les Troyens* in the works; the San Francisco Opera plans a staging of *La damnation de Faust*. (Yes, I know it's a cantata, not a stage work, but if you want to see a really stunning if off-the-wall *DamFaust* staging, check out the DVD from the 1999 Salzburg Festival, on the ArtHaus label, with a Mephistophélès from Willard White that'll curl your toes.)

His music, as I was saying, doesn't resemble anyone else's. The most obvious reasons have to do with its sound. His grandiose orchestral effects are deservedly famous: the four huge bands of brass and percussion that converge for the "Tuba mirum" of the Requiem; the brass, winds, and gibberish-shouting chorus as Faust and his tormentors fall into the infernal flames; the howling of winds and unseen demons as the storm overtakes Dido and Aeneas in *Les Troyens* and causes them to fall in love. Equally amazing are the small sounds, sometimes at the far end of audibility: the radiant "Alleluia" and the concluding "Amen" sung offstage in *L'enfance du Christ*; the astonishing merging of high flutes and low trombones—with three octaves of emptiness in between that stand for a vision of eternity—again in the Requiem; the amazing moment in the *Symphonie fantastique* as woodwind-playing shepherds serenade one another from distant hilltops while four timpani harmonize in soft, haunting, menacing thunder.

Paris's most beloved music in Berlioz's time was nothing like any of this. Audiences who had taken slowly to the shock waves of the "Eroica" were even more reluctant to deal with the shaggy-haired new upstart. What they flocked to, instead, was the solid, blocky orchestrations and harmonies of Luigi Cherubini's resolutely academic grand operas and of Giacomo Meyerbeer's even emptier lyrico-historical spectacles, the spaghetti westerns of their day. This was the crowd-pleasing fare that filled seats at the Paris Opéra, while Berlioz wept as his far grander, far more deserving scores went a-begging—the stunning *Les Troyens*, which has only now come into circulation; the magnificent, still-neglected *Benvenuto Cellini*, from which only the *Roman Carnival* Overture has gained any attention.

Berlioz's harmonies, too, are like nobody else's. The guitar was the only instrument he truly mastered; the familiar image of a composer at a piano working out inspirations in full four-part harmony doesn't apply here. His chords often have one or two notes missing, which produces an interesting earthiness; listen to the mountaineer's song in *Harold in Italy*. Above all, however, the wonder of Berlioz's art lies in that supreme command of the ardent, heartrending, long melody: Romeo's soliloquy in the *Roméo et Juliette* Symphony, the merging of that tune into the Capulets' party music, and then—wonder of wonders!—the sublimity of what ensues as the lovers meet one another among Verona's dark shadows. (Find Giulini's recording with the Los Angeles Philharmonic recording if you can.)

Similar marvels form the essence of the Christmas music which began our Berlioz observance two weeks ago. *L'enfance du Christ* is one of Berlioz's smaller miracles—smaller, that is, in terms of the reduced orchestra and the disarming simplicity of much of the music. (Another of the small wonders is the chamber opera *Béatrice et Bénédict*, an elegant condensation of *Much Ado about Nothing*; pray that it's on somebody's agenda during the anniversary year.) Berlioz's text tells of the Holy Family's escape from Herod's massacre and its flight to Egypt. He tells it as a folk tale in simple, quasi-peasant language, similar to what John Adams and Peter Sellars have created, with the same dramatic context, in their *El Niño*, due here in March. Wonderful, quiet, disturbing music, it seems lit through candlelight and stained glass. That rich, earthy harmonic sense suffuses the entire work: the familiar (and weepily beautiful) Shepherds' Chorus, Mary's Lullaby, even the charming throwaway chamber music for flutes and harp.

The performance under Salonen was full of love and reverence, although I might have wished for a smaller contingent of Master Chorale members to match the somewhat cut-back orchestra. The solo group couldn't have been better: Vinson Cole's slightly reedy (and, therefore, very French-sounding) narration, Susanne Mentzer's adoring singing as Mary, and—a newcomer, at least to me—the excellent French-Swiss baritone Gilles Cachemaille in diametrically opposite roles as the evil Herod and the Ishmaelite father who offers the Holy Family shelter, and whose few lines in the latter role might just be the world's most comforting music.

[January 2003]

Schoenberg: The Best Music Composed in Los Angeles

There was a time when the world of classical music revolved around Los Angeles, when the streets of gold were trodden upon by the giants of the creative world—all of them refugees from other lands where gianthood had become dangerous. Arnold Schoenberg played tennis in Brentwood, Igor Stravinsky sipped tea in West Hollywood, Hanns Eisler's songs bemoaned the moral squalor of his adopted Hollywood, where Erich Korngold and his expatriate pals counted their handsome take-home pay from the studios. Under the warm California sun, composers waxed prolific, which is not the same as stating that they all set about producing instant masterpieces. Rather a large percentage of California's music in the time of giants was, in fact, rather small-scale, as if its creators had, indeed, succumbed to the lure of the lotos. Few of Stravinsky's California works attained the stature of, say, his *Symphony of Psalms* or *Oedipus Rex*, of his earlier time. One that came close, his *Symphony in Three Movements*, which actually incorporated bits and pieces from a failed film score, might pass muster as *almost* the best music ever composed in Los Angeles.

But Schoenberg held firm. The last of his four string quartets, which he composed here in 1937 under the patronage of the great Washington patron Elizabeth Sprague Coolidge, proved to be his chamber-music masterpiece. Sixty-six years later, it remains the strongest, the most emotionally powerful, and—yes—the best music ever composed in Los Angeles. Its musical language is not immediately lovable; the work is composed along the strict rubrics of the "technique of composing with twelve notes" that Schoenberg had formulated in Europe in the 1920s. Yet there is much to love here; its melodic materials (yes, melodic) are so strongly identified that we recognize them on every recurrence. The slow movement—deep, dark, mysterious, and yet utterly clear—takes hold. In just a few seconds short of half an hour, it takes you somewhere strange and exciting and returns you a better person.

[December 2003]

Cartesian Coordinates

Elliott Carter has been in our midst for most of this month, as a resident fellow at the Getty Institute—ostensibly to complete a number of compositions (a fifth string quartet, an orchestral work for the BBC, another for the Chicago Symphony), but also to be on hand to take bows at performances of a number of his compositions. He turned eighty-five last month, and no other American city is honoring that event as extensively as Los Angeles, where Carter has been generously feted by the enterprising EAR ("experimental and recent") Unit, the Southwest Chamber Music Society, the Philharmonic's New Music Group, and, later in the season, the Philharmonic itself. Major European music centers, he ruefully noted in one of his talks here, honor him this way all the time.

He has a point. My guess is that European new-music audiences, especially in Germany and England, find more of a kindred spirit in Carter's music—the bristling counterpoint, the intricate if usually inaudible structural details—than in most American music that makes its way across the Atlantic. His most ardent champions, at least in the last twenty years, have been European: the conductors Pierre Boulez (who conducted Carter's *Penthode* here last fall) and Oliver Knussen (who leads an all-Carter Green Umbrella concert here next week), Britain's Arditti Quartet, and the critic Andrew Porter. "If there were to be an international poll to nominate 'the greatest living composer,'" Porter wrote in the *New Yorker* in 1979, "Carter's name would lead all the rest."

If the "greatest living composer" is the one most skilled in the manipulation of materials, most eloquent at writing about the inner workings of an extended composition—the way theme A, when played upside down and backward, generates themes B, C, and D—so that scholars and journalists can report on these processes for page upon page while sidestepping such "alien" concepts as beauty of expression and communication, then Carter probably merits all of the praise flung his way. Reading, in Carter's notes for the Double Concerto on next week's Umbrella concert, that "the antiphonal groups are partially separated musically by the fact that each emphasizes its own repertory of melodic and harmonic intervals" and that "each of these intervals is associated...with a certain metronomic speed" is enough to strike fear into any listener hoping to uncover the basis for Carter's "greatness" in the sound of the music itself. What happens, we are entitled to ask, when we cannot detect these processes when we listen? Do we fail the test for the Elliott Carter merit badge, doomed to a lifetime admiring the clear structural processes of Mozart?

The Southwest program at the Pasadena Presbyterian Church ended with the first local hearing of Carter's Quintet for Piano and Winds, coupled on the program with Mozart's masterpiece for the same instrumentation. Even in a shaky, uncoordinated performance, the Mozart shamed the Carter utterly. Into one ear went the sublime understanding of the way a single instrumental melody or a loving conversation among instruments can wring the heart; into the other went twenty minutes of fuzz and squall. The EAR Unit concert at the County Museum, all of it wondrously played, began with early Carter—the Cello Sonata of 1948 and the Sonata for Flute, Oboe, Cello, and Harpsichord from 1952—graceful, eclectic works (neoclassical, Stravinskian, even somewhat jazzy), designed to charm and successful at it. It ended with the Triple Duo of 1983, dense, abstruse, and bloodless. ("Riveting," wrote Porter.)

There is, I admit, something irresistible in the sheer intellectual content such works as the First Quartet, from the early 1950s (which the Southwest plays this weekend), and, above all, in the astonishing, complex density of the 1961 Double Concerto due at next Monday's

Umbrella. That concert, all Carter, begins with the Cello Sonata and also includes the 1981 song cycle *In Sleep, in Thunder*, a memorial to the poet Robert Lowell. You may find yourselves wondering how Carter's path led from the open-handed expressivity of the Cello Sonata to the dry, point-by-point dissection of Lowell's poetry, with the bristle and scratch of the Double Concerto along the way.

Carter hasn't disowned his early works, which also include a powerful and genuinely expressive Piano Sonata that several adventurous pianists are now taking up. (Among them is the excellent local pianist Scott Dunn, who played it at an invitational concert last week.) Just the opposite, in fact; in a discussion at the New York premiere of the Triple Duo, Carter suggested that increasing familiarity with his early works should make the newer works more approachable, more openly expressive. He described the succession of his works as "the wish to constantly explore more vivid ways of presenting the musical vision in all its freshness." Maybe so for him, but not for me.

[January 1994]

THE OLD

It was Noah Greenberg and his New York Pro Musica, back in the 1950s, who first spread news of the spark of life in music before Bach, of the joy in Josquin and the laughs in Landini. Maybe his message went too far; somehow the over-interpretation of the arcane scribblings of the Holy Hildegard bears some resemblance to those who detect the visage of the Virgin in a tortilla. Yet the Long Beach Opera brings Monteverdi operas to life set among a motorcycle gang, and a heroic impresario named MaryAnn Bonino plants some of the world's finest early-music interpreters—Anonymous 4, say, or the Tallis Scholars—in latter-day Los Angeles church buildings and transports our souls. I call what she does a class act, and she's been producing these concerts of Chamber Music in Historic Sites now for thirty years. Tell me about fly-by-night California culture!

Chants: The Religious Rite and Wrong

The game of chants is on, and the stakes are high. You walk into one of those Grand Canyon–sized disc emporiums up on Sunset, steeled against the usual aural assault as the aficionados gather around the stereo and gibber on the relative merits of one Allan Pettersson symphony versus another (there are none) or of Maria Callas before and after the weight loss. Now, instead, all is tranquil, even chill; over the mile upon mile of display racks there wafts the evening prayers of monks in some Iberian backwater, or the quietly ecstatic visions, going on 1000 years old, of the Blessed Hildegard von Bingen. You take in the sounds of salvation, aware that Holy Trinity for the 1990s consisted of an entente between God and the record producers, and that this is the stuff—no longer the Beethoven symphonies or the *Amadeus* soundtrack—that makes it to the charts these days: classical, crossover, even Christian. To talk of *Carmina Burana* currently is to evoke not Carl Orff's monster chorale, produced for the delectation of Hitler and his pals, but the original medieval songs and dances unearthed in some Bavarian monastery and sung to authentic shawms and sackbuts. Peace: it's wonderful; it's also ambient. Chill along with Hildegard.

You can trace this newly hatched passion for the ancient musical arts as far back as you care—to candlelight soirees in the 1930s, for example, when the soft, sweet sounds of Safford Cape and his Belgian Pro Musica Antiqua dispensed the doctrine that anything very old was also very fragile. In the 1950s there was rebuttal, in the joyous outbursts of Noah Greenberg's New York Pro Musica, which dug up medieval religious plays and Renaissance motets and performed them as if all that early stuff might possibly be fun—to sing and to hear. At a time when much of life revolved around potted Tchaikovsky on Muzak, the crystalline sounds of Guillaume de Machaut's polyphony or John Dunstable's fauxbourdon provided a refuge for the ears and the soul. When Greenberg produced the twelfth-century *Play of Daniel* in an appropriate setting at the Cloisters in Manhattan, it became the second hottest ticket in town, right after *My Fair Lady*. Greenberg died in 1966, but his musicians continued his advocacy; several of his disciples now play in the Waverly Consort, which comes through here every so often.

Skip ahead. The early-music passion seems to have flared up again with the advent of the CD in the early 1980s. England produced the Tallis Scholars and the Hilliard Ensemble; Spain had Jordi Savall's Hespérion XX; the United States could claim Sequentia, based in New York and Cologne, and the Boston Camerata. A pardonable misconception justified the work of these diverse ensembles (as it had Noah Greenberg's a generation before): the notion that even music meant for private prayer or church service could somehow also stand on its own as a concert experience. One thing exonerated the intrusion into the private precincts of faith: the fact that these ancient chants and counterpoints were often extremely beautiful, or at least could be made so in respectful performances.

And then came Hildegard von Bingen, poet, mystic, abbess of a women's religious commune—and composer. To compose in the early twelfth century meant to create single melodic lines, whose distinctiveness was limited by the restrictions of the style. Rightfully noted in church annals for her steamy descriptions of apocalyptic visions, Hildegard figured hardly at all in music history—she went unmentioned in any of the standard texts—until an ecstatic entry in the 1980 *New Grove Dictionary* restored her to world awareness. The timing was right. The reborn Hildegard was the answer to contemporary prayers: a figure of high intellectual stature, an author of texts of strong visionary appeal, a woman composer of more than minimal competence writing music intended to be sung by women (the eighteen nuns of her own convent in the Rhineland town of Bingen).

The floodgates opened. The first Hildegard recording, released on Hyperion in 1982, bore the alluring title *A Feather on the Breath of God*, which happened to be one of Hildegard's several ways of describing herself. It enlisted the services of such early-music heroines as the angelic-voiced Emma Kirkby, and it sold and sold. So did ensuing discs, many by the excellent Sequentia, which lost its collective heart to Hildegard sometime around 1985. "Would Hildegard be such a commodity if she were a dead European white male?" asks the CalArts choral conductor Paul Vorwerk. The answer comes loud and clear, in the comparative sales of Sequentia's Hildegard discs versus the group's dozen or so recordings of far more interesting medieval repertory.

None of this pretty, pretty music made any pretense toward authenticity, of course—toward recreating the composer's sounds exactly as conceived. The blurred and inconclusive manuscripts of Hildegard's time and centuries afterward require modern interpretive decisions as to tempo, rhythm, even pitch. The latter-day record-biz evangelists tarted up Hildegard's primitive single vocal lines by adding instruments and extra voices, even an occasional harmony. It sounded archaic, even when it sounded wrong. There was no stopping her; she made it to the charts and to KCRW's "Morning Becomes Eclectic," where the slender, angelic tones of her music paved the way for that program's later love affair with the spacey religious minimalism of Henryk Górecki's Third Symphony and of Arvo Pärt, 800 years newer than Hildegard's music but in many ways similar.

Hildegard's destiny also befell her churchly brethren. Some months later the monks in the Benedictine abbey of Santo Domingo, near the small Spanish village of Silos, joined their bionic sister on the medieval parade of hits. The well-named Angel records produced a disc called, simply, *Chant*, a program of Gregorian chant—the liturgy of the Roman church. which was maybe or maybe not assembled (according to what you read) in the sixth or eighth century at the instigation of a couple of popes who may or may not have been named Gregory, but which in any case was formalized and published around 1000 A.D. There had been Gregorian recordings before, some by the Silos gang in their echoey, hooty style ("musically distrait and slapdash," wrote Berkeley's gadfly musicologist Richard Taruskin in the *New York Times*) and still available on Deutsche Grammophon budget discs. Angel's release is a single-disc condensation of a two-disc set on Hispavox that sold a quarter of a million copies in Spain, gussied up with fancy cover art and enough echo-chamber remastering to transport your ears to the high altar of St. Peter's. It's not a patch on the Tallis Scholars' elegant, dedicated Gregorian disc of a few years back, called *Sarum Chant*, on the Scholars' own Gimell label. Guess which of the two discs has gone platinum.

Like the Hildegard discs of a few years back, *Chant* was a matter of the right sound at the right time. "There's a New-Age kind of connection," Paul Vorwerk suggests. "Many of the people who buy Gregorian Chant may 'listen' to it in the same way they listen to recordings of birdsongs and surf, to elevate their consciousness or put them in the appropriate space." The juicy new remastering helped, of course, as did the accompanying leaflet, which raised the concept of sanctimoniousness to heights hitherto unscaled. However the marketing of *Chant* may have distanced itself from the sounds of serious liturgy, it has extended the blessing of the Almighty upon the ambience scene.

"I don't mind that people are 'chilling out' to chant," said the medieval scholar MaryAnn Bonino, whose Chamber Music in Historic Sites series has given Los Angeles more early-music events than any ten impresarios you can name anywhere else:

> How nice it would be to imagine that millions of people were listening to this music with some kind of cognitive understanding. What really bothers me about the chant phenomenon is its affinity with the

New Age, supermarket spirituality, the religious equivalent of dress-for-success, chant on the charts. It's a shame, because even unbelievers can experience its genuine spiritual dimension, can be moved not only by the musical beauty of chant but also by an accumulation of spirit that accompanies it.

The late Joseph Spencer, who ran Berkeley's Musical Offering, a record store–*cum*–café–*cum*–performance space (a class act if ever one was), sadly concurred. "Discussions with record company people invariably concentrate on the saleability aspect, while we who have loved this music for many years may squirm a bit. We are uncomfortable with profitability. But before we get too condescending and self-righteous about it, let's remember the real mission: to spread the beginnings of an appreciation of old music among those who have known only pop forms."

Does it work? You decide. Here is a quick overview of the current hottest "chill-out" items, over a range from great to ghastly, sacred to profane. None of them are likely to stir vibrations among the Religious Right as more recently defined; this is one area of contemporary culture that is unlikely to draw their attention or their scorn. Thank heaven for that, at least.

Gregorian

Chant (Angel): The Benedictine Monks of Santo Domingo de Silos in their sexy, smudgy singing style, their disc still high up on the Billboard 200, now joined not far below by a new Christmas collection. A mail-order catalog from something called the Music Stand lists this as "America's Newest Pop Music Phenomenon" and offers a sweatshirt with a Gregorian manuscript emblazoned on the front.

Eternal Chant (Atlantic): Three discs, handsomely packaged, with the formidable Taruskin as annotator. The performances, mostly splendid, are from several monasteries in the south of France, recorded on the French "Studio SM" label between 1960 and 1992. Three hours of Gregorian isn't what you want to contemplate in one wad, but the arrangement of materials on the three discs has been intelligently planned.

Chantmania (Rhino): It had to happen. The seven "Benzedrine Monks from Santo Domonica" inflict a Gregorian style on "The Monkees' Theme," "We Will Rock You," etc., ending with "The Monks' Vow of Silence" (pure John Cage). Ben Bagby, co-founder of Sequentia, tells me that their manner of singing is pure, authentic Gregorian.

Tampering

Officium (ECM): Britain's superlative Hilliard Ensemble, whose Old *Hall Manuscript* disc on EMI is one of the high points of the repertory, sings chant and early counterpoint, and Jan Garbarek's tenor and alto saxophones weave an ecstatic improv counterpoint in and around their work. The spirit survives; this is an example of the enlightened opening up of ancient treasures.

Vision (EMI): And this is the exact opposite: a conflation of some of Hildegard's pretty songs with the generic sounds of synthesizer, drums, and some modern instruments played by Richard Souther. The singer, Emily van Evera, was on the *Feather on the Breath of God* disc; the booklet shows some of Hildegard's psychedelic paintings and her famous cures. But the final product has little to do with either the real or the imagined Hildegard. It's just a trashy exploitation venture in the tradition of musical hype.

Hildegard, Etc.

Canticles of Ecstasy (Deutsche Harmonia Mundi): Sequentia's extended Hildegard homage in their Complete Works of...series. It's more of the same, the music imaginatively spread out for superb, dedicated modern voices, artfully sidestepping the ongoing controversy as to the authenticity of the music or its historical value.

Love's Illusion (French Harmonia Mundi): the four women who call themselves Anonymous 4 (after an unnamed medieval journalist!) lend their marvelously pure voices and impeccable style to yet another milestone in the annals of "women's" music, a thirteenth-century codex that superimposes love lyrics atop fragments of chant, better in the hearing than the telling.

Codex Las Huelgas (Deutsche Harmonia Mundi): Sequentia again, performing works from a medieval manuscript of chants and sacred songs from the Cistercian Convent at Las Huelgas de Burgos in Spain, full of extraordinarily moving music—laments, rejoicings, and prayers—produced by the ensemble of solo and conjoined singers in a manner to wring your heart.

Next?

Now that Atlantic Records has scored with the Three Tenors and now with three discs of Gregorian chant, nothing remains but a melding of their resources: The Tenors Go Gregorian. They could call it "Fat Chants."

[December 1995]

Anonymous 4: Past Pluperfect

For anyone given to living in the past, February was a month full of rewards. It began with two programs by Anonymous 4 presented by UCLA at the United Methodist Church in Westwood, continued with the Hilliard Ensemble at Ambassador, and ended with Paul Hillier's Theater of Voices at St. Basil's. While the fashioners of the grand noise busied themselves in larger halls with Dvořák and Sibelius, here was balm for the ears and the spirit.

What do we get from listening to music six or seven centuries old, set to harmonies lacking the drive and logic known to us in, say, Bach's musical language; to archaic poetry dense with impenetrable symbolism, small-scale and lacking the cumulative dramatic urgency we find in a Beethoven symphony? The very strangeness of the music is one attraction. The program by Anonymous 4—four women who take their name from a medieval scribe whose writings are a trove of information about the times—was a case in point. It bore the title "Love's Illusion" and was the second of the two the group gave—the first conflicted with the Music Center's *Pelléas*, an agonizing choice—consisting of chivalric love songs from medieval France. The range of dissonance in this pretonal music would have driven an audience out to the streets if it had been billed as the latest from Karlheinz Stockhausen. Instead, it hit the ears like an icy restorative shower of fantastic musical invention.

The level of contrivance is, in itself, wonderful in some of this very old music. Again in the Anonymous 4 concert, several of the pieces were compounded out of a daring kind of counterpoint: one or two texts of secular poetry sung simultaneously, while a third line presented the notes, widely spaced out, of a fragment of Gregorian chant. All three (or sometimes even four) lines worked together on a musical basis as a dense contrapuntal conflation. They also worked together in that the lines of poetry were interrelated: the upper parts seemed to comment upon one another and upon the text of the bit of chant in the lower parts as well.

I have no interest in arguing whether any or all of these concerts were "authentically" performed; such arguments at this late date make no more sense than the angels-on-a-pin controversy. All three groups performed with splendid clarity, a fine sense of how ancient Latin, French, and English might have been pronounced, and, above all, a realization of the beauty of their music that came into every sound. The additional assurance that in the remarkable choral works of Tavener and Pärt something of this ancient spirit has been captured and translated into contemporary visions bodes well for the next thousand or so years of music.

All three concerts drew good crowds; even though most of what Anonymous 4 sang is on their Harmonia Mundi disc, people know that hearing their music, even the secular songs, in a church just seems right and this was the right place. The Theater of Voices, led by Paul Hillier, who also founded the Hilliard Ensemble some years back—apologies for this tangle of names!—sang in St. Basil's downtown (also sold out), where the visual dualism between the Gothic design and Franco Assetto's earthy Stations of the Cross bas-reliefs uncannily reflected the contrast of archaic (Palestrina and Tallis) and contemporary neo-archaic (John Tavener and Arvo Pärt) on the program. Trust MaryAnn Bonino and her Historic Sites series to get the right music into the right place.

The Hilliard at Ambassador Auditorium—four British guys singing Renaissance madrigals and part-songs, elegantly and wittily—drew less well. There was something wrong about the setting this time;

Ambassador's glitz—not to mention the fundamentalism of its Church of God management, which forbade any sacred music on the program—set the soul in conflict with the ear. (The Hilliard had wanted to present their wonderful *Officium* program with Jan Garbarek's saxophone improv, which still graces the charts. "Not on our stage, or any other in these parts," said Ambassador, invoking its exclusivity rights. We rightly mourn the closing of the auditorium, but not the passing of its management.)

[March 1994]

Machaut: 700 Years Old, Still Cool

If I tell you that my favorite disc of recent months contains over an hour's worth of three-minute bursts of the same kind of music, seven centuries old and built on principles in no way related to anything else in our repertory experience, you may want to change stations...but wait! Know first that the disc is on ECM, one of the more trustworthy of surviving classical labels, and that the performers are the Hilliard Ensemble, that lively and questing group—countertenors, tenors, baritone—whose lust for stylistic exploration is apparently boundless. Here they sing a collection of motets by the fourteenth-century poet, philosopher, musician, and churchman Guillaume de Machaut, music whose strange, distant beauty is much enhanced by the typical ECM treatment: haunting, softly echoey sound that bespeaks the cold stones of the small Austrian church that their microphones have resanctified, and the dark, mysterious distances in the accompanying booklet's artwork. There aren't many class acts left in the recording industry; ECM, along with Nonesuch and Harmonia Mundi, bravely holds the fort.

The Machaut motet is a different concoction from the polyphonic motets of Palestrina and his Renaissance pals. It is a form built up in layers, sung simultaneously. The low voice (tenor, from *tenere*, to hold) sings a very short text, maybe just a couple of words, in long, sustained notes. A higher voice above him (the motetus) sings a much faster melody, with words that relate to the tenor's text. A third voice (the triplum) sings faster still, with a third text again related to the other two. In the first Machaut motet in the ECM collection the tenor's entire text is "I sigh"; the motetus begins "with sighing, suffering heart," and the triplum has what amounts to a whole sermon on what to do when you fall in love. This all creates a hopeless jumble of text, of course, and you have to wonder whether Machaut or any of his numerous colleagues had any interest in having this music performed, or whether these pieces were more like philosophical designs set to music. Many of the motets have religious connotations; some will have a hymn of praise to the Virgin Mary in the lower voices, coupled with a fairly carnal encomium in the upper voice to the girl next door.

But then there's the music. As I listened the other night a friend asked if this was Arvo Pärt; he was off by 700 years, but right on as well. We cannot, of course, hear this music with fourteenth-century ears, but the weight of history can be a marvelous enablement for discovering a whole new level of freshness in this music. Is it so wrong to hear Arvo Pärt or Bartók or Charles Ives in the cross-references and false cadences in Machaut? It would be equally wrong to hear this music as any kind of primitive, to miss the high level of poetic daring in the textual or musical crossovers, the sheer beauty in the sinuous melodic lines. This is a hypnotic, stupendous disc.

On NPR last week a music guy told *Talk of the Nation*'s Neal Conant that he uses these motets—along with Peruvian tribal chants and other assorted exotica—as "buttons" between news items on *All Things Considered*. Things being what they are in classical music these days, we take what we can get.

[April 2004]

Landini: Time Traveling

Happily adrift in the enchanting pseudo-Renaissance fakery of UCLA's Powell Library, my ears coddled and cozened by the authentic Renaissance harmonies of Francesco Landini's music interspersed with the raptures of Dante's poetry, I beheld my own kind of vision. It revealed to me the golden message that some things very old in years are actually very new in spirit.

Landini and Dante, the musician-poet and the poet-musician: the one reached beyond the agony of blindness to shape musical forms exactly the color of their poetry; the other translated the agony of love's rejection into words as close to music as music ever gets. Anonymous 4, in one of the Da Camera Society's bewitching Historic Sites events, filled the evening with the high art of their time: fifteen of Landini's *ballate*—songs mostly above love's joys, love's torments—alternating with short readings from *La vita nuova*, Dante's account of his early love for the fragile and unattainable Beatrice. Perhaps neither composer nor poet envisioned his words and his music sung by four women to large audiences, in rhythms and pitches exactly fixed by serious musicology and a vibrance that accomplished a blend of the antiquarian and the high-spirited contemporary; these men's times didn't always call for optimism. The best early-music ensembles of today, a group to which Anonymous 4 definitely belongs, make of their chosen fields of specialization an entertainment so joyous, so contemporary—and yet so honest, in the best sense—that years and dates and footnotes in dusty tomes no longer matter.

A great wave swept through the music of the fourteenth century. Composers in the great cathedrals had found ways to enhance the chants of the liturgy with all kinds of interesting harmonic devices: two or three lines sung simultaneously but with different texts, or the almost dance-like virtuosity of the counterpoints composed at Nôtre-Dame in Paris. Then the pope stamped his papal foot, church music was ordered back to its pristine one-line-at-a-time chastity, and even the most devout composers went over to the secular side. The 150 or so surviving love songs of Landini (c. 1335–1397) detail the shape of that wave, from the austere expanse of the first works to what we begin to recognize as the early stirrings of classical harmonies in the mature songs. Dante instilled the human heart into his poetry; Van Eyck's *Adoration of the Magi* revealed the way to create perspective on a flat painted surface; Landini's harmonies brought passion into music. Early or late, for a single voice or four voices intertwined, what still amazes us in his wonderful repertory is the closeness in mood between the tunes and the poetry they enhance—most of it by authors whose names no longer exist. Half a millennium before the flowering of art song in the hands of Schubert, that same sensitivity guided another pen to other kinds of music. Anonymous 4, by the way, has recorded this Landini garland on a Harmonia Mundi disc called *The Second Circle*.

[March 2002]

Let's Hear It for Ockeghem

Listening to very old music demands a confrontation on shaky ground between the imaginations of the long-dead composer and the presumably living listener. However pious the press releases may read on the subject of "authentic performance practice as the composer might have heard it half a millennium ago," the impression is inescapable that an interlock of artificialities is in operation. There is no way that today's performance of, say, a mass by Johannes Ockeghem can be made to resemble what the composer had in mind—let alone what he was able to extract from whatever amateur choral forces his church might have been able to afford. We wouldn't like it if it did; over five centuries, ears and expectations change.

Instead, our ears are bathed in a thoroughly modern contrivance: the richness of medieval and Renaissance repertory newly repainted to fit today's conception of past practices: not the Parthenon of Athens, but the ripoff in Nashville. In the last couple of weeks we've been visited by excellent early-music specialists whose performances, besides being gorgeous to hear, bore some cachet as "authentic" or that more satisfactory epithet "historically informed," time machines devised for escorting latter-day throngs back through olden times in mellow modern comfort. The British group Magnificat made its local debut performing sixteenth-century Spanish polyphony in a church setting—vaguely Spanish, vaguely Renaissance—built in 1923. A week later came four women of the hot-ticket New York ensemble Anonymous 4, along with the six men of the group Lionheart, performing a complete mass service by Ockeghem in UCLA's Royce Hall—a secular venue inspiring secular behavior. (Despite an appeal in the printed program, some in the audience succumbed to the need to break the continuity with applause every three or four minutes, thus widening the gap between listening to music circa 1999 and inventing music in the time of Columbus.)

Two major Renaissance figures, born 130 or so years apart, formed the substance of these programs: Magnificat sang music of Spain's Tomás Luis de Victoria (1549–1611) and his countrymen: dark, passionate, sideslipping into passages of the startling dissonance we tend to ascribe to Gesualdo. Anonymous 4 and Lionheart labored on behalf of Ockeghem (1410–1497). Together, these two sublime composers form the bookends for the century that saw man and God sharing the composer's worktable and turning out music that told what the world needed to know about both.

Ockeghem is the "where-has-he-been-all-my-life" of my recent years. Not a note of his existed on records during my student years in Berkeley, so we were left unaware of his existence. Like Monteverdi, Beethoven, and, arguably, Mahler, he straddles a major musical upheaval, from the chaotic mannerisms of the early fifteenth century to the infusion of triadic harmonies and sweet, shapely melody as the century neared its close. At Royce there was the music of Ockeghem's *Missa Mi-Mi* with others of his works inserted as they would be in a church service. The flow of expressive devices—strings of first-inversion triads called fauxbourdon that sound as if the had been born long ago in a distant galaxy; wrenching shifts of harmony; beautifully spaced-out counterpoint games (a tune sung in one voice against its mirror image in another)— is astounding enough; the sheer beauty of the music is beyond description. Ockeghem's music is somewhat recent for the usual tendencies of Anonymous 4 and their "brother" ensemble; it could be that this venture into new repertory—or the rude applause—brought on the occasional unsettled-sounding passage at Royce that afternoon. At the end there was the lament on Ockeghem's death by his most illustrious pupil, Josquin Desprez (1450–1521), music that seemed to capture the breath of anyone within earshot and the surrounding air as well.

[May 1999]

Monteverdi's *Ulysses*

The program book for the Los Angeles Opera's magnificent staging of Monteverdi's *Return of Ulysses* strikes a defensive tone at times: Glen Wilson's musical edition "will doubtless come as a surprise," and there is an apologetic bow "to listeners wanting more variety." It's a preemptive strike, in other words, at an audience expected to rise up in protest over being denied the usual warm soup of Puccini sound. Yes, the audience did rise up at the two performances I've seen so far, but only to cheer the glories of the performance and to inform the company's timid leadership that there is still room for entertainment that engages both the gut and the mind.

It's late in the day to plead the cause of baroque opera. The Long Beach Opera has delivered excellent and acclaimed productions of the three extant Monteverdi operas along with Purcell's Dido and Aeneas. The Los Angeles Opera had a smashing success with one Handel opera (*Xerxes*, gorgeously produced) and a fair success with another (*Alcina*, in the company's first season). *Ulysses*, written in 1640, had its first modern publication in 1922. Three years later that dreariest of French academics, Vincent d'Indy, produced a performing edition for full d'Indy-size orchestra; I can only shudder. There were later versions; Glen Wilson's edition, which he prepared for the 1990 Netherlands Opera production—ecstatically received, several times revived, seen at the Brooklyn Academy of Music and now here—comes closest yet to what survives of Monteverdi's conception.

The legend about this repertory, that Monteverdi's surviving manuscripts represent only a skeleton of his intention, needs a new version as well. Our expectation from classical and romantic operas, of singing surrounded by orchestral support, still lay at far horizons in 1640. Monteverdi's *Orfeo* of 1607 had called for a large gathering of instruments, but these were used mostly between the vocal numbers to create atmosphere—the mass of solemn brass sonority to usher in the scene in Hades, for example. But *Orfeo* was produced under special circumstances in the lavishly endowed Mantuan court, which could afford a full roster of instrumentalists. In Venice Monteverdi wrote for smaller forces, which were all that box office–supported theaters could afford. (*Plus ça change*....) The singers were supported only by the continuo—harpsichord, lute, organ, perhaps a bass viola da gamba—which supplied the bass line and, therefore, the harmony. The orchestra—here, a splendid group of strings, lutes, and a couple of recorders from Michael Eagan's Musica Angelica, discreetly amplified—plays in the intervening interludes and a few dance-like moments. To Monteverdi the most important thing was the words and the passions they represented; an orchestra between those words and the audience would serve as an extraneous, audible scrim. At one moment in the current production Glen Wilson does introduce orchestral tone around a singer; it comes at the crucial moment, when Ulysses describes to Penelope the coverlet over their bed (which only he could know about), and thus breaks through her disbelief that he is who he claims to be. A soft halo of low string tone surrounds his words, resolving three hours of operatic conflict in a most electrifying way.

Wilson, along with the director Pierre Audi, has cut the score rather drastically but not fatally. One whole dimension has been removed: the council of the Olympic gods, where the outraged Neptune—whose son Polyphemus Ulysses had blinded—argues bitterly against a happy resolution. (Jupiter is missing, but at least his eagle is not. A remarkable creature named Marimba shows up on cue to strike terror into the treacherous gang of suitors and to earn the evening's only intruding burst of applause.) Absent this council, which near the opera's end determines to prolong Penelope's grief even after Ulysses' return, you might think that her reluctance to accept a happy ending suggests that she has actually been enjoying her twenty-year lamentations, an explanation that Oprah might sanction but not necessarily Homer.

I've gone on at length about this opera because of its extraordinary beauty, which has been matched by this performance. Even though no opera had existed before his time, Monteverdi came to his art with a full awareness of what the solo voice could accomplish, the taut unity that words, melody, and harmony could achieve. His vocal lines are sinuous and enchanting; they move from arialike tunefulness to agitated recitative with the ease of human speech transfigured to a higher level of eloquence and richly colored from a broad harmonic palette. One moment of many resounds in my head as I write this: a trio of rejected suitors sings of love and of sighing while Monteverdi moves the harmony down a slithering chromatic scale. The startled listeners look at one another almost in disbelief. Think of the eerie, haunting music we hear as Wotan puts his beloved Brünnhilde to sleep; it's unlikely that Wagner heard a note of Monteverdi in his lifetime, yet at such moments they are indisputably linked. "Sì, sì, sì," the reunited couple sing to each other (as sang Molly Bloom to herself in yet another *Ulysses*), and the opera simply ends; no big orchestral blam, no grand finale. Is there another operatic ending so simple, so haunting, so right?

I've left myself scant space to exult over the Penelope of Frederica von Stade, the one "heavy" role she has taken on (and currently owns) after all the airy-fairy delights of her Cherubinos and Rosinas; the splendid, strong Ulysses of Thomas Allen; the iridescent elegance of Paula Rasmussen's Minerva, John Duykers's Clown, and a supporting cast with nary a blemish. Glen Wilson's musical direction is sure and responsive. He has the good sense not to "conduct" (in the sense of throwing cues to singers) but instead molds a plastic, energetic performance that respects the music's own momentum. And I've no space left for the look of the production: Pierre Audi's insinuating, intelligent direction, Michael Simon's stageful of abstract shapes, in which the visual plasticity becomes an exact mirror of the music, Jean Kalman's lighting design, which confers an ultimate radiance. In this altogether splendid evocation of opera's legendary past, our company offers a compelling view of what the art can (or did I hear a "should"?) be like in the future.

[March 1998]

Morimur: Is There Sex after Bach?

Morimur is up there on the charts, the latest implausible release from ECM, one of the few remaining labels to turn implausibility into solid musical virtue—and perhaps into a few euros along the way. The title is something Latin about dying, and the message from the disc is that thoughts about dying were the principal fuel for J. S. Bach's phenomenal creative energy. A German scholar named Helga Thoene has discovered tunes—or, let's say, melodic turns of phrase—in Bach's secular music that also turn up in some of his sacred chorales. Therefore, Dr. Thoene would have us believe, some of these secular works, specifically the famous D Minor Partita for solo violin, with its implausibly beautiful chaconne, fairly bristle with secret messages. This partita, she points out, was published in 1720, the year that Bach's first wife, Maria Barbara, died. Therefore, we must regard the work as some kind of elegy. We must, of course, look beyond the fact that some of the other works in that same published set of solo violin works are downright jolly.

On the new disc the violinist Christoph Poppen delivers the chaconne in a rather juicy manner that might set proponents of historically informed performances to dark mutterings. Then the Hilliard Ensemble, the splendid British quartet of astonishingly wide repertory, sings a selection of Bach's chorale settings, including the poignant "Christ lag im Todesbanden" from a Good Friday cantata; these are interspersed with Poppen's playing of the other movements from the partita. Then we get the chaconne again, this time with chorale melodies woven into—or perhaps pushed up against—the violin solos. The whole thing is very sad, very deep, and, I have to admit, damned irresistible; the acoustical setting, in an echoey Austrian monastery, enhances the effect.

It is also, I regret to inform you, very fraudulent. Perhaps it doesn't seem that way in the context of its companions on the aforementioned charts: Andrea Bocelli, Charlotte Church, and a newcomer (to me, at least), Russell Watson, whose vibrato nearly knocked my stereo off the shelf. The process of imposing veils of sexy romantic sadness across well-meaning baroque creations goes way back: the Pachelbel Canon (a legitimate small piece made morose in unscrupulous performances), the Albinoni Adagio (a pseudo-archaic piece of nineteenth-century fakery), and, of course, all the rainbow bridges from Bach to Wagner created by Leopold Stokowski's orchestrations of organ works, choruses, even the long-suffering chaconne.

Yes, there are points of resemblance between some of the minor-key chorales and articulations in the chaconne and countless other instrumental works. Tune detectives can have a fine time tracking these down from one work to another, and when they've finished they can link arms with the people who find the face of Jesus in the burn marks on tortillas. There was a vocabulary of turns of phrase in Bach's time, as in Mozart's and beyond; composers knew them, and the best composers knew what to do with them. In order to make this work some of the chorales had to be transposed to fit the D minorness of the partita. That in itself violates an important baroque principle, wherein particular keys take on particular personalities. Don't get me going on this, or I'll put you all to sleep.

At violinist Andrew Manze's splendid recital last week, one of the Historic Sites events, a Bach sonata began with a close relative of the "Erbarme dich" melody from the *St. Matthew Passion*. Bach ripping off Bach? Secret message? Or merely a sublime composer drawing upon the musical language of his own time and celebrating its infinite variety?

[November 2001]

Bach at Carmel

Old J. S. Bach, in his infinite variety, took over my ears these past few days. On Tuesday of last week they were laid siege to by his best-known organ work, blown up into Hollywood Bowl–sized proportions. My week ended at the Carmel Bach Festival, culminating with the *St. John Passion* in a vivid, powerful "authentic" performance to engage both hearts and minds.

Many of us past a certain age first learned about Bach through the romanticized distortions inflicted by certain self-proclaimed "experts." The harpsichordist Wanda Landowska (a.k.a. "The Bach Auntie") began her career playing Chopin on the piano, then brought the worst aspects of the Chopin style—the roller-coaster rubato, the oh-so-expressive stops and starts—to what we were made to believe was the "authentic" instrument for Bach. Albert Schweitzer played and recorded Bach's organ music on the groaning and moaning French organs that had served César Franck. When I started collecting records, in the 1940s, there were only two Bach cantatas available, recorded by a huge church choir in Barcelona and sung in Catalan.

The D Minor Toccata and Fugue, which Matthias Bamert and the Los Angeles Philharmonic played at the Bowl, roared forth in the Leopold Stokowski orchestration familiar as the curtain-raiser in the Disney *Fantasia*. Bamert, furthermore, did a pretty good job at imitating

Stokowski's overwrought phrasing. For whatever this implies, it was the most interesting performance in his two nights of otherwise logy music making. Anytime the Philharmonic decides on a sabbatical for the *1812 Overture* this portentously oversized venture in uncomprehending megalomania could supply the fireworks in equal measure.

In a sense, the history of the Carmel Bach Festival follows the evolution of public awareness of the nature of Bach's music itself. My own personal involvement began around 1950. Gastone Usigli, the music director from 1938 until his death in 1956, was the kind of romantic, otherworldly musician who could drive board members bananas with desire in those innocent days, and probably still can. Gloriously mustachioed, with an Italian accent you could spoon over pasta and a conducting manner reminiscent of certain Italian traffic cops—the guy in the traffic circle in Rome across from the Victor Emanuel Monument, remember?—Usigli was something of a throwback, even in his time. I remember writhing through a much-truncated *St. Matthew Passion* and a Mass in B Minor around 1953, the choral sound a little like wet blotting paper, the phrasing more suitable to a late-romantic tone poem. The audiences loved him.

They also loved Sandor Salgo, the successor to Usigli, who retired in 1991. He came with a Hungarian accent at least as warm and caressing as Usigli's Italian. Salgo's notions about Bach performance were approximately a century fresher than Usigli's had been; Salgo at least knew about harpsichord continuo and baroque ornamentation. He expanded the scope of the festival to include Mozart and even Beethoven. His performance of Mozart's *Magic Flute* in, I think, 1980 hangs in the memory. It used the wise and adventurous W. H. Auden translation; why doesn't everybody? But Salgo still had to deal, as Usigli had, with an orchestra and chorus of local sit-ins; the playing in his last years at Carmel was tired and ungiving, a comedown from the vitality of his early years.

Enter Bruno Weil, diminutive, somewhat given to pudge, decidedly uncute, his German accent only a thin veneer over a businesslike English. Yet he is currently Carmel's heartthrob; he could probably become mayor just for the asking and would do at least as good a job as that Eastwood chap. In its years under Weil the Carmel Bach Festival has become musically important, not only to the doting townspeople but worldwide. The orchestra and chorus are recruited from world-class professionals and they, too—concertmaster Elizabeth Wallfisch, for one—also reap their fully deserved share of municipal adoration. They don't play the authentic-instruments game, but they play their modern instruments with authentic style and spirit. Weil has recorded profusely, mostly for Sony with the Toronto-based ensemble known as Tafelmusik; Wallfisch records, mostly baroque violin concertos, on the Virgin Classics label.

Over last weekend I heard three of Bach's most jubilant cantatas, two religious and one secular, a hilarious and noisy number about the wind god, Aeolus, calling off his wintry blasts after a promise of some snuggypoo from the goddess Athena, all wonderfully sung by the splendid chorus, a solo vocal group that included a magnificent fiery basso new to me, Christòpheren Nomura, and some meticulously controlled grand noises from the orchestra. I can't remember hearing better playing of any part of the violin repertory than Wallfisch's performance of the A Minor Concerto. In the middle of Saturday's Bach program, however, came an implausible interloper, one of Respighi's suites of *Ancient Airs and Dances*, nice old Renaissance and baroque tunes reharmonized and rescored, full of gooey romantic chord progressions. Next to Bach, it all sounded somewhat...well, dirty. Sunday afternoon's *Passion* took full account of the surging unrest that underlies this extraordinary score, with David Newman a powerful Evangelist and Nomura once again to sing the harrowing bass arias.

Some things in Carmel have changed; who'd have ever dreamed of a Saks Fifth Avenue in the middle of this seaside Brigadoon? But at least all that Munchkin architecture still survives without house numbers, the arrival of stop-and-go lights remains a far-off nightmare, and the continued well-being of venerable trees still enjoys priority rights over the street planners. The Bach Festival, as always, is a nonstop event: major evening programs, morning and afternoon chamber music, lectures and runouts to other venues including Carmel's spectacular restored mission, most events given three times over as many weeks. And the main concert room, the 738-seat Sunset Auditorium, with its vaulted ceiling that was once the domain of a certain "Johann Sebastian Bat" (and may still be), houses some of the best music civilization has produced.

[July 1996]

THE NEW

Early in my California time I was asked by a local NPR station to produce a radio series on California composers past and present, and the first question I asked everybody was simply this: what makes a composer Californian? Most of them, like me, had come here from somewhere else; that made it easier to define the specialness of this place. "We don't have to be afraid of being pretty," said Lou Harrison. "When you get right down to it," said Robert Erickson, "what a composer does is compose his environment"; Erickson incorporated Sierra brooklets and Pacific waves into his music. Terry Riley and John Adams caught California's spaciousness (and perhaps its spaceyness as well). These all created an atmosphere uniquely welcoming toward visiting composers who worked in other musical languages, as unalike as the formulas of Elliott Carter and the mysteries and ecstasies of György Ligeti. CalArts (the culmination of Walt Disney's dream) spun off the EAR Unit, which later found refuge in the Los Angeles County Museum of Art. That splendid arts repository, too, harbors the Monday Evening Concerts, a series of thinking-man's concerts that began as Evenings on the Roof in an aficionado's rooftop studio in 1939 and has continued uninterrupted ever since. The Philharmonic's Green Umbrella concerts (whimsically named by the former manager Ernest Fleischmann) are among of the best-attended new-music series anywhere in the land. When I ask myself what could have possessed me to give up a power job in New York (plus a nice house on the Hudson, good friends, and all the rest) to remake life on these far shores, it's the creative buzz here in Los Angeles, above all, that must take the blame: the artists who make it happen and the loyal audiences who support it.

Tuning In, Tuning Out

Toward the end of a recent symposium celebrating hard-core musical creativity, someone asked what seemed to be a sensible and important question: How can a listener, confronted with a new and abstruse piece of new music, recognize what's going on? How do we, in other words, determine from our ears' evidence whether this is a piece of chance composition, an open-form work, twelve-tone, or, for that matter, a latter-day update of one of the time-honored classical forms?

Nobody had an answer. Nobody, in that distinguished aggregation of composers, scholars, educators, electronic aficionados, and a critic or two—gathered together under auspices of the Getty Institute and CalArts to celebrate the legacy of the legendary pianist/composer/guru David Tudor on the occasion of the Getty's acquiring Tudor's archives—seemed to attach much importance to whether the music and musicianship under examination was ever intended to be received, understood and welcomed into the worldwide repertory of masterpieces. The works in that repertory, from the past or even the recent present, survive on an audience's ability to recognize their mix of inspiration and process: not only the beauty of the theme of Bach's *Goldberg Variations*, say, but the adventures that theme undergoes; not only the shape of the tone row in Schoenberg's Fourth String Quartet, but the power it generates as its music unfolds. Sometimes it takes a generation or two for the world to catch up with some works of a particular creative genius, but it eventually happens.

At the Getty I was assaulted and appalled by Tudor's twenty-nine-year-old electronic work called (or un-called) *Untitled*. What disturbed me wasn't just the aggressive ugliness of the piece; in my line I encounter plenty of that. What disturbed me more was that the work—whose twenty minutes could have been twenty hours—seemed to be only about itself, closed off and impenetrable.

There's an irony here, because a couple of nights before at CalArts, there was another Tudor creation from about the same time that was most of all about reaching and involving an audience. *Rainforest IV* invites the crowd to wander through a roomful of gadgetry—an old car door, a sculpture of toilet floats, an inverted barrel, you name it, all wired and vibrating, all adding up to a three-dimensional experience exhilarating in its own wacko way. Here, too, was a creation that was basically about itself, but with the extra dimension of sharing that was denied to the beset audience sitting still in the Getty's darkened auditorium. The Getty concert—Tudor and his orbit, including John Cage and Morton Feldman—had its moments, however, above all Vicki Ray's exquisite reading of some of Feldman's small piano works. Here there was sharing, inviting a listener to lean toward the music to savor every near-silent detail, as we do with the *Goldberg Variations* and with Schoenberg's Fourth Quartet.

You couldn't name two American originals farther apart in style and outlook than Tudor and Harry Partch; yet, within ten days both were handsomely celebrated in local halls: Tudor for his archives, Partch for the upcoming centennial of his birth (June 24, 1901). For twelve hours last Saturday at UCLA's Schoenberg Hall there was Partch on film, Partch in photographs on walls, Partch manuscripts (extraordinary, the elegance and exactitude of his notation, of music that strayed so enchantingly beyond the limitations of mere written notes!) and, finally, Partch's music on the stage. John Schneider—guitarist, composer, baritone, microtonal guru, and host of KPFK's *Global Village*—put together a concert mostly of works Partch composed early on for himself to, er, sing, and delivered a pretty good facsimile of the old boy's stentorian growl. Some of Partch's instruments were on hand: originals, re-creations, and, in one case, a keyboard programmed to reproduce the forty-three-tone scale of the original "chromelodeon"; the performers, members of Schneider's Just Strings, managed their exotic gadgetry with appealing skill. On video there was larger, later Partch as well: the dance piece *Delusion of the Fury* and Betty Freeman's short documentary *The Dreamer That Remains*. Arriving home, I put on something in C major, and it was startling.

Nobody cared more than Partch about reaching an audience. On Freeman's film he talks about the need for his players to look good—"not like a bunch of California prune pickers"—and move well on the stage. At the afternoon's symposium there was talk of producing more copies of the instruments Partch himself designed and built to manage his one-man tuning revolution—whose originals are now in the care of the composer Dean Drummond in New Jersey—to enable more widespread hearings of the music. That is certainly preferable to recent attempts to hand the works over to "normal" players, as a recent stab at Partch's *Barstow* by Philharmonic players at a Green Umbrella concert (even with Schneider's recitation) sadly proved.

Yet there is a dead end here, similar to what I sensed at some of the Tudor discussions. The music Partch wrote for his strange and fascinating array of instruments—some two dozen, originally—stands as the audible emanation of one whole, ornery, cantankerous, innovative spirit. The instruments provide the visible counterpart. Nobody else in his right mind could compose for these instruments without cloning that whole spirit. As long as there are John Schneiders to recreate passably the sounds of Partch—like all those jazz bands claiming to rekindle the sounds of Ellington—we'll have a tenuous grip on this fascinating, unique byway in the annals of American innovation. But Partch remains inimitable, in both the best and worst sense.

[May 2001]

Ojai: Finnish Touches

Between Ojai's verdant valley and the dour woodlands of Finland, some distance intervenes. For a time last weekend, however—the occasion of the Fifty-Third Ojai Music Festival—you could have sworn that miles had shrunk to inches. The Finns came, wonderful musicians bearing remarkable music; they charmed and they conquered.

Here in Los Angeles we live with testimony, in the presence of Esa-Pekka Salonen, of Finland's emergence in the last couple of decades as a major musical power. Not only has Salonen's conducting created an aura around the Los Angeles Philharmonic that currently crowns it the most irresistible of American orchestras; he has added to that glow the work of a composer of extraordinary gifts for whom no limits are easily discernible. At Ojai there was music by Salonen and by two near-contemporaries, all three onetime classmates at Helsinki's Sibelius Academy—all three, for what the information is worth, currently living outside Finland.

Sibelius's music is, and will remain, the rock on which Finland's eminence rests; his music, of necessity, maintains an obligatory presence at any celebration of that country's music. The music that opens his First Symphony, the clarinet solo off in the chill grayness over muffled drums—which Salonen, the Philharmonic, and the irreplaceable Michele Zukovsky performed at Ojai's first concert on Friday—is some kind of magical mood-painting which nothing that ensues in this logy, overstuffed sofa of a symphony ever again matches. After Sibelius there was a generation, perhaps two, of composers apparently content to labor in his shadow, conservatives like Einojohani Rautawaara—the excellent Sakari Oramu performed a short work of his with the Philharmonic last month—and Aulis Sallinen, whose opera *Kullervo* had its world premiere here in 1992. Then came a vastly different generation, students at Helsinki around 1980: Salonen, Magnus Lindberg, and Kaija Saariaho, all by now familiar here through the efforts of Salonen and the Philharmonic and represented at Ojai by works either brand-new or at least new to American ears.

A weekend of new music from Finland cannot answer all questions about the musical state of that land; the Finnish government is also remarkably supportive of new opera, and there was none of that at Ojai. What there was, however, if any generalities can be spun, was music strongly narrative, bristling with jagged, deeply coloristic masses that often seemed to jar against one another: Kaija Saariaho's *Amers*, for one, with its prominent cello solo set against the gently rackety orchestra. The weekend's most sensational work was Lindberg's *Kraft* composed and recorded (on Finlandia) in 1985 but never before performed in the United States. Outbursts of brutal, crushing blows on gongs spread around the audience area, moments of ethereal calm as a gathering of twittering piccolos seemed to make common cause with Ojai's resident avian population: this is some sort of nihilistic masterpiece, wonderfully scored (including an assortment of auto parts and old railway-car springs to enhance the percussion). The piece seemed exactly fashioned for Ojai, where performers (including Lindberg himself) could easily hurtle from onstage noisemakers to more gadgetry among the trees that ring the audience area.

Salonen's own new work bore another kind of beauty, profound and luminous. His *Five Images after Sappho* sets fragments of several Sapphic love poems (in translations by Paul Roche) to music of fluid, plangent grace. Some passages in the small orchestra take on the urgent purling of, say, the Daybreak music from Ravel's *Daphnis et Chloë*; the richness and easy flow of the melodic line suggest a mastery of vocal writing that should make anyone impatient for the opera that will soon occupy Salonen's full attention.

If the music was extraordinary, the performances were even more so. Salonen had composed his songs for Dawn Upshaw, who then had to cancel for emergency spinal surgery, and another American soprano, not yet as well-known, sang the music as if it were her own. Remember her name: Laura Claycomb. By some distance, however, the weekend's performance laurels were earned by Toimii, the fearless seven-member new-music ensemble founded in Helsinki in 1981 by Salonen and Lindberg and often led by Salonen on recordings. Individual members of the group were prominent on almost all the concerts: the supremely gifted cellist Anssi Karttunen (the way those Finns waste letters!) making his unerring way through a Lindberg concerto and the Saariaho and the delightful clarinetist-sprite Kari Krikku. No less impressive was Toimii's morning "family" program, in which all members joined forces to eradicate the institution of opera once and for all through a boisterous and mettlesome spoof that even included a high note or two from the august Salonen himself. Our own Los Angeles Philharmonic New Music Group, founded the same year as Toimii, was also on hand in a program that ended with a reminder of what a solid, beautifully planned work is John Adams's *Chamber Symphony.*

Things are happening at Ojai. Ernest Fleischmann's first year as artistic director brought changes, including an expansion via three short Sundowner concerts earlier in the week. There is to be a yearly young-composer competition, financed by a local foundation, with the first winner included in next season. Next year's conductor, by the way, is Sir Simon Rattle, and the solo list includes the incomparable Lorraine Hunt. It's not too early to reserve.

[June 1999]

Berio: Impurity with Impunity

You can fly the nine hours from Los Angeles to Paris for less money than for the seventy-minute hop from Paris to Milan; still, it seemed foolish to be in one exhilarating musical center and ignore the other. Milan is currently immersed in a lavish festival of the music of its distinguished sometime resident, Luciano Berio, rounding out a year of celebrating his seventieth birthday: three weeks of concerts, recitals and discussions, mostly at La Scala, and the world premiere of his opera *Outis*. In true Italian fashion, the opera came in as a cliffhanger; a musicians' strike at La Scala (reportedly a protest not against working conditions but against Berio's music itself) forced a postponement of the first performance, threatened the entire festival, and then resolved itself as if on predetermined schedule. I got to the opera's second performance, and also to one concert that included Berio's astonishing twenty-five-minute *Sequenza* for solo bassoon and his ravishing, intense, hourlong *Coro* for singers and orchestra.

Berio's generation also includes Boulez and Stockhausen; his own teachers, Luigi Dallapiccola and Bruno Maderna, were the forces that firmed his Italian self-awareness, the secret of blending a passionate, surging lyrical sense into the European nontonality that claimed Anton Webern as ancestor. The glorious cascade of orchestral sound that raises the curtain of the new opera, romantic melody insistent and irresistible, brought to mind not Webern but his warmer-hearted colleague Alban Berg.

The individuality in Berio's musical manner stems in large measure from his mixtures, his way of merging vocal and instrumental lines, often involving poetry in several languages presented simultaneously into extraordinary, original textures whose power seems to derive from their very impurity. The "collage" movement from the 1968 *Sinfonia*, his best-known work, stirs words from graffiti and the writings of Mayakovsky and Joyce into a pastiche of orchestral snippets from the familiar repertory to create a bristling, breath-stopping dozen or so minutes of high if indefinable adventure. The 1976 *Coro* does much the same, on a grander scale; the forty singers—not massed as a chorus, but scattered through the orchestra—deliver a text that blends lines from Pablo Neruda into a vast assemblage of fragments from folk poetry: Sioux, Persian, Sicilian, Hebrew, and so on. The mix of sung words and orchestra ferments into a stream of consciousness out of which recognizable elements bubble up now and then out of an unstoppable onward flow.

Outis accomplishes somewhat the same, and magnificently. Its title—Greek for "nobody"—is the name Ulysses assumed when he confronted and wounded the giant Polyphemus. The opera is a series of speculations on Homer's *Odyssey* and the lights it has cast on the human condition over its three millennia. Again, its text is a multilingual assemblage: fragments from—among others—Catullus, Shakespeare, Melville, and Auden interspersed into a libretto by Dario Del Corno and Berio himself. There is no linear plot; each of the work's five "cycles" starts with the murder of Ulysses by his son Telegonus ("the fashioner of endings") and then veers wildly into other realms. Among the most memorable moments: an auction, a circus-*cum*-striptease, horrifying war games enacted by children, and a final scene in which time and place disappear and singers and pianists in concert clothes give a formal recital. Similarly, the music careens from manner to manner: jazz, a corny waltz, some deep and dark lyricism, a little doo-dah dispensed by the Swingle Singers—whom Berio has used before, always brilliantly. The opera lasts just over two hours; it left me with the sense of having witnessed a stunning and convincing demonstration of creative omnipotence. It also left me with the reminder to start packing for the next Berio opera production, the 1983 *Un re in ascolto*, scheduled for the Chicago Lyric Opera late next month.

The *Coro* was properly dealt with by the visiting London Sinfonietta and the BBC Singers under Simon Joly. Pascal Gallois got through the bassoon *Sequenza* with a stupendous outlay of breath and technique. *Outis* was conducted by David Robertson (Santa Monica born but only recently honored in the United States after a brilliant orbit through European new-music circles), staged by Graham Vick and sung by a huge cast led by the Outis/Ulysses of Alan Opie. In the gorgeous room where Maria Callas had sung, where Verdi's *Otello* was first heard, a Milanese audience stamped and cheered this latter-day affirmation that opera still lives.

[November 1996]

Boulez at Ojai: Fifty and Counting

Three pillars support the uniqueness and value of the Ojai Music Festival. Lawrence Morton, who died in 1987, directed the festival for more than thirty years, commanding its flights into unknown but important musical areas, resisting with all his power any hint of diluting the strong brew of his programming merely to appease the box office. Igor Stravinsky, who died in 1971, came frequently to Ojai at Morton's bidding, sat in on performances of his prickliest music and—in this unlikely rural setting of orange groves and horse farms—became a household name. Morton also brought Pierre Boulez to Ojai, first in 1967; this was his sixth time as the festival's music director, celebrating the fiftieth anniversary of this precious, implausible, cherishable annual event.

The affinity that has developed between Boulez, the austere, intense perfectionist—in his attitudes as a conductor and in his own music—and Ojai may seem outwardly curious; actually, it forms an ideal blend. Before Boulez's American involvement—in 1960, if I remember correctly—Leonard Bernstein had led one of Boulez's early works and told the New York Philharmonic audience that "fifty years from now everybody will be listening to this music." But Bernstein himself did nothing to lead audiences toward that time, toward an acceptance of innovation, with the result that even now, when orchestras pretend to play the music of their own time, they usually end up with the dances from *West Side Story* or ten minutes of John Adams. When Boulez took over Bernstein's podium, he struggled against daunting odds to bring the whole institution of the symphony orchestra into its own time and soon learned the folly of subjecting subscription audiences to the abrasions in his own music.

Boulez has never won that fight. In his frequent visits to the Los Angeles Philharmonic, he has delivered spellbinding performances at subscription concerts of composers close to him—Debussy, Ravel, Messiaen, and Mahler—but very little of his own music. Not the wonderful *Mallarmé Improvisations*, for example. These he has reserved for special settings that attract smaller but more adventurous audiences: the Green Umbrella concerts and Ojai. In this past week we have had both: a stupendous closing event at the Umbrella and a weekend at Ojai. At both events the greatness of Boulez was readily assessed, in the two short pieces that go by the name *Dérive*, the delirious instrumental fancy known as *Eclat* (played only at the Umbrella) and, above all, the stupendous...*explosante-fixe*..., a work first revealed in embryonic form in 1972 that has now grown into one of the glorious monsters of our time.

The original...*explosante-fixe*...("...beauty shall be an immobile explosion...," wrote André Breton), which I heard at a Lincoln Center performance in 1973 and described in words of which I would not now be proud, consisted of a single page of music and six pages of instructions dealing with ways of expanding the instrumental sounds; the work took about half an hour. Over the years, as the piece has constantly assumed new and newer shapes, Boulez has experimented with, and later rejected, other electronic processors. Now there is new equipment, from Boulez's own associates at the Institute for Acoustic/Musical Research and Coordination (IRCAM), his fabulous Paris toy shop; the work has grown to thirty-seven minutes of tense, intricate sound patterns, somewhat terrifying but suffused with a disturbing, indefinable beauty. The piece is run by a solo flute that activates electronic processing through a MIDI interface; two more flutes front a twenty-two-member instrumental ensemble.

The Boulez work bristles with confrontations, both between the flutes and the ensemble and within the components of that ensemble. The work hangs suspended in space; banks of loudspeakers, fed from the computerized processing of the live sound, surround the music on stage. At the Japan America Theater the space was, of course, defined by the walls of the room. Outdoors in Ojai's Libbey Park, the sounds seemed to blend into trees and, beyond them, the full moon. At moments the score calls for blacking out the stage, and at Ojai at those moments you could very well find yourself circulating among the planets.

The piece is undeniable gritty at times, full of the busy-busy chatter that has become a Boulezian trademark. I picked up the sounds of outrage in some of the lunchtime conversations around Ojai the next day. For offended ears, the two *Dérives* provided greater solace; the second of the pair (listed as No. 1 but played in reverse order) flowed out to merge into the moonlight like a sublime, whispered near-silence, no more resistible than any Chopin Nocturne. At his talk before the Umbrella concert, Boulez and his sound designer, Andrew Gerszo, delivered a fearsomely detailed description of how the electronics were supposed to work in the . . . *explosante-fixe*. . . . But near the end, Boulez assured the (probably, by then, thoroughly intimidated) crowd that they were welcome to forget the whole mass of scientific description and try to trust their ears.

He wouldn't have made such conciliatory statements in years past. The Boulez who, during his New York years, pulverized the spirits of Juilliard composition students with one merciless tongue-lashing after another, has mellowed. He now conducts music you wouldn't have thought he'd have touched with a long pole in years past: Strauss's tone poems, Ravel's *Bolero* and *La valse*—not always triumphantly, need I add. On opening night at Ojai he made Mahler's Fifth Symphony more rickety and ill-tempered than even that rickety and ill-tempered music deserves to be. At the final concert, however, he delivered *La valse* as if to waken the dead and set them all to dancing. He even—imagine!—took off his jacket to conduct. Sure, it was ninety-seven degrees that afternoon; even so, you'll live a long time before the spectacle of a shirtsleeved Boulez again looms before you.

There was more. The divine Mitsuko Uchida played half a program of some of Schubert's most heartrending piano works: two Impromptus and the B-flat Sonata, music so sublime, and so sublimely played, that I must devote an entire column to them next week. She also played the Ravel G Major Concerto on the final program, an exhilarating romp. The Juilliard Quartet played Beethoven (Op. 135), the Carter Second Quartet, and an early Schubert: the C Major Quartet from his sixteenth year, a work full of remarkable invention and even more remarkable prophecy. As for the Carter, the meandering, desiccated patterns of this work made any of Boulez's most frightening outbursts sound, in retrospect, positively romantic.

[June 1996]

Henze: Sanitary Sanity

Hans Werner Henze weighs on my conscience. Colleagues whose opinions I value write about his music with respect merging into love. Paeans of praise ("luminous," "full-blooded," "exuberant") resound from the five volumes—bedtable companions all—of Andrew Porter's collected *New Yorker* writings. "His music is the real thing in a plastic world," writes Ned Rorem, himself a master fashioner of high-quality plastic. It is common practice to deplore how seldom Henze's operas are staged or his symphonies performed; they are the products of a keenly literate intelligence that proclaim high faith in the survival of civilization and ought—for that reason if no other—to be kept close within reach. Still...

Even in absentia, Henze was an identifiable presence here for a time last week. His forty-five-minute *Kammermusik*, composed in 1958 and with an epilogue added in 1963, constituted the second half of the latest Green Umbrella program; his shadow, actually, fell over the entire program, whose guest participants—alongside the expectedly excellent contingent from the Philharmonic's New Music Group—were young performers who often operate in the Henze orbit.

Henze in 1958 was king of his world, overwhelmed with more commissions he could possibly manage, widely greeted as the savior who would rescue European music from the twin curses of residual Nazi dogma and total serialism. He had already had his immersion in Schoenbergian atonality and had climbed out; now, in his adopted Italy, he would allow the southern sun to restore the warmth to his soul and his art. In his new world there were no doors (not even on the closets); all people were welcome, and all musics. Stravinsky, jazz, Monteverdi, Asian ritual, dissident chantings of all political and social stripes, Berg, Bach...it all went into the same pot, blended with elevated, exquisitely sensitive taste.

The *Kammermusik* simply throbs with taste and intelligence. Its core is a string of poetic fragments by Friedrich Hölderlin, whose own outlooks—like those of Henze a century and a half later—were shaped in a meld of a German upbringing and a passion for matters classical and Greek. The poet's terminal madness—which clouded his last forty years—affects the disequilibrium of the poetry; the composer's stubborn sanity restores the balance. A further extension of that exquisite sanity binds the imagery onto an artistic framework in which six song settings alternate with six instrumental movements which, if you insist, can be thought to reflect upon the words.

It's all very sane; the tracery is exquisite, the balances meticulously arrived at. My own flaw—which, I have to confess, affects my view of Henze's music over all and which, therefore, may also be terminal—is that I find it sanitized beyond any power to hold my interest. Here is poetry of fragrant imagery, of flickers of ecstasy mingled with great sorrow; there is music that is all straight lines immaculately drawn. I had kind words for the Long Beach Opera's skill—not to mention bravery—last season in producing Henze's *Elegy for Young Lovers*, without my once being reached by the chill musical setting of its moving, melancholy tale. I admire the physical impact of his *The Bassarids*, an operatic setting of Euripides' *The Bacchae*, and would travel any reasonable distance to see it staged, but draw little heartsease from the actual music Henze has contrived to advance the marvelous plot.

At least his music seems to gladden its performers. The visiting Henze-Jugend—the "improbably young" (so read the program note) pianist/composer Thomas Adès and the not-much-older conductor Markus Stenz and guitarist David Tanenbaum—participated with commendable skill. Jon Garrison sang the Hölderlin texts acceptably, although I would have preferred a sweeter, more persuasive tone—that of Neil Jenkins, for example, on the Koch-Schwann recording. Two works by Adès himself were also included: a piano solo called *Traced Overhead*, elegant, vibrant, and gorgeously played by the composer; an ensemble piece called *Living Toys*, something about childhood visions, sour and rather off-putting (in a Henze sort of way). Better than any of this were the two short works by the enigmatic György Kurtág: a set of tiny crystalline moments gathered as an homage to Robert Schumann and his *Grabstein für Stephan*.

Here, in this last-named work, was something that revealed what music is all about, and what it can accomplish in an interlock with a hearer's soul. The music hangs suspended, mostly in silence punctuated with ghostlike sounds from players spread widely through the house; a guitarist (Tanenbaum) strums on open strings. A couple of weird blasts from airhorns, up in the balcony, adds further punctuation. Its nine minutes pass all too quickly; wisely, Stenz led his assembled forces in an immediate reprise. Still too little known—although his presence at Ojai in 1986, during three wondrous days of his music, was a presence not soon forgotten—Kurtág achieves in his lapidary, enigmatic music an intensely pure communication that others aspire to with lesser results. At seventy, he is one of the giants of our time.

[April 1997]

Glass: Faux Pas

Jean-Pierre Melville's film version of Jean Cocteau's *Les enfants terribles*, first released in 1949, has finally made it to video. A two–laser disc package from Water Bearer (distributed by Image Entertainment and also including Cocteau's own version of his *Les parents terribles*) appears in time to underline the folly, the arrogance, and, I might as well add, the sheer wrongheadedness in Philip Glass's notion of turning the elegance of Cocteau's ethereal fantasy into a scaffold for his own bland and meandering music. If these words suggest that I had a rotten time at the Wiltern Theater last Friday night, when the UCLA Center for the Performing Arts presented the Glass Ensemble's production of *Les enfants* (or "Children of the Game," as the program identified it), they have been properly chosen.

See the film; watch, as the tortured game playing of these obsessed almost-grown children unfolds like some long and devious baroque melody. Listen, as Melville's (or Cocteau's?) actual choice of music— J. S. Bach's transcription for four keyboards of a Vivaldi concerto for four violins, performed in the bloated "big-band-baroque" manner that passed for authentic early-music practice in 1949—mirrors uncannily the hermetic world of these game players. Listen, too, to the one slender, comforting line, as Cocteau's own suave, bland narration leads us with almost imperceptible insistence from scene to scene.

Did Philip Glass and the director/choreographer Susan Marshall (remembered, not exactly fondly, for her inane dance numbers in the Los

Angeles Opera's *Les Troyens*) really believe that even their finest efforts could in any way translate the eerie cloud formations of Melville/Cocteau into something worthy to replace, or even to stand beside, the original? Does Glass himself, for that matter, dare to presume a place in the firmament for his "operatic" treatment of Cocteau's *La belle et la bête*, which lumbered in and out of town (also under UCLA's auspices) a couple of seasons back? (I have so far not seen the third of these Glass/Cocteau buddyings, based on *Orphée*; this does not, I firmly believe, forfeit my claim to have truly lived.)

Claustrophobia rules the film; it reeks of unaired bed linen, and we choke in empathy. Marshall's whizzing, zooming characters—three dancers and a singer to each of the major roles—create an effect exactly the opposite, to no apparent artistic gain. They aerate the stage like zany, errant breezes, leaving vast spaces where music might fill in. But Glass's music goes nowhere. The best of his works—*Einstein on the Beach*, *Satyagraha*—call less for singing than for a kind of half-spoken intonation. More than any of his previous stage works, *Les enfants* seems operatically conceived; there are arias, duets, attempts at creating vocal lines for singers. "Attempts," I said, not "accomplishments"; the saddest news about this new concoction is that its music is grindingly. achingly dull. It meanders past the beginnings of tunes without taking hold; its nurdling instrumental accompaniments evoke memories of "Einstein on the Fritz," P. D. Q. Bach's deadly accurate takeoff. You have to wonder if perhaps Glass himself, or his attendant Muse, isn't also in need of repair.

[October 1997]

Salonen: Doing Himself (and Us) Proud

Everyone thought he would, and he did. Esa-Pekka Salonen's *LA Variations*, commissioned by and dedicated to the Los Angeles Philharmonic and given its world premiere last week, is some kind of great work, marvelously conceived and shaped and, for all its craggy musical style, remarkably communicative. At the first performance, on Thursday night, the audience gave it the kind of cheering, standing ovation usually reserved for flamboyant soloists in familiar concertos. "I've been with the orchestra twenty-six years," the cellist Dan Rothmuller told me after the performance, "and I've never seen this kind of ovation for the premiere of a brand-new piece." I heard the piece again the next night, and the reception was the same.

Years before he entered the roster of internationally acclaimed conductors, Salonen had already earned notice as a serious composer, one of a group of young Finns—whose numbers also included Magnus Lindberg and Kaija Saariaho, both now well-known—anxious to escape the shadow of their conservative ancestor Jan Sibelius and go their own innovative way. Still, a full-time conductor with composing aspirations faces a clear and present danger: how to purge both the conscious and the subconscious from memories of other people's music and avoid turning out mere pastiches. On the flip side, however, a conductor's mastery of orchestral balance can also light a composer's path. *LA Variations* demands formidable orchestral forces, including a synthesizer and a vast array of percussion; so beautifully planned is the disposition of orchestral parts that, even at the premiere in the acoustically inferior Dorothy Chandler Pavilion, individual voices were clearly defined: a solo flute or a harp glissando, say, against a massive brass outburst.

The work lasts twenty-one minutes. Here, as in Salonen's best-known earlier scores (several of them, including a cheeky concerto for alto saxophone, available on the Finlandia label), faint reminiscences from his own musical heritage do surface fleetingly from time to time, to no detriment. Several whirring, swirling, buzzing clusters of string tone, for example, stir memories of similar passages in Sibelius; in the Salonen they whoosh forward with a furious, exhilarating energy far beyond the reach of the older master.

That energy, in fact, imparts itself to both players and audience. Salonen's music takes no prisoners. Its sense of harmony stems from an intricate interweaving of chords built out of all twelve notes of the familiar scale—plus some imaginative collaboration from a synthesizer that stretches the harmonic bounds even farther. Wisps of folklike melody surface and disappear, almost subliminally. Now and then the fury subsides, and a gleaming moment of old-fashioned harmony seems almost like a dissonant intruder. The ending—muted strings and a piccolo at the quiet edge of audibility—summons visions of distant stars.

[November 1997]

In one of those imponderable ironies by which the music industry slowly but surely succeeds in cannibalizing its own, the Deutsche Grammophon recording of Esa-Pekka Salonen's *Wing on Wing* will be made not by Salonen's Los Angeles Philharmonic (for which it was written) in the Walt Disney Concert Hall (whose architecture it celebrates), but half a planet away, in Helsinki, by the Finnish Radio Orchestra. The reason, it should not surprise you to learn, is money.

I don't have the exact figures involved in this case, but I do for a parallel situation reported in last week's *New York Times* Sunday magazine. The

New York Philharmonic management recently learned that John Adams's *On the Transmigration of Souls*, which he composed for that orchestra in 2002 as a memorial for 9/11, was slated to be recorded by a London orchestra rather than its own, since the cost differential would be something like $40,000 as against $95,000. In that case an enraged New York Philharmonic patron came up with the difference. I would not hang by my thumbs expecting a similar resolution in Los Angeles, especially since the DG recording also includes two other Salonen works, one of which (*Insomnia*) hasn't yet been heard here. (I would, of course, be delighted to be proved wrong.)

This is all part of a dark cloud that overhangs classical music these days. Domestic orchestral recording by the major orchestras on the major labels has all but stopped; what persists are the few projects of individual orchestras producing their own labels—as in San Francisco—but, of course, without the blockbuster promotion that RCA and Sony were once able to accord the Boston, New York, and Los Angeles orchestras. The irony aches especially in the case of *Wing on Wing*, since the piece comes wrapped in so many layers of pride—with, at the core, music of exceptional beauty and delight.

Reading through the printed score, as I was privileged to do for several days before the two performances I heard, that sense of pride was as clearly visible as the notes themselves in the care with which Salonen had mapped out the movements of the solo musicians—the two singers and the two deep-toned wind instruments, which impersonated some kind of marine specimen. The voice of Frank Gehry intrudes now and then, as part of the obbligato of pride that pervades the work. No matter how clear the tape, will that voice, that pride of identity, transplant to a Finnish recording studio? Against the complexity of other works—the hugely successful *LA Variations* and the manic turmoil of *Insomnia*, which I've heard on a pirate disc—this is, for Salonen, a lighter piece; it has some of the cold, clear wind of his homeland, without the murk that his musical ancestor seemed fond of stirring up. It does him proud, and us, too. The real matter at hand on these two programs and a third one yet to come (on February 24) is the beautifully designed, well-fitting second hat worn by Salonen himself as one of our time's major, serious composers. Conductors who compose are nothing new on the landscape. Elephantine bloats by the likes of Wilhelm Furtwängler and Bruno Walter belong among the sorry items cited two paragraphs back; Leonard Bernstein's symphonic ventures will gather dust while his stage shows continue to flourish. Salonen came to Los Angeles with a commendable repertory of a young man's smart, craftsmanlike pieces that showed the touch of good teaching and good companionship. His music since his arrival has taken enormous forward strides; it is some of the most important music being composed anywhere in the world today, and the remarkable thing is that it gets better right along with his strengths as a conductor.

The *LA Variations* of 1997 was his giant step; it is now a repertory piece. It is the work of a master of orchestral practice, a knowing testimonial to the excellent state to which he had brought his own orchestra at that time. But it is also a work of *musical* mastery, a process piece that holds you in its grip as the variations unfold. The three works on the current 3 × Salonen Mini-Festival follow logically. (I heard the first two, *Wing on Wing* and *Mania*, at last week's concerts, and *Insomnia*—which is on the third program—from the new Deutsche Grammophon recording.)

Wing on Wing was wonderful to hear again live, breezing through the same hall and by the musical forces for which it was written, saddening to hear in its inferior preservation with its cramped, studio sound on the DG disc. I love its sparkle, its cold clear wind. Wherever it may travel, with its lovely intrusions by the sampled voice of Frank Gehry, it remains *our* piece, Disney Hall's piece, lightest of this "festival's" three works, but a treasure. *Mania* draws the phenomenal cellist Anssi Karttunen into the mix, removing most of the orchestra (strings, especially) from his manic path.

When I first interviewed Salonen, soon after he began his career here, he seemed anxious to downplay the image of Sibelius as ancestral shame, the dark secret borne by all living Finnish musicians. The sense I get, in both *Mania* and the imperfect hearing of the thrilling *Insomnia* on disc, is that Salonen has found a way to extract at least one valuable aspect of Sibelius's orchestral style, the wonderful headlong dash in, for example, the end of the first movement of the Fifth Symphony or again in the Seventh. Both these new pieces, it seems to me on early acquaintance, seem to have found the way to make Grandpa respectable once again in polite society. That takes some doing.

[October 2004]

Ligeti: Clouds and Cuckoos

Finally, there is *Clocks and Clouds*. I have entertained a private passion for György Ligeti's fourteen-minute gathering of moonbeams and distant thunderclaps ever since Esa-Pekka Salonen performed it with the Philharmonic in 1993. It was scheduled for inclusion in Salonen's complete Ligeti survey on Sony; the release is assigned a number in the discography in Paul Griffiths's splendid biography. It never happened; a new recording from other sources, out this month on Teldec, is the first ever. The new disc includes the Violin Concerto, which was also on that Salonen concert (along with Debussy, a memorable matchup). The performances are led by Reinbert de Leeuw, with his Amsterdam-based Schoenberg Ensemble; Frank Peter Zimmermann is the phenomenal soloist in the Violin Concerto.

"Better than any other living composer," I wrote in 1993,

> Ligeti defines the full panorama of contemporary musical possibilities. At sixty-nine (now seventy-nine) his catalog is not large, but his modest legacy embraces the thinking of a man completely in command of the grammar of music and its expressive scope.... *Clocks and Clouds* is [a] work of high delight. Its basic plan sounds simple in the telling: instrumental music of meticulous, metronomic exactitude (i.e., clocks) gradually melting into a nebulous, cloudlike flow, with a superimposed line for a small women's chorus that reverses the flow. Little side-trips along the way form a constant web of surprise.

The title stems from an essay by Karl Popper on the philosophy of science, but Ligeti's setting transforms scientific images into poetic. The women's text is notated in the International Phonetic Alphabet, and serves to define rhythm more than melody.

This is a small piece, compared to the twenty-seven-minute Violin Concerto, but the two share an important facet of Ligeti's particular genius: his joy in opening his musical language to all kinds of intrusions beyond the limits of the European systems in which he was raised. In the Violin Concerto there are wonderful, manic outbursts from, of all strange devices, an ensemble of ocarinas and slide whistles, instruments that hoot and chortle in outer-space harmonies that have nothing to do with do-re-mi. The women's chorus in *Clocks and Clouds* accomplishes some of the same, slipping and sliding into some kind of cloud-cuckoo land. Listening to this can be unsettling to ears nurtured on C major; on a tape I sneaked when the work was done at the Hollywood Bowl in, I think, 1998, some yahoo in a nearby box can be heard booing his head off. Sad, how some people simply resist the process of delight.

I suppose it's even possible to resist the delight in the final music on this Ligeti disc, *Sippal, dobbal, nádihegedüvel,* a set of seven tiny songs for mezzo-soprano (Katalin Károlyi) and percussion based on poems by Sándor Weöres—some of them gibberish, some folksy, some word games—but I cannot. Wonderful, serious fun, mingled with that infectious wisdom that seems built into this cherishable composer. *Clocks and Clouds* dates from 1973, the *Sippal* songs from 2000. A sense of humor and delight can endure over twenty-seven years only if buttressed by a sense of infinite wisdom, and that Ligeti surely possesses.

There is more Ligeti, and more wise humor, in a recent disc in Deutsche Grammophon's Echo 20/21 series of reissues and remasterings of major landmarks from the company's ongoing service to new music. From 1962 come the two sets of play pieces, *Aventures* and *Nouvelles aventures,* in which wisdom and sheer hilarity play off side by side. The language here, too, often lapses into gibberish, as three vocal soloists have at one another in conversations that rise to high expressive levels without once revealing what they're about. "The characters," writes Paul Griffiths, "sing, play games, charm each other, fight, and hope for some response.... They are a little like children. They are a little like us." Pierre Boulez conducts the performance; if, as some have, you doubt his ability to manage genuine humor, even wit, you don't know this disc. The disc also includes some of Ligeti's works for organ, performed by Gerd Zacher. If, like some (myself included), you find the idea of humorous organ music something of an oxymoron, this is the disc to set you straight.

This Deutsche Grammophon series, by the way, is one of the few remaining evidences that someone in the record industry still cares about preserving the world's musical heritage. The catalog lists some thirty items so far, including the Berio *Sequenze* I wrote about last week, Messiaen's *St. Francis*, three discs of Boulez, and such inexplicable items as André Previn's *Streetcar Named Desire*. Berio's *Coro*, a recent issue, is one more disc I would describe as indispensable.

The work was completed in 1977, written for the Cologne Radio Chorus and Orchestra who perform it here under Berio's direction. The name means, simply, "chorus"; it belongs among the generically named works—*Opera*, *Sinfonia*, etc.—that form the pillars of Berio's catalog. Forty chorus members sit among the same number of orchestra members, creating a sound far more homogeneous than the usual orchestra-down-front, chorus-upstage arrangement. A Pablo Neruda poem forms the backbone of the hourlong work: "The pallid day appears...come and see the blood in the streets." Texts twined around Neruda's lines are mostly drawn from primitive sources: Peru, Polynesia, Africa, Native American, Hebrew. Berio's music reflects various native chanting techniques; the pileup of information and emotion is astonishing at times. Now and then you become aware of a German chorus struggling with other languages: "a-VAKE LOFF in dis POY," but Berio apparently clings to his originators. He's entitled.

[February 2003]

Lou Harrison: Borrowed Finery

"Cherish the hybrids," Lou Harrison used to say, and say again as a kind of mantra. "They're all we've got." Two big works of Lou's, nearly forty years apart in the infinite variety of his legacy, were on hand last week, each a different kind of mix and, as it happened, each a different kind of marvel. What they shared was that cherishable quality that we are only now coming to discover about Harrison, its beauty and its strength.

That latter quality in particular eludes some listeners. Harrison never concealed his fondness for writing pretty music and some of it, to be sure, simply melts in your ear. The final moments of *The Perilous Chapel*, which the University of Southern California Thornton Contemporary Music Ensemble performed at last week's Green Umbrella concert, fades out in a haze of pure diatonic velvet for which no better word than *pretty* will suffice. But the music in context, as the resolution to previous barbarous goings-on—all scored for soft-spoken ensemble of harp, flute, cello, and small drum and, therefore, sounding off in the distance like a bunch of garrulous toys—is exactly the proper sweet resolution.

That music dates from 1948. Harrison was in New York; his circle included Virgil Thomson and John Cage, and he had made a name for himself editing and performing the Third Symphony of Charles Ives and guiding it toward recognition forty years overdue. Some of that work's naive and folkish melodic style rubs off on the young (thirty-one-year-old) Harrison's work, but the sound of this early piece, the wonderful "open" scoring of those solo instruments, points unmistakably ahead to the fascination with matters exotic and otherworldly that would seize his imagination many years later.

The Double Concerto for Violin, Cello, and Javanese Gamelan dates from 1981 and reveals that fascination in full flower. Harrison had by then journeyed around the Pacific Rim and absorbed the languages of its musics until he could make those languages his own. He then set himself up in California as a missionary, teaching college kids fresh off the beach how to compose in the tuning systems of Bali and Java, how to build and tune their own gongs and drums and form their own gamelans, and yet—this is important—how to merge these sounds and these harmonic systems into their own Western melodic and rhythmic instincts. Cherish the hybrids, he taught, and become them. His own music led the way.

This Double Concerto, which concluded a splendid XTET program at LACMA in a burst of glory with Susan Jensen and Roger Lebow as soloists and Bill Alves's Harvey Mudd American Gamelan from the Claremont Colleges, is pure mongrel, and wonderful of its kind. The background is, of course, the rich, subtle sounds of the excellent small gamelan—and that's already a sight, five very undergrad-looking kids whomping away at devices from a culture half a world and half a millennium away. Against this the solo instruments play an almost continuous rhapsodic line that seems to have both shape and no shape at all. There is other music like this: some of Terry Riley's long works for the Kronos Quartet, but there the melodic impetus seems more Celtic than Pacific.

It's probably pointless, however, to seek out resemblances; there are just so many notes in the world, after all. What has happened here, and it is more delightful than anything else, is that Harrison has accomplished an overlay of Western concerto principles onto this alien foundation, made it adhere in some strange and cockeyed way, and turned out something close to a masterpiece. This exhilarating Double Concerto is just that. It's easy to make the distinction, in dealing with new music, that diatonic harmonies plus tunes equals conservative and that abstruse harmonies plus bristling melodic lines equals progressive. But those equations break down constantly in the real world, and they do with Lou.

[May 2004]

Precious Perle

George Perle turns eighty in a few weeks. He is probably better known for his books than his music, but that should change. Among his writings are several books on the music of Alban Berg; they belong in the small company of scholarly works that have as much to do with the love of music as with knowledge. He lived in California for a time, and taught at the University of California, Davis in the 1950s but later escaped back to New York.

The pianist Michael Boriskin played Perle's Six Etudes at his recital at the County Museum last week; he has also recorded these pieces, along with Perle's Second Piano Concerto, on a newly issued Harmonia Mundi disc: marvelous, strong music that speaks with its own voice while proudly honoring its stylistic past. Perle has composed steadily for most of his life, but there is a renewed strength in his music from the mid-1970s to the present time that suggests a kind of self-rediscovery, a sureness of expression that the earlier works only sporadically attained.

The etudes, composed between 1973 and 1976, vividly proclaim this new gathering of strength. Fiendishly difficult to play, they seem less like studies in piano technique (as with Chopin) and more like a series of explorations into the techniques of cajoling the limited resources of the piano into saying different and important things. In that expressive quality they summon up the marvelous (and too little known) etudes of

Debussy, and—even more—the astounding works of György Ligeti that were played here during the composer's memorable visit two years ago.

What attracts me the most in this music is its sense of play, of challenges presented to the hearer's powers of observation and assimilation and of rewards when those challenges are met. I know of almost no other living composer—Ligeti is the sole exception—who comes as close as Perle does to using an abstruse artistic language to impart so much delight. Like solving a tricky British crossword, you work your way through Perle's intricacy and come out refreshed, even euphoric.

That power—to engage the mind in the euphoria of problem solving—is communicated many times over in the nineteen-minute Second Piano Concerto, which dates from 1992. Refreshing, bristling music, its energy level is sometimes overpowering, mitigated only by its wit. The slow movement provides some relief: ethereal wisps of melody that seem suspended in deep silence, giving off tiny points of light as they make contact with one another.

Perle describes his musical language—quite accurately, I think—as "twelve-tone tonality." Perhaps his early identification with Alban Berg's music brings this about; in his Violin Concerto Berg seemed to have found his own way of blending twelve-tone devices into a distinctly G-minor tragic aura. But Perle has the unique ability to rip pages out of many books and make them sound like his own original style, evoking Stravinsky in the jagged rhythmic clashes in the first movement, Ravel in the ethereal dark aura, pierced by tiny beams of light in the slow movement. Drawing that blatantly on the surrounding world is a dangerous practice for any composer; Perle makes it work.

[March 1995]

Reich: Less Is More

Steve Reich's *Drumming*, which figured on his marvelous program at UCLA's Wadsworth Theater a few nights ago, turns twenty-five this week; its first performance, in New York, was on December 3, 1971. By that time Philip Glass had begun work on his *Music in Twelve Parts*; a new recording of that work has just come out on the Nonesuch label. By 1971 Terry Riley's *In C* had been around for three years, on a successful Columbia disc, and people were beginning to discover that, even without a little help from their friends, this piece maintained its power to surprise and delight. The performance of *Drumming* at Wadsworth presented only two of the four movements, about forty minutes' worth, but it made its point; the two available recordings of the complete work clock in at fifty-seven minutes (on Nonesuch) and eighty-five minutes (on Deutsche Grammophon); the four recordings of Riley's work run from twenty-six to seventy-six minutes; the Glass recording, on three discs, runs three and a half hours. None of these figures mean very much, except that all three of these ancestral pieces of the style commonly but erroneously known as minimalism create their own sense of time, which has no relationship to any other system of measurement. (The differences in timing in the various recorded versions stem from the leeway the composers allow performers to choose how many times a certain element is repeated, and at what tempo.)

The "minimalist" epithet became attached to this music because of the need for journalists to create easy pigeonholes; some similarity exists between the succession of fragments in, say, *In C* and the succession of abstract, hard-edged elements in an Ellsworth Kelly canvas or one of Richard Serra's massive, static blocks. Listening to *Drumming* the other night, I was caught up once again (as I always am) by the music's constant forward impulse. By the normal stopwatch, things happen slowly; a phrase hammered out by the tuned bongos or the mallet instruments may repeat verbatim four or seven or however many times, and then there comes a slight, almost subliminal change: a note overstressed, another note sort of oozed in, a tiny but perceptible glitch to destroy the music's even pulse. Amateur musicians I've heard sometimes think they're writing minimal music by going "bong bong bong bong, bong bong bong bong" for hours or weeks, repeating identical four-note patterns so that the music simply stops. What amazes me in Reich's and Riley's music, or in the early works of Glass before he went slushy, is the strength of its momentum.

Above all, listening to this music becomes a wonderful cleanout process for the ears. In the placid, undulating landscape laid out in these works at the start, the smallest change—the introduction, say, of a mildly dissonant F-sharp into Riley's C-major tonal horizon, or a shift of rhythm in one of the modules that make up Reich's music—becomes as much a cataclysm as the collapse of Valhalla at the end of Wagner's *Ring*. You learn to listen, rather than merely to hear, and the effects of this cleansing process can last for a lifetime.

Meanwhile, Reich has moved on. His program here—with most of the participants the same crew that has played his music from the start, freelance players who also play other gigs but return to Reich's music for refreshment—was a sweep in time from *Drumming* through the exhilarating Sextet (percussion and keyboards) of 1985 to the brand-new *Nagoya Marimbas* (a slight work) and *Proverb*. The Sextet is justly famous. Like the *Desert Music* of the year before, it proclaims its structure proudly, its sections set apart by a summoning short motif, its finale a sort of resume of what had come before. *Proverb*, available on the latest Reich disc (on Nonesuch), is delightful sport: a short epigraph, intoned by the splendid singers of Paul Hillier's Theater of Voices, spread out and dealt with in a style both new and old, edgy and innovative but also reminiscent of complex medieval polyphonies from the time of Pérotin's pioneering work at Notre Dame Cathedral: eight centuries of musical style artfully comprehended and condensed into an ecstatic quarter hour of sheer inventive chutzpah. For Reich—as for Luciano Berio, whose music I've also been ecstatically rediscovering this fall—I see no horizons close at hand, rather a reaffirmation of music's ongoing power.

[November 1996]

Stravinsky: Even Ludwig Nodded

My oh my, how the mail has poured in! "How could you?" their writers fairly scream, as if I had turned my back on motherhood, America, and a hot lunch for orphans—which, by the way, I haven't. What I have done, in all innocence and, I think, all honesty was to note my displeasure at being subjected to just short of a full hour of Igor Stravinsky's *The Soldier's Tale*, complete with narration, dancing, and what has always struck me in this work as an agonizing tendency to pad by repetition. Minus the story line—whose garrulousness suffers greatly in translation from the folksy French—and the music's tendency to chew its cabbage once or twice too often, *The Soldier's Tale* boils down to a twenty-three-minute suite: not top-drawer Stravinsky, but bearable. At the Ford Amphitheater the cabbage was expertly sliced by Esa-Pekka Salonen and a state-of-the-art ensemble, but we still were served the whole head to try to digest.

This is my statement on Stravinsky, definitive as of this morning but—as with all my statements—subject to change at the drop of a downbeat. I admire above all the pleasure in his own technique that his music radiates, his own great joy in the act of composition. *The Rite of Spring* remains his supreme score, most of all for the sheer arrogance that enabled its creation. It stands—beside Michelangelo's Sistine Chapel, Beethoven's "Eroica," and yours to name—as one of the truly brave, inexplicable, forward steps in the arts. Stravinsky never lost the motive power that his arrogance provided. It led him in time to the creation of other excellent scores, alongside a large repertory of intellectual flim-flam that, had it not flowed from the pen of the composer of *The Rite*, would surely have languished in limbo long ago. Not since George Frideric Handel had a major composer produced so high a proportion of trash to masterworks. One of the ongoing astonishments about Stravinsky comes when you try to equate, say, the triviality of the *Four Norwegian Moods* with the fervor of the *Symphony of Psalms*, the desiccated gestures of the Violin Concerto or *Oedipus Rex* with the elegant inventions in *Orpheus*.

I admire his continued intellectual curiosity. *The Soldier's Tale* came from a time, near the end of World War I, when awareness of America's music had begun to inundate European imaginations. American ragtime caught on quickly, more so at the start in Europe than in the United States. It conquered Stravinsky early in his game; there is some of it in *The Soldier's Tale*, and there are also two other ragtime pieces from 1918–19, both of them truly awful. In a career spanning over half a century he seemed obsessed with trying his hand, at least once, at every new musical style that came down the pike, and in those between-the-wars decades there were plenty of new styles to try.

The failure rate may have been high. I don't hold much hope for the claims to eternal-masterpiece status of most of the hybrids: the pseudo-baroque works like *Pulcinella* and the chamber concertos, the pseudo-atonal works like *Abraham and Isaac*, the pseudo-medieval Mass, or the pseudo-Tchaikovsky *Fairy's Kiss*. About the pseudo-Donizetti *Rake's Progress* I change my mind with every performance I witness. Yet we can read into the best of these works—or, let's say, the least bad—the process of a vigorous, questing mind investigating the vast panorama of his chosen art and trying it all on for size. That's a time-honored process; Bach studied his contemporaries by copying out and adapting their music, and Mozart did the same with Bach.

[August 2002]

Adams in Houston and at the Beeb

This first part was the last assignment of my four-year stint as Newsweek's classical-music editor. It never ran; this is its world premiere. Newsweek ran a Bruce Springsteen feature in its place.

They never hired another classical-music writer.

For a few glorious days last month the crossroads of the operatic world shifted to somewhere other than its usual place: not New York's Metropolitan, not Milan's La Scala, but all the way to Houston. Three new productions by the Houston Grand Opera, ranging from the grandly traditional to the off-the-wall wacko and including a much-anticipated world premiere: that's impressive enough for a week's work. Set it all in a gleaming new $70 million opera house boasting not one but two performance spaces. For all that only a word of pure Texan will do: wow.

The massive centerpiece in a three-acre downtown city site hard by Houston's well-known Alley Theater, the Wortham Center (named for the late insurance magnate Gus S. Wortham, whose $20 million donation topped the list of private donors) trumpets its greetings afar, through a massive eighty-eight-foot entrance archway that dominates architect Eugene Aubry's brightly lit brick-and-granite façade. Its two auditoriums, bearing names of other major donors—the 2176-seat George and Alice Brown theater and the 1066-seat Lillie and Roy Cullen—underscore the versatility of the Houston Grand Opera itself. In fifteen years under the master impresario David Gockley the company earned praise in both the crowd-pleasing grandiose repertory and for out-of-the-way operas in smaller-scale, experimental stagings.

In the latter regard, Houston's success in 'unlikely, even implausible operatic areas dwarfs that of most other American companies. Even last week's world premiere of John Adams's *Nixon in China* wasn't the company's first go at an American political figure. That honor goes to Carlisle Floyd's 1981 *Willie Stark*, whose Willie is a thinly disguised stand-in for the 1930s Louisiana demagogue Huey Long.

But *Nixon in China* is something else again; when in the world did composer and librettist project an opera whose characters are not the gods or deathless heroes of customary lyric lore but true-to-life personages still living or recently dead? "The myths of our time," composer John Adams has said, "are not Cupid or Psyche or Orpheus or Ulysses, but characters like Mao-ze Dong and Nixon." And the theatrical wunderkind Peter Sellars, who devised the original scenario and staged Houston's virtuosic production, supports the notion that political events as recent as 1972 "are ancient history already."

In any case, the subject of *Nixon in China* is exactly what the title suggests, a musical re-creation of the historic visit to lands where no American president had gone before, an intellectual confrontation between Eastern and Western leaders incredible in its social and political resonance. From the facts of that confrontation, the Chicago poet Alice Goodman has constructed as libretto a poetic fantasy that is, on its own, a masterpiece of psychological insight. President and Chairman first meet; in the space between the two men words slip past one another but never connect. Mao talks of philosophy; Nixon, of Taiwan. Pat Nixon visits schools and a pig-insemination lab; her well-rehearsed platitudes—"I treat each day like Christmas"; "I used to be a teacher many years ago, and now I'm here to learn from you"—ring poignantly, pathetically.

In a final scene worthy of romantic operatic tragedy, the Maos and Nixons join at a farewell banquet. Each couple drifts off into a private reverie, their words far apart yet contrapuntally linked: Madame Mao lost in the strains of a sleazy foxtrot with a husband young and dashing; Nixon and Pat back on war-torn Guadalcanal, dishing up hamburgers in an improvised canteen. "They called it Nick's snack shack," he remembers. "The smell of burgers on the grill made strong men cry...."

Haunting, powerfully resonant, this oddly evocative poetry...and Adams's lithe, observant music adds yet another level of distinction. Now forty and based in the San Francisco Bay Area, the New England–born Adams has emerged in recent years as the most romantic of the so-called minimalist composers, the one most ready to mingle the austere chug-chug of doctrinaire minimalism with a ragtime lick or, in his huge orchestral piece *Harmonielehre*, even a touch from such a currently out-of-favor composer as Sibelius. Still, nothing in his most successful music up to now paves the way for the mastery of musical drama that lights up scene after scene of *Nixon in China*, the variety of musical devices, here the familiar patterns of minimalism, there a soaring aria bringing a character fully alive. Here the obsessive repetitiousness of minimalism brilliantly underlines the sad dilemma of Nixon, trapped in his catch-phrases and mumbo-jumbo. (The opera has already spun off one successful separate item. The Maos' foxtrot from the final scene, fleshed out by Adams as a separate orchestral piece called *The Chairman Dances*, has made its way into the pop-concert repertory. Eat yer heart out, *Wozzeck*.)

Given the tough road ahead for any serious musical theater piece nowadays, *Nixon in China* cannot by itself be considered a breakthrough. What is truly remarkable here, however, is that Adams, with the considerable help of Goodman's words and the nonstop theatrical sense of the astounding Sellars, has fashioned that rare commodity, an opera (in Sellars's own words) "in a contemporary musical language that is not cheap, is also profound, and which also does the things that opera does." A piece for singing, in other words, a wonderful toy for a gifted director, a skillfully waged campaign against audience resistance to the new and the challenging: in these ways *Nixon in China* fully lived up to the hype and hoopla attendant on its conception and birth over the past several years.

[October 1987]

Adams at the Beeb at the Barb

On September 11, 2001, John Adams was in London, rehearsing vocal forces for the film version of his ten-year-old opera *The Death of Klinghoffer*, which was released later. By coincidence, the BBC was also preparing the work for its first-ever British hearing, at a John Adams weekend scheduled for the Barbican Centre the following January. "The news arrived in early afternoon," the fifty-four-year-old Adams later remembered:

> I walked out into the lobby, and there was all this television about the World Trade Center catastrophe. It only took a few seconds to realize that my opera had suddenly developed some built-in problems. Later that afternoon I met with the cast and the chorus to talk about whether we should cancel the performance or move on. Their message, and I think it was unanimous, was that they wanted to go on, that the opposition of inflammatory messages in Alice Goodman's libretto actually offered a special kind of solace. After all, *Klinghoffer* has lived on the edge of the cliff since its first performances in 1991. There were people then who hated it enough to want to kill it. Now I imagine they wish they had tried harder.

Like the earlier *Nixon in China*, the first collaboration with Adams, Goodman, and the high-flying stage director Peter Sellars, *The Death of Klinghoffer* was a venture in turning actual headlines into an operatic commodity—"CNN opera," as the genre soon became dubbed. Its action was the hijacking of the Italian cruise liner *Achille Lauro* by Palestinian terrorists in the summer of 1985 and the gratuitous murder of an American

Jewish wheelchair-bound tourist, Leon Klinghoffer. The opera surrounds the event with a series of deeply emotional elegiac choruses in which hypothetical groups of exiles, Muslim and Israeli, give personal voice to the conflicts and atrocities that divided their lands then and still do. Those thoughts are further echoed by participants in the drama—the confused, undermotivated Palestinians most of all. "America," snarls one of them, "is one big Jew." The major sin of the opera, as detractors have been trumpeting for ten years, now more loudly than ever, is that Adams's music and Goodman's words—many of them lifted straight from biblical lamentations—give the personages on both sides of a murderous conflict a genuine, lyrical personality. That wasn't always the plan, however. "Peter's scenario," Alice Goodman recalled, "was to tell the Klinghoffer story in the first act and then turn the tone into satire. We realized early on that this wouldn't work. In a sense, you could say that John and I hijacked the opera away from Peter." (Beaming as usual, Sellars was in London to hear his hijacked baby. "I wouldn't have missed it for the world," he chortled.)

Klinghoffer's would-be killers at the start included most of the East Coast press. I'll never forget the hot words during the bus ride back from the Brooklyn Academy after the premiere; another couple of blocks and there might have been a reenactment of the murder itself. Both the San Francisco and Los Angeles Operas were among the co-commissioners. The San Francisco performance in 1992 drew pickets from a Jewish information center; the Los Angeles performance never happened. By the time the Nonesuch recording came out, the opera was, by all accounts, already dead. Michael Steinberg's program note for the recording contained an ironically prophetic note: "On whichever date you read these words," he wrote concerning the tragedy of Leon Klinghoffer, "there will be a new installment in the morning paper."

Came September 11, Steinberg's words took on a new impact. So did the opera. In early October Mark Swed eloquently wrote, in a Calendar cover story in the *Los Angeles Times*, that the work had assumed an enhanced relevance that ordained a revival. A month later, however, the Boston Symphony Orchestra backed out of a performance of the inflammatory choruses—scheduled, of course, long before 9/11—for reasons diametrically opposite to the impulse of the London singers. On December 9 the *New York Times* carried a verbose polemic by the firebrand musicologist—if that isn't an oxymoron—Richard Taruskin to the effect that it would have shown "reprehensible contempt" for the Boston Symphony to have fulfilled its commitment. Back and forth flashed the letters of praise and condemnation; they still do. The BBC's concert performance at the Barbican Centre last weekend, triumphantly sung and powerfully led by Leonard Slatkin to begin a spellbinding three-day bash of Adams's music, was London's hottest ticket. On the same weekend the opera was also being performed in Italy at the Communale in Ferrara, in an English-language staging slated to make it to video. There, too, there were protesters outside the first performance. For the moment, *The Death of Klinghoffer* has become the world's most important opera.

In the years since *Klinghoffer*'s early travails, Alice Goodman has abandoned her Jewish upbringing and been ordained an Anglican minister; she now preaches to a largely Palestinian congregation at a church in London's outskirts. Adams, too, has moved explosively ahead, as London's weekend emphatically demonstrated. Still, the apparent resuscitation of his "problem" opera has brought back memories, which he enlarged upon in a breath-catching moment during his wall-to-wall celebration. "We knew we had a difficult subject," he recalled:

> Alice immersed herself in the Koran—in English, of course—which isn't what nice Jewish girls in Chicago naturally do. Like most American non-Jews, I had a vague idea about Jewish history. In the bookstores there was plenty to read on the subject from a Jewish point of view. Except for the writings of Edward Said, a powerful writer of Palestinian background, there was almost nothing from the other side. We read essays on the conflict, but we resolved to stay away from television and all the stereotyped interviews. What we wanted to do most of all—and this is where we had to part company from Peter's conception—was to give those terrorist

hijackers inner lives, through music and words. But that was enough to turn me into an anti-Semite in the eyes of very many people.

In some of my very old copies of Britain's *Gramophone* there are reviews of American composers—Bernstein, Copland—that ridicule the very oxymoron. How dare these upstart colonials, wrote the august Compton MacKenzie and his confrères, aspire to the sacred precincts of composition and demand space alongside our beloved Elgar? Even within the last decade the noted and notable film documentarian Tony Palmer (he of the nine-hour *Wagner*) was refused BBC support for an Adams documentary that eventually became the superb, privately funded *Hail Bop!* Times have, apparently, changed; the looks of the crowds that pushed into the convoluted precincts of the Barbican and stood in long queues in hopes (usually dashed) of turned-back tickets for concerts, even for pre-concert lectures, were widely spread from collegian to codger. If John Adams is any proof, the American composer has in British eyes advanced from curio to superstar.

Adams is, of course, a special case, a product of great creative skill and exquisite timing. Tarred with the academic rectitude of a Harvard education, he seemed to know when to walk away, when to blend the sounds of the real world into his acquired rigid Schoenbergian precepts. Academic purity was still the air of choice around 1971, but Adams had already learned to pollute it with alien accents: rock, jazz, and the freedoms preached by John Cage. The 1977 *Phrygian Gates*, the first music Adams acknowledges, is also his purest minimalist work: twenty-five minutes of richly colored throb all in one place, broken only near the end by a wrenching shift to somewhere else.

Adams remembered. "Minimalism was, for me, the greatest restorative force from the structures and the abstruse language of, say, Elliott Carter and the tone-row people, who were holding music in a death-embrace. It had that freshness, and it was listenable. At the same time, there was this stasis in early Philip Glass and Steve Reich. The music never went anywhere, and I wanted momentum. " That, indeed, is what begins to happen in the unfolding of Adams's meteoric career: the great swoop down from a holding pattern into a gut-busting outbreak of E-flat in the *Grand Pianola Music,* which drew boos at its 1983 New York premiere but survives as an early landmark in an illustrious career; the energy explosively uncoiling in twists and turns in the 1992 *Chamber Symphony*; the great hootenanny that takes over at the end of *Hallelujah Junction,* the glorious two-piano romp that Adams fashioned as a gift to Ernest Fleischmann last year.

The marvel of Adams splendidly, exhaustively (and, I have to confess, exhaustingly) surveyed in the Beeb's thirty-plus hours of music, film, and enlightened discussion—is his astonishingly gift for combinations, his exquisite skills at commanding the blending of a broad musical vernacular into a bristling newness. It doesn't always work, of course. *Guide to Strange Places*, a brand-new twenty-four-minute BBC commission (inspired by a travel book) that ended the weekend, came off as a somewhat drier reworking of the *Chamber Symphony*'s manic convolutions. *Century Rolls*, the piano concerto for Emanuel Ax that was played in Los Angeles last season, does tend to roll off the edge.

The Adams outpouring honored a BBC tradition: a weekend in January given over to a single composer, with everything broadcast (most of it live). Last year's honoree was Alfred Schnittke; Kurt Weill was celebrated the year before. Think of just that for a minute: a nation's prime radio facility given over to an in-depth exploration of important contemporary creativity. (Could, or would, KUSC? NPR?) The BBC Symphony is neither a superbly tuned nor an accident-proof orchestra; yet under Slatkin and, in the final concert, Adams himself, it still sent some brave and forthright playing out into the acoustically tricky Barbican Hall. (And, while I blush for entertaining such thoughts in a hall where Peter Sellars also sat, I found the *Klinghoffer* as a concert performance, with the chorus delivering its mighty and stirring invocations full face, a more profound experience than when staged.)

Mighty and stirring, to be sure; yet I don't think I am the only one to carry away and cherish memories as well of smaller sounds during the Barbican's Adams immersion: the wistful plangence of the Clarinet Concerto called *Gnarly Buttons* in Michael Collins's wonderfully colored performance; the phenomenal depths in Leila Josefowicz's playing of the Violin Concerto; the deep, lush sorrows in *The Wound Dresser*, the haunting Whitman poetry sung by Christopher Maltman; Rolf Hind's staggering delivery of *Phrygian Gates*.

One more memory. This one is of Adams before a capacity crowd at a pre-concert talk—dealing, as I remember, with the basic question of what music is, or ought to be.

"Something beautiful," said John Adams, "that tells the truth."

[January 2002]

Erickson: Local Sounds

Several years ago, in a rare burst of journalistic zeal, I tried to work out a clear definition of what it means to be a California composer. I interviewed electronic composers, neoromantic movie composers, pop-versus-classical fence-straddlers (i.e., Dave Brubeck), resolute serialists who had studied with Arnold Schoenberg and some who hadn't. I made the tapes into a radio series. I had probably known before I began the series that Robert Erickson would emerge as the archetypal California composer, and nothing in my travels changed my mind.

Erickson turns seventy-nine next week. He has been flat on his back, in his home north of San Diego, for most of the last ten years; a horrendous form of lupus—a disease that turns connective tissue into jelly—has rendered him virtually immobile in body, but not in mind and spirit. His composing has slowed, but not stopped, and he spends a lot of time immersed in detective novels. Two books have just come out that celebrate his life, his work and his influence. One, *Music of Many Means* (Scarecrow Press, edited by John McKay), consists mainly of the autobiographical and contemplative essays that Erickson himself has been writing over the years. The other, *Thinking Sound Music* (Fallen Leaf Press), is a biography-plus-evaluation by the critic and composer Charles Shere, a former Erickson student.

Among my most cherished possessions is the pile of tapes of my talks with Erickson over the years, conversations not so much about his own ego (which is minimal) but about the musical world at large, real or hoped for. "What we do more than anything else," he told me, "is to compose our environment." It's an irrefutable statement, whether it applies to a composer's physical environment (for Erickson) or the intellectual (Bach, Mozart, Schoenberg, you name it). The sounds of California fill many of Erickson's works. A piece called *Summer Music*, for example (available on a Musical Heritage Society disc), uses a tape of the babbling of a noisy brook in Sequoia National Park, processed through a system of filters and resonators (including organ pipes of various length that Erickson built by welding coffee cans together) so that it resembles the lulling patterns of a gamelan—and then uses the result as accompaniment to a solo violinist. Another, *Pacific Sirens*, mingles the crashing of surf at Pescadero with an ensemble of wind and brass instruments: "the music the Sirens might have sung to Ulysses," as Erickson puts it.

But Erickson's stature as a California composer doesn't only come about because he has taped and processed the sounds of the place. Something about his own life defines the difference between what composers do (or can do) here, the variety of accessible influences, including Asian, as opposed to the Europe-facing, serialism-tinged establishment beyond the mountains. "I was in and out of twelve-tone music before most composers had discovered it," he asserts. Moving to California (from his native Michigan) in 1953, he soon fell in with the generation of composers discovering that all the musical sounds they had grown up on were just a patch on the iceberg. The first electronic music had begun to circulate. The then-unknown Pierre Boulez first came to California in 1957, and in his luggage was a ten-inch LP from the Cologne electronic studio of Karlheinz Stockhausen's *Song of the Holy Children*, which got passed from hand to astonished hand. Meanwhile, John Cage and his pals had discovered the music embedded in brake drums and thunder sheets, further liberating musical expression from the confines of the diatonic scale.

As music director at KPFA, the first of the free-form, noncommercial Pacifica stations, Erickson put young composers on the air, including the ancestral minimalists Terry Riley and La Monte Young, before they had begun to dream about someday becoming famous. Bay Area radio, thanks to his pioneering efforts and his advocacy, became a wonderful public laboratory where we could all observe the phenomenon of musical progress. Under Erickson's guidance, some of the younger ardent innovators—Morton Subotnick, Steve Reich, and Pauline Oliveros among them—devised the San Francisco Tape Music Center, incorporating the Cage dictum that "music is whatever we say it is."

The philosophy here was truly Californian, not only in sound but in aura: a musical outlook free of, perhaps even contemptuous of, the academic serialists. Erickson, who taught at the University of California, Berkeley and the San Francisco Conservatory, was the ideal paterfamilias, passionate about expanding the limits of musical sounds but still aware of the disciplines that go into the making of all kinds of music. His first book, *The Structure of Music: A Listener's Guide* (Noonday, 1955) proposed a manner of listening to contrapuntal textures in music old and new without losing track of emotion and beauty. A later book, *Sound Structures in Music* (University of California Press, 1975), went even deeper into the way the manipulation of pure sound—never mind tonics and dominants and sonata form—can determine the effect on the hearer of a piece of music old or new.

In the late 1960s Erickson moved on to the University of California, San Diego, where he and a few like-minded colleagues founded a new kind of music department—"a place," he says, "where composers could feel at home the way musicologists feel at home at other schools." Music students at U.C. San Diego studied voltage control regulation and the use of synthesizers. In music-appreciation classes kids went out with tape recorders and created their own compositions out of natural sounds—as Erickson had done—rather than learning the dates of dead composers. Erickson designed, and composed for, instruments consisting of tuned rock slabs you could bang on and metal rods that you could stroke to make sounds like nothing else on earth. The performers at U.C. San Diego were as experimental in their outlook as the composers; with the phenomenal trumpeter Ed Harkins Erickson created *Night Music*, a piece in which the soloist bends his tone away from the normal notes, creating a shaft of audible moonlight that seems to shimmer through the surrounding instrumental ensemble. When I need to convince someone that it is still possible to create beautiful music this late in the century, the tape I usually play is of Erickson's *Night Music*. (There is no commercial recording on CD at the moment; the LP on CRI, which also included *Pacific Sirens*, cries out for reissue. A recording of one of the metal-rod pieces, *Taffytime*, is packaged with the Charles Shere book.)

Erickson is not as well-known as he deserves; during the time when he was recreating the whole concept of college-level music education, ransacking the landscape for new sounds for his own musical use, and turning them into music with instruments and gadgets of his own invention, he didn't bother much with playing the establishment game. Now, when he has more time on his hands, he has neither the strength nor the stomach to send out press releases or give TV interviews. Someone needs to rebuild his revolutionary instruments—which were damaged when the university's music department moved into new quarters—so as to revive the whole repertory of cool fantasy that they were designed to play. There are four string quartets in need of recording; the Kronos played them once, but doesn't anymore. There are big orchestral pieces—*Auroras* for one, a handsome work full of sunshine and the exultation of birds—that demand admission to the repertory.

His music, the art of the state, is also the state of the art.

[March 1996]

The Life of (Terry) Riley

Thirty-three years ago (my lord, really that long?) a twenty-eight-year-old, hitherto little known Bay Area composer named Terry Riley created a work called *In C* and thereby reinvented the whole process of listening to music. For centuries it had been a given (in the artistic outlook of the Western world, at least) to think of music as a structural process involving performer and listener in an ongoing progression toward a climax. A three-minute song or an hourlong symphony began somewhere, moved onward and upward through a gathering of tension to somewhere else, and then subsided to a point of resolution whose logical placement the audience could recognize in brain, heart, or gut. *In C*—and its innumerable progeny to which the convenient but not necessarily appropriate term minimalism has been attached—challenged that perception; here was music essentially static, a series of short musical "loops" anchored to an unchanging pulsation, with no ostensible goal except the arbitrary one set forth by the composer—that the performance would stop after all the players had gone through all fifty-three of the loops a stipulated number of times.

The impact on the hearer was (and still is) like viewing a cataclysm through the wrong end of a telescope. Where Beethoven tingles the scalp with a full orchestra thundering out a violent change of key, a single small dissonance—an F-sharp intruding into Terry Riley's placid C-major trance—can do the same. The details—the number of players, the order of the events, tempo, and dynamics—were to be decisions of the moment. Currently available recorded performances of *In C* run from twenty (Piano Circus, on Argo) to seventy-six (Good Sound Ensemble, on New Albion) minutes' duration; others have been known to last three hours. Riley claims that he wrote the whole work—the fifty-three separate fragments centering around the note C and the performance rubrics—during a trip on a San Francisco bus to his bartending job, as "something that all my friends could perform in, whatever their skills."

Some composers have been known to disown their firstborn (Pierre Boulez, for one); not Riley. He never again composed anything exactly like *In C*; don't expect to hear many traces of it at his County Museum joint concert with the fantastic Italian double bassist Stefano Scodanibbio next Monday. On the phone from the rural retreat in Gold Rush country that has been his home for the past twenty years ("four hours from the nearest symphony orchestra," he says with some pride), Riley sketched the impact the work had on his own life. "I had worked with other music involving repetitions, gradual shifts and pulsations," he recalled,

> but I always thought I had to write everything out exactly the way it had to be performed. *In C* showed me that I didn't have to. That discovery, in turn, got me to be thinking about music more in a solo mode, something that I could play at the piano, or sing and, most important, could improvise upon. Gradually, I got away from notating music at all, although I did some experimentation with graphic notation—John Cage's ideas, or Earle Brown's. In the Bay Area in the late 1960s everybody was discovering Indian music. A sitar player in Berkeley named Krishna Bhatt taught me about ragas and the way they worked. We had a lot of fun playing together, because we had two vocabularies which we could exchange. Incidentally, he tuned his sitar to C-sharp, so you could say that I had worked my way up the scale by at least one semitone.

From the psychedelic, out-of-body motionlessness of *In C* to the cumulative, improvisational energy of the raga was, for Riley, a crucial forward step. The Indian influence has remained a life force in his music, where it mingles easily with the jazz styles he absorbed over the years from working with the likes of Chet Baker and Bill Evans. There's a magical new disc, released last year on New Albion: a live recording of a piano concert by Riley in Lisbon in July 1995—a few weeks after his sixtieth birthday; in seventy minutes the music threads its way through the fullness of the life of Riley, pausing now and then for a delighted sampling of his many vocabularies, translating into radiant and serene sound the essence of the soft-spoken, smiling, bearded figure who created it all.

One thing, however, is missing on this particular disc. A fellow Berkeley student, La Monte Young, was also monkeying around with exotic musical influences—Japanese court music, Balinese gamelan, music built on stasis rather than progression—at about the same time as Riley. When Young moved to New York in the 1960s—the story persists that the Berkeley faculty gave him a scholarship just to get him out of town—he formed an improv group that investigated, among other things, the old tuning systems known collectively as just intonation, with intervals formed from the pure ratios (C to the G above = 3:2, C to the F above = 4:3, etc.) set down by Pythagoras, free from the compromises of "equal temperament" that came into European music around Bach's time, which created "impure" intervals but allowed composers to write in all keys. Riley joined Young's Theater of Eternal Music ensemble for a time and absorbed Young's fascination with the purity of just intonation. His *Harp of New Albion*, on a two-disc Gramavision set, is a piano solo in just intonation lasting just under two hours—puny in size, however, compared to Young's own five-hour *The Well-Tuned Piano* (also on Gramavision). The Lisbon recital, however, is performed on an equal-tempered piano. "It's just too much trouble, lugging a specially tuned piano all over the world," Riley told me. "It's a lot easier to reproduce the intervals on a synthesizer."

Working with other musicians—with Scodanibbio, say, as Riley has done in turn-away concerts in several European cities and New York and will do again next Monday at LACMA—won't that require writing down the music to keep the two players in synch? "Not at all," Riley said:

The sounds Stefano draws out of his instrument, especially the high harmonics, come out exactly in just intonation, and so I just tune my synthesizer to his intervals. When we first played together I thought I'd better write something down, but when we started working together we both found it was a lot easier just to play to one another. Once I taught Stefano the improvisation principles in playing ragas, we found our own synch. We don't waste time discussing what we're doing. It's better to let it happen. What's particularly great about working with him, on this improv, ragalike basis, is the way we constantly discover new things. Sometimes they happen when we least expect it.

The founding fathers of minimalism (whether they accept the title or not)—La Monte Young, Steve Reich, Terry Riley, and Philip Glass—have all turned sixty in the last few months; only John Adams dawdles a decade behind. Is sixty a frightening age? I asked Riley. "Not at all. Oh, sure, you realize that there's not as much time to do what you want to do, so you'd better go ahead and do it."

I think that living out here, surrounded by nothing but space, has had a lot to do with my music, as well as my outlook over all. I don't think of it as isolation, rather as the freedom to choose what I want to do, what I want to hear, what I don't. I don't try to isolate myself from other kinds of music, either. I grew up listening to Mozart, and I still do. And Bach, too. When I first started working with ragas, around 1970, I thought it was going to be a lot different from all the music I grew up with. But, without stretching a point, I immediately noticed a kinship between the way a piece by Bach can unfold, gradually getting bigger, more complex, and what happens when a superb Indian musician unfolds a raga. There are a lot of connections in music, maybe more than some people realize.

[March 1997]

Home Brew

At the County Museum these weeks, the eye and the ear are beguiled with evidence of creative urges irradiated by the California sun. Through vast and noisy rooms we are confronted with pictures of painted orange crates, Japanese internment camps, and platinum-blonde movie queens. In the museum's Leo S. Bing Theater the music of Californians, adopted and native, eloquently contradicts the outside world's image of the state as beach-blanket banality. Even the Los Angeles Opera's current offering, Puccini's *La Bohème*, has its local connection: its first-ever American hearing took place in October 1897 at the Los Angeles Theater downtown when a touring company from Italy, heading for a gig in Mexico, ran out of travel funds and landed here instead. To native son and voluntary immigrant alike, there is reason in this area's musical history for pride of place.

In 1936 George Antheil could write of Hollywood as "the Mecca of young American composers." In the current programming, fortunately, we are being spared the kind of cheesy stuff Antheil was grinding out by then, long after his brief zoom across the horizon. LACMA's Focus on California series began with the percussion concert I wrote about (glowingly) two weeks ago. Last week's program was compounded of sterner stuff, most of it from the European contingent that settled here (beginning with Arnold Schoenberg, in 1934), supported its own pastry shop

(Benes, on West Third Street, still flourishing), and sought to transplant its own musical ideals into alien soil.

There was nothing the least bit warmed by the local sun in Hanns Eisler's 1943 Third Piano Sonata, which Leonard Stein played earnestly to start the LACMA concert; how could there be, when Eisler's only truly California-inspired work was a set of songs vividly detailing his hatred for the place? Schoenberg's String Trio of 1945, his last major twelve-tone work and as eloquent a statement as any of the expressive power of that style, could have taken shape in pre-Hitler Berlin. Ernst Krenek's *Aulokithara* of 1971, originally composed for oboe, harp, and orchestra and dolled up a year later by transferring the orchestral accompaniment to what passed for electronic sounds ("whoosh-whoosh, plink-plank") at the time, could pass for anyone's overextended academic exercise, anywhere in the world, anytime from 1930 on. Igor Stravinsky would later make his own accommodation to local musical language, but his 1944 *Elegie* for solo viola, small-scale but elegantly fashioned, was again a work of no time or place.

That left Ingolf Dahl's 1946 *Concerto a tré* as the evening's one unmitigated charmer, as though old Benes himself had been standing at the door handing out his renowned *Apfelstrudel*. Otherwise, the evening's major delight was the high quality of performance, from the iconic Stein; the string players Maiko Kawabata, David Walther and William Skeen; the oboist David Sherr (ambulating through Krenek's prescribed stageful of oboes in a vain search for interesting music); the harpist Amy Wilkins; and the smiling clarinetist Gary Gray, whose smile rubbed off onto Ingolf Dahl's piece and became a positive gleam.

[February 2001]

That Other '70s Show

Having served us nobly, for the past thirty years or so, in resurrecting both the music of the distant past and its surrounding ambience—baroque chamber music in a baroque-ripoff Pasadena mansion, say—MaryAnn Bonino's Da Camera Society have now brought their explorations to within shooting range of nowadays. The substance on a recent sunny Sunday was some of the musical monkeying around that had been perpetrated hereabouts in and around the 1970s. The chosen venue was the reconverted railroad freight depot that now houses the anything-but-retro enclave of architectural wisdom known as SCI-Arc (Southern California Institute of Architecture). For baroque gimcrackery, substitute raw concrete. The entertainment, too, was solid.

Ah, the '70s! In New York the movement known as Fluxus had served to rekindle the anything-goes spirit of Dada of the recent past: the topless Charlotte Moorman playing her cello (not too well); Nam June Paik mooning the audience (sparse, I'm happy to report); La Monte Young and his smashed (cheapo) violins. Something of Fluxus emigrated to CalArts in its early days, back when it was the only enclave of human habitation up on the hills above Valencia. Most of the membership of the current EAR Unit—which performed at the concert two Sundays ago—were students at CalArts in those days. You could trace their Fluxus inheritance right at the start, as the group distributed the afternoon's printed programs to the crowd in the form of paper airplanes. Later on, indeed, a violin or two got smashed.

There was greater substance in other of the afternoon's music, but not necessarily greater quality. There was Henry Brant, doing then what he does now, trying to enhance the impact of some basically academic note spinning by spreading the performers around the space. There was some of Frank Zappa's indigestible goulash, stirring half a dozen kinds of music (rock, blues, twelve-tone, misunderstood Varèse) into one cacophonous proclamation that Unplayable Is Preferable. There were early pieces by composers on their way up—Jim Tenney, Steven Mosko, Daniel Lentz—in show-off styles they would soon disown. And there was one piece, Mel Powell's serene, fragrant *Immobiles* for instruments delicately surrounded by electronic murmurings, that on the criterion of pure quality was of greater worth than anything else that day.

But the concert wasn't so much about quality as spirit. Everything that was happening in the '70s—at least everything that was sampled at this one exhilarating event—seemed to be happening for the first time. Electronic music was a brand-new box of toys only recently opened. Other composers—Iannis Xenakis, for one—would invent more interesting uses for space than Henry Brant had found. Mel Powell would create a more extensive, even more beautiful legacy than this one small jewel. As the low man in the critics' hierarchy at the *New York Times*, I was assigned to most of the Fluxus events at Carnegie Recital Hall and other low-rent venues way back when, but I don't remember any of them as being as much fun, or as loaded with as much truly smart joyousness, as the EAR Unit provides these days. It was fun being *there* for that one afternoon—and the SCI-Arc building, teeming with young, creative impulse, was surely worth the trip—but I prefer being *here*.

[March 2003]

PEOPLE

I have shaken hands with all but one of these people. All have, in some way, enhanced my own sense of closeness to some part of the musical world. There are magical people in that world: the wizards on podiums who draw Beethoven and Berlioz out of the tip of a stick, the pianists who do that with the tips of their ten fingers. There are composers who take dictation from mysterious higher powers and transcribe it into half-hours of inexplicable mystery and beauty. There are the organizers who can make all this happen: the managerial types who bring musicians together in enchanted venues and make it imperative that the world turn up at their feet; the real working stiffs who move from one freelance gig to the next, can switch musical styles (Bach to bop on a moment's notice), and see to it that our hills are truly alive with the sounds of music. I've known people—the New York Times editor who hired me, for one—who loudly proclaimed that any critic who hobnobbed with other people in the profession was leaving himself open to charges of corruption, selling out, and colluding with the enemy. Bushwa; I love my job because I love the people in it. Most of them, anyway.

Armen Ksajikian: Akbar of the Armadillo

Some scenes from the life of Armen Ksajikian:

A limo hurtles along the Florida Keys Causeway; the driver, who looks like the Middle Eastern terrorist of your worst nightmares, frantically blathers over the car phone, while Arnold Schwarzenegger hangs overhead from a helicopter. Then the car and driver are blown to smithereens.

The Hollywood Bowl Orchestra, formed three years ago to take on the lighter side of summertime Bowl programming, comes onstage; one cellist out front bears a striking resemblance to the terrorist in the car.

The Armadillo String Quartet, whose members are among the city's top-flight freelance players, performs some of the more serious music of Peter Schickele, sometimes also known as P. D. Q. Bach, in a downtown concert. The quartet's cellist is, once again, a dead ringer for that walking monolith from the Crimson Jihad.

A backup band plays with the Eagles at one of their recent concerts. People in the audience spot the cellist and start to chant "Akbar! Akbar!! AK-BAR!!!" Others look around in annoyance. "There's nobody named Akbar with the Eagles," a man proclaims. That night, however, he's wrong.

Armen Ksajikian was playing with the Hollywood Bowl Orchestra in the summer of 1993 when a studio casting director picked him out through her binoculars and decided that he was exactly the monster director James Cameron had been searching for to play Akbar, the lead terrorist in *True Lies*. It mattered not that Ksajikian had never acted in his life; the fate that once befell nubile starlets at the Schwab's Drugstore soda fountain, only a few blocks away, now claimed a thirty-six-year-old, 300-pound-plus, Soviet Union–born freelance musician. (The job also afforded Ksajikian an overdue honeymoon. On the Hollywood Bowl Orchestra's Japanese tour a year before, Ksajikian had found common cause with the tour publicist Vanessa Butler; they were married on the Bowl stage a few months later.)

Curious contrast: Akbar on the screen, the menacing, glowering countenance, framed in a forest primeval of dark beard; the soft-spoken, serene musician in his hillside garden in Eagle Rock, cultivating prize roses for a hobby. Once he was taken onto the *True Lies* team, Ksajikian got his acting lessons—"mostly in the art of standing around and looking evil" and some further training in handling an Uzi or an AK-47. Better yet, he was also hired to participate on the music track, including the chance to accompany his own death scene. The double life has its amusing moments. "I drive around in my trashy old Cadillac with the 'AKBAR' license plates," he told me. "People pull alongside to see if it's really me, but when I smile at them they decide it couldn't be, so they drive off."

He has no immediate plans for a further film career, along the line, say, of *Akbar's Revenge* or *Truer Lies*. At the moment Ksajikian is doing just fine in his other world, one of the steadily employed freelance players who move from gig to gig, from studio to recording job to the Bowl. In one recent week he played for two upcoming movies, *Batman Forever* and *Nine Months*, worked on a demo recording for the jazz pianist Chick Corea, played with the bluegrass-turned-jazz composer Richard Greene, and took a day off to celebrate his birthday with some work in the garden. The movie jobs were especially tough. "Laying down the music track is usually the last thing that happens. You're working less than a week before release date, and there's tremendous pressure to get everything right the first time."

On the other hand, the current situation for studio musicians is better than it has been for several years. The trend now is once again toward big, heavily scored epics; the new Batman movie used an eighty-member, symphony-sized orchestra. "That wasn't the case a few years ago," Ksajikian remembered. "Synthesizers were putting live musicians out of business; more and more movies and series were being scored out of people's garages. Then there was the invasion from the orchestras in Eastern Europe, who would work for peanuts. But you kept hearing stories of orchestras in Hungary, or wherever, who just couldn't cut the music. Now we're working again."

In 1976, at nineteen, Ksajikian and his parents emigrated to the United States from Abkhaziya, part of the former Georgian Soviet Socialist Republic. "I had studied cello for seven years at the conservatory at Sukhumi, but I had little other schooling and not a word of English. Somehow I knew that I had to get into the Musicians Union right away, and so I started pulling down little jobs: $30 for a gig with the orchestras in La Mirada or Downey or at a senior citizens' home. Gradually, it began to add up."

Gradually, too, the name began to get around. Freelance musicians—in Los Angeles and everywhere else as well—get their assignments through union contractors (who are not always musicians and don't always choose on the basis of musicianship). "A lot depends on whether you're liked," Ksajikian said, "and that depends on how long you've been around and what you were willing to accept at the start. You can come to town with a big career behind you—Sidney Weiss, for example, the former Philharmonic concertmaster, but now a freelancer—but you still go through a long process to get to that inner circle":

> The best thing a freelancer can have is the ability to move quickly through a lot of different styles: to play with the Bowl Orchestra, then do some jazz and bluegrass, and get it all right the first time. The next best thing is drive; you learn to accept everything, even if it means ten to twelve sessions a week. I try to arrange my movie dates so as not to conflict with the Bowl, but I know that a good movie engagement can pay as much as a whole Bowl season. I know one guy who works with me in the studios, and during lunch he goes across the street and records jingles.

And when the timing gets too tight, he sends his wife to play, because she's also good.

But then I know another guy who turned down a jingle, which would have meant thirty-five minutes of work. Several months of residuals later, each of the people who worked on that jingle had received 128 checks, $58 each: nearly 7500 bucks for a half-hour's work.

Even with cutbacks in studio activity and the virtual demise of the local recording industry, Southern California is still a paradise for free-lance musicians—once, that is, that they break into the inner circle. Players work by day in the studios, for movies, TV series, commercial jingles, recording dates. At night they salve their artistic consciences by playing more demanding—but far less lucrative—dates with the Los Angeles Chamber Orchestra, the Pasadena and Long Beach Symphonies, the Hollywood Bowl Orchestra, or a chamber ensemble at the County Museum. The steadiest employment in town is, of course, with the Los Angeles Philharmonic, which has a fifty-two-week contract, but it doesn't leave its players much leisure time for outside activities.

To Barry Socher, even that small amount of leisure time is important. A member of the Philharmonic's first-violin section, Socher was one of the founders, in 1979, of the Armadillo Quartet, with the violinist Steve Scharf and the violist Ray Tischer; Ksajikian joined in 1982, replacing the original cellist, Roger Lebow. Socher dreamed up the name after a visit to the Armadillo World Headquarters in, of course, Texas. Currently the group is working up a demo CD in hopes of a recording contract and planning its next annual concert of Peter Schickele's considerable cham-ber-music legacy. "I worked with Peter in the P. D. Q. Bach days," Socher remembered, "and even dreamed up a few skits of my own: the composer Wolfgang Amadeus Schwartz and his oratorio *Irving in Egypt*." The security of the Philharmonic job is comforting, but the Armadillo Quartet is, to Socher, no less important. "In twenty-five years I have never been without a string quartet."

Like Ksajikian, Socher started life in the maw of the Los Angeles freelance machine. "But I got to substitute with the Philharmonic on a regular basis, and accepted the invitation to join on the strength of Carlo Maria Giulini's brand of music-making." But doesn't the security of the Philharmonic job also bring a certain sense of routine? Not necessarily; even faced with the upcoming routine of Hollywood Bowl, with its emphasis on the familiar masterpieces and the downplaying of the adventurous repertory that Esa-Pekka Salonen brings to the winter season, the players have their own ways of devising diversions. Every June for several years, for example, Barry Socher and several other Philharmonic members have cruised some of the most dramatic Western rivers (the Colorado in the Grand Canyon, for example) on a huge raft, tying up here and there to play chamber music in natural outdoor settings for tour groups that sign up for the series.

To Armen Ksajikian, the one non-Philharmonic "outsider" who tags along on these river cruises, his own life has been a year-to-year avoidance of the kind of routine a Philharmonic job might entail:

> I'm just afraid that, however good that permanent orchestra might be, there comes a time when resentment, or just weariness, might set in. I remember a situation from years ago, when the New York City Opera used to play the Music Center, and they'd hire a few freelancers to fill out their orchestra. The New York cellists were so hostile to one another that they refused to share music stands; we had to cram the orchestra pit with extra stands. That, to me, is the end result of people playing together too long. Here is what I like about freelance playing. It's the sense that this is *my* gig, and that I'm the one who can make it happen.

The Hollywood Bowl Orchestra starts its season on June 30 and plays almost every weekend through September. Watch for the big guy down front among the cellos, making it happen. Just don't offer him a movie contract; that has already gone by.

[May 1995]

Mary Ann Bonino: The Best of Site and Sound

MaryAnn Bonino comes into the room, and her smile is like the lighting of a hundred crystal chandeliers. She welcomes the crowd, most of them by name. The scene is timeless: a grand room in some home or public building of great beauty, with a gracious hostess greeting the guests, who have come for an evening of splendid music. It could be at the Medici Palace in Florence in the Renaissance, or at Count Esterházy's palace in Austria with Joseph Haydn as composer in residence. It happens to be, however, one of the Da Camera Society's Chamber Music in Historic Sites concerts in the Los Angeles of here and now; the main difference is that, instead of taking place in the demesne of some particular well-heeled noble patron, these concerts happen all over the local map.

If you ever needed proof that we live in the best of all worlds, you need only drop in at one of these Historic Sites events for reassurance. It's one thing to take in a musical event at any of the functional concert venues in the area: the corporate-boardroom blandness of the Chandler Pavilion at the Music Center, the glitz of the Disney Concert Hall, the academic conservatism at Royce. It's quite another to hear medieval vocal music in a church setting where the decor seems to form an embrace around the sound, or chamber music in the spacious rotunda of a restored downtown mansion whose builders a century ago had designed the room for exactly that purpose. It's one thing to pile out of a concert hall and immediately onto a freeway in this most centrifugal of cities; it's another to linger over drinks and desserts after some exceptionally rewarding program of out-of-the-way music from some corner of the distant past, swapping impressions with fellow concertgoers.

Bonino, herself a musicologist, a former musical commentator on KUSC-FM in its enlightened bygone days, and now and then a pre-concert lecturer at the Philharmonic, first combined her architectural passions with her musical evangelism nearly two decades ago. Mount St. Mary's College, where she hangs her professorial shingle, has as the centerpiece of its downtown campus the ninety-three-year-old Doheny mansion, whose original owners took great delight in welcoming distinguished musicians to perform in their grand, glass-roofed rotunda. Never mind that the room's marble floors and vast dome created something of an acoustical horror (and still do); the point is that music in such a handsome space can look the way it sounds, which is something that could never happen at the Music Center.

Bonino started her Da Camera Society in 1973 for invitational musical events at the Doheny mansion, programs of chamber music by local artists and a few big-name visitors who could be convinced of the value of playing in agreeable surroundings for small audiences, as compared with the faceless thousands in the big halls. "People loved the idea," she remembers, "and they kept suggesting other places in town where music could again take on that extra glow." The "historic sites" idea emerged in 1980, when the Los Angeles Cultural Affairs Department suggested a one-shot series of concerts in several historic venues as part of the city's bicentennial. Now it's twenty-five years later, and that one shot remains one of the city's hot-ticket cultural attractions.

One of the problems brought on by the relative newness of the Los Angeles area—relative, that is, to the Parthenon of ancient Greece or the pyramids of even more ancient Egypt—is that people aren't instinctively responsive to the history of the local scene. "History is always somewhere else," as Bonino put it over waffles at a woodsy Santa Monica hangout a few days ago. "I grew up in Los Angeles, and the problem here has always been our tendency to isolate ourselves from our environment, to get in a car and drive off. Even with the efforts of groups like the Los Angeles Conservancy and the Pasadena Heritage, we need to remind people more vigorously about the great buildings here, the wonderful old homes, the churches, the public buildings."

Bonino sees her Historic Sites concerts as aiding that awareness:

> You can give people a guided tour through an old building, and that's fine. But if you fill that building with music, so that you direct people's senses to the entire dimension of the space, the echoes from the corners and the reverberations down the halls, that's even better. Take that Fine Arts Building downtown—Seventh and Flower or thereabouts—with its great Ernest Batchelder tiles and its Gothic arches that make you think of twelfth-century architecture. Sure, it's all WPA Romanesque rather than truly venerable, but it's actually modeled after a particular old church in Italy. And so, when I brought in the group called Sequentia, which specializes in twelfth-century music, including the works of that amazing mystical abbess Hildegard of Bingen, and set them up in that Fine Arts Building, the effect was overwhelming. You want "authentic" performance practice? Well, there it was!

Talking to Bonino, you can't help admiring the wonderful time she must be having, working out those imaginative matchings of site and sound that make these Historic Sites concerts the hot ticket that they are. My own memories of her presentations over just the past couple of years include a wondrous variety of musical experiences. Take, for example, England's Tallis Scholars, the best early-music specialists around, whom Bonino has presented here not only in old-style churches but also once in the great vertical space of the City Hall rotunda. Take a great weekend on Catalina a few years ago, with chamber concerts jammed into nearly every lavish mansion in sight, and a spectacular night of silent movies and movie-palace organ music at the Avalon Theater. Take another weekend last year at Murieta Hot Springs, where you could drop in for a concert, drop out for a mud bath and massage, and drop back in again for more music.

"The idea of these concerts wasn't *supposed* to work," says Bonino with the assured smile of one whose idea has, indeed, worked. The concerts are pricey, up to a $56 top for the Los Angeles Guitar Quartet, playing next March at the brand-new, deliciously wacko Lawson-Westen House in West Los Angeles. ("The first concert to sell out this season," gloats Bonino.) Given the amenities, however—the settings, the splendid informality that often includes catered post-concert refreshments, the chance to mingle with the artists, and, above all, that welcoming Bonino smile—the price seems exactly right.

This season's offerings add up to the typical Da Camera mix: four Friday nights of chamber music at Doheny, more chamber music in great hotel ballrooms (the Biltmore and the newly restored Ritz-Carlton Huntington), three nights of ancient vocal music in church and synagogue settings. The great Odetta sang her throbbing folksongs not long ago at the First A.M.E. Church; the jazz saxophonist Teddy Edwards brought a combo into—why not?—Union Station. And, on the matter of matching settings to music, consider the Ying Quartet, four siblings named Ying, who play serious chamber music in a few weeks at a downtown *dim sum* palace.

Beyond question, Bonino's enterprise over two decades highlights all the old clichés about the relationship of architecture to music. "Sure, architecture is frozen music, everybody knows that," says Bonino. "It seems to me, however, that these concerts prove that the arts really combine. After twenty years of this, I've gotten to the point where eyes and ears, seeing and hearing, become part of the same impulse. And I don't think that's so bad."

[November 1992]

Chen Yi: The Gang of Four Invades Orange County

There was a time in China, Chen Yi remembers, when playing Paganini on your violin—or Mozart or Beethoven—could land you in a labor prison, your instrument confiscated or burned. "I was about thirteen," she says, "and I remember that I had to play with heavy blankets over the windows and a big iron mute over the strings to mute the sound."

That began in 1966, at the time of the infamous Cultural Revolution (which was anything but cultural), organized to support the artistic policies of Mao Zedong and his nihilistic wife and carried forward by the formidable Red Guard and their up-front Gang of Four. One astonishing relic from that sorry page in Chinese history, however, has been the emergence of yet another gang of four: four composers of extraordinary talent, born within four years of one another (between 1953 and 1957), all of them with the same history: early musical talent, crushed by governmental forced labor for a time, emerging all the better for their experience to gain international fame. All four—Chen Yi, her husband Zhou Long, Bright Sheng, and Tan Dun—managed the transition to American acclaim (and green cards) in the 1980s.

This latter-day gang of four is in Orange County this week to participate in the Pacific Symphony's annual American Composers Festival (which has now and then been "American" by a stretch; two years ago it was Dvořák). That event starts off on March 1 with a concert and demonstration of indigenous Chinese instruments at the University of California, Irvine's Barclay Theater, featuring music old and new including works by the attendant composers. On March 7, at the small Founders Hall underneath Costa Mesa's Segerstrom Hall, art historians will link recent developments in Chinese painting to the striking emergence in that country's music by the four visiting composers plus Pasadena's own Joan Huang. The festival reaches its climax on March 10 and 11 at Segerstrom Hall, with music by all four composers performed by Carl St. Clair and the Pacific Symphony, including the world premiere of Chen Yi's *Ballad, Dance and Fantasy for Cello and Orchestra*, with Yo-Yo Ma as soloist.

On the phone from her home in Brooklyn, just back from performances of her *Chinese Myths Cantata* in England—a characteristic work combining indigenous instruments and men's chorus (Chanticleer)— Chen Yi is her usual *sparkle*, sounding very much like her piece of that name that stole the show at a Green Umbrella concert not long ago. Her message, however, is anything but sparkly as she reminisces about life under that other Gang of Four:

> I think my life was even more miserable than the other composers, because my parents were really, *really* bad—in the eyes of Madame Mao, that is. My father was a doctor, which meant that he had contact with all kinds of Western medicine—*very* bad. My mother worked in a hospital. When the Red Guards came first to our building, in 1966, our neighbors tried to tell them that we were all good people and that they should leave us alone, and so they went away for a while. But in 1968 they came back. My mother was made a prisoner in that hospital, and I was taken out to work, to plant vegetables—barefoot—and to carry 100-pound loads of stone and mud up the hill, maybe 20 times a day.

It's only recently that we have come to realize the impact of that horrifying decade in Chinese cultural history: the destruction of an entire educational system and of an educated generation. Throughout that overpopulated nation for an entire decade, young people raised in good middle-class homes were forced to abandon their career ambitions and shanghaied into labor camps and youth gangs in the Chinese countryside. We know their story only because of the few happy endings—the four surviving composers brought together by favoring circumstance being one small example.

Yet the benefits from just this small composer group have already had an impact on the contemporary musical scene. From all four composers there has emerged a substantial repertory of striking, original music: the delightful sound creations (involving water, paper, and all manner of toy creations as well as large-scale devices) that sent Tan Dun high onto the charts; the wrenching musical memoirs of Bright Sheng; and the remarkably vivid works of Chen Yi, with their rich, colorful combinations of large-scale Western orchestral tone and the dark mysteries of sinuous Chinese melodies.

Somehow fate—or the ancient gods of music—intervened in the case of all four young musicians, all of them initially dragged off toward a destiny similar to Chen Yi's. Dog-tired as she was by her daily exertions, she still found time to entertain her co-workers with revolutionary songs on her violin at night. "I felt a big release," she says, "in being able to exercise some creativity in making something out of these circumstances. Frankly, it wasn't until the Cultural Revolution that I found my roots, my motherland, and really appreciated the simple people of the earth. I found my own language when I realized that my mother tongue is really the same as what the farmers speak." Off in Mongolia, her future husband, Zhou Long, in another labor camp, experienced the same epiphany, driving a tractor by day and playing the accordion for folk dances at night. Bright Sheng taught himself piano at a work farm in Qinghai province. Tan Dun, youngest and mostly completely self-taught of the four, planted rice in a commune by day and sought out musical sounds in rocks, water, and paper by night.

"In 1970," Chen Yi remembers,

> Madame Mao had composed a revolutionary opera, a big piece that needed a Western-style orchestra. But all the Western-style musicians in Beijing had been fired and sent to prison camps, so they needed a new orchestra and very quickly. So suddenly I had a job playing my violin, out in the open! Not only that: I had to compose a lot of music, very quickly: overtures, dance pieces, songs. Now I had a job, and most of the other composers came to work with me in the Beijing Opera as well. We had a company that toured through many cities, and that made life a little better.
>
> By the time the Cultural Revolution was over and the Chinese conservatories could be open again—1977, I think it was—I had a huge pile of compositions to submit, from the music that I had composed for the operas. No, it wasn't very good, and no, I don't want to use any of it now, but everybody was amazed that I had such a large pile. Still, I had to start at the beginning, to learn orchestration techniques and harmonies and to do all the straight things that I had been doing just by instinct. In 1986 the Chinese Central Philharmonic gave a whole concert of my work. But I had gone as far as I could at the Beijing Conservatory, so I applied to Columbia and was accepted. I got a visa in one week—imagine that!
>
> Also I got to travel with Tan Dun on a project to collect folk music in Chinese villages. We would travel some distance on a bus, and then we would walk, maybe ninety miles, to where there was a singer or a musician that we could record.

This was the same thing that Bartók had done, recording the folk music of his native Hungary, and it helps to define the particular strength in the music of Chen Yi. Listen to her latest disc: *Momentum*, a thirteen-minute orchestral work on Sweden's BIS label, or the *Chinese Myths* on New Albion; not packaged exotica on the Rimsky-Korsakov level, these are strong, confrontational pieces in which the strands of Chen Yi's own concerns stand forth in stark relief.

If anything can be said about music's direction in this new century, it could very well define itself in a new language typified by these taut, intense sounds brought to us by Chen Yi and her countrymen: a language in which the dominant European tendencies that have moved music through past centuries mingle easily with the sounds and sound ideals of the far side of the Pacific Rim. Many other composers seem to be experimenting with this new stylistic mix—Asians and Americans as well. There will be much to hear, and to learn from, in Orange County these next few days.

[February 2004]

The Gould/Bernstein Brouhaha

Legends die hard, in music as in the real world. They flourish like hardy garden growth, spreading and changing their shape from generation to generation and profiting now and then from a touch of the pruning shears. Once in a while even the hardiest of legends may die; the wise gardener will dig them up and leave room for the stronger plants nearby.

Glenn Gould, himself one of music's supreme legends, is in the news these days, not yet three years after his untimely death, at fifty, in October 1982. No fewer than three books on or by him have appeared recently, including the *Glenn Gould Reader* (Knopf, $20), a marvelous, extensive collection of essays compiled by the critic Tim Page, writings on a profusion of subjects (Bach, Mozart, twelve-tone music, the Canadian North as love object, critics as the butt for well-earned ridicule, etc.) that reveal one of the great original minds—iconoclastic, if you will—of our times. Another book, shorter but equally brilliant, contains the far-ranging interview with Jonathan Cott, *Conversations with Glenn Gould* (Little Brown, $15.95), that originally ran in *Rolling Stone*, a model of mind-speaking by two intelligent, concerned individuals, an object lesson to any musician cornered by a journalist or talk-show host. Moreover, CBS has begun a reissue of most of Gould's major recordings, which cover the ground all the way from Bach's *Goldberg Variations* to Gould's own transcription of Wagner's *Meistersinger* Overture.

Here was a musician celestially endowed, or so it sometimes seemed, both to play the piano and to generate legends with prodigious skill. Like him or not—and neutrality didn't come easily—you couldn't help *knowing* about him: about his strange dress habits, which included overcoats on summer days and half-gloves while playing; his slouch at the keyboard, his nose almost touching the keys; his sing-along that threatened to drown out the notes; the glass of water at hand and frequently resorted to.

I did an interview with Gould back in 1959 after one of his San Francisco appearances. I had primed myself on the extant legends, especially the one about his aversion to physical contact, but I had neglected to brief my recording engineer. After the interview the engineer did the most normal thing: He reached over to shake Gould's hand. I froze in horror, expecting the floor to open at our feet. Not at all; Gould returned the handshake even as you or I. I ventured one myself. It felt like...well, like a handshake.

Above all, there were the great fight stories: the lawsuit against the Steinway piano people because an employee had ventured a friendly tap on the back, the squabble with George Szell that resulted in Szell's turning the podium over to an assistant (and Szell's later comment that "that nut's a genius"), and, above all, the Bernstein Brahms brouhaha. It is on that last legend that some vigorous pruning is long overdue.

"All Worked Up" over Brahms

In April 1962 I was one of the underlings in the music section at the *New York Times*, mostly covering debut concerts at Carnegie Recital Hall and knocking out an occasional interview for the Sunday Arts and Leisure section. The top critic was Harold C. Schonberg, and among his personal legends was his omniscience in all matters of the piano and pianists (both of which, I suspect, he truly believed he had invented). In those days critics reviewed the Friday matinee concerts by the New York Philharmonic; the Thursday night events, at which Leonard Bernstein sometimes gave talks about the Inner Meanings of the music at hand, were considered "previews" and, thus, immune from the press.

On Friday afternoon, April 6, Harold got back from the Philharmonic in a mood that might be described as "all worked up." Glenn Gould was the soloist that day, in the D Minor Piano Concerto by Johannes Brahms. Two years before his sudden retirement from the concert stage, Gould was at the height of his popularity and of his ability to stir up controversy. Harold was not what you'd call an ardent admirer; in his book *The Great Pianists* Gould doesn't even rate a whole sentence, just a few words tacked onto a sentence about some other pianist. Between Schonberg and Gould there was simply a chemical mismatch; it could happen to anyone.

At this Friday concert Bernstein had decided to make another speech. There had been disagreement, he said, between him and Gould about tempos, dynamics, virtually every interpretive point in the Brahms. Still, since Bernstein regarded Gould as "so valid and serious an artist" he had decided to grant him his "rather unorthodox" vision of the concerto, a vision that he himself, however, disclaimed. Then had come the performance, and then, the next morning, Schonberg's review. "Such goings-on at the Philharmonic," it began, "I tell you, Ossip, like you never saw." Harold had invented an old buddy named Ossip (as in Gabrilowitsch, a bygone pianist who fares a lot better than Gould in Schonberg's book) and cast his whole review as a letter to pal Ossip in a conversational broken English. "So then the Gould boy comes out, and you know what, Ossip? ... [He] played the Brahms D Minor Concerto slower than the way we used to practice it. (And between you and me and the corner lamppost, Ossip, maybe the reason he plays it so slow, is that his technique is not so good.)"

The review became famous, almost a battle hymn in both the pro- and anti-Gould camps. (There is no mention of Schonberg in *The Glenn Gould Reader*, at least by name. He does show up as "Homer Sibelius," critic of the *New York Square*, in a satirical piece on a critics' conference which, praise be, took place only in Gould's imagination. I'm there too, I think, as "Alain Pauvre" of the *New York Witness-Centurion*.) To the growing fund of Gouldiana was added the legend that Gould had played the entire Brahms concerto at excruciatingly slow tempos (which got slower and slower at each retelling), that Bernstein had washed his hands of the whole affair, and that Schonberg had handed Gould a long-overdue public spanking. People who had never heard the performance could still describe it note for note, like the two or three million people who swear they were at the Polo Grounds on the day in 1951 when Bobby Thompson's home run won the pennant for the New York (sob!) Giants.

The legend persisted for twenty years and more. Now comes a book called *Glenn Gould Variations* (Quill, $12.95), and in lead-off position is an essay by Leonard Bernstein called "The Truth about a Legend," the subject being, of course, that Brahms performance. Revisionist history has here wrought its masterpiece. Bernstein makes much of Gould's having changed the tempo of the first movement from an "allegro" to an "adagissimo." He writes of the entire performance having lasted "well over an hour." He writes about Schonberg's review as being a Sunday think-piece, instead of the daily critique it was, and comes up with a "quotation" in which Schonberg's Germanic accent becomes an even more impenetrable Slavic ("Dear Ossip, you vill nyever guess vat last night in Carnyegie Hall hhappent!").

The Truth Comes Out

Being the soul of honesty, I have to admit that I didn't hear that performance at Carnegie Hall, nor its broadcast two days later. Now, in the throes of my own rediscovery of Gould through Tim Page's *Reader* and the new record reissues, I decided to hunt down a tape of the event. [It is now available on a Sony CD, by the way.] My source came through, as I knew he would, with a tape that began with Bernstein's speech of bemused "renunciation" loud and clear and ended with James Fassett's announcement: that this had been a recording of the Friday performance, the very one Schonberg had heard. What a document!

And you know what, Ossip or Vladimir or Wladziu Valentino Liberace or whoever you are? That tape also contains some pretty spectacular Brahms playing, technically flawless (it goes without saying), shaped with an impressive imagination, a few minor details worth raising an eyebrow at (for one, a charming, lyrical approach to a murderous passage in the first movement in double octaves that is strewn with the bones of a few less proficient pianists) and on the whole a fascinating example of a persuasive mind at work on music that doesn't give up its secrets easily.

And what about those famous tempos and that one-hour-plus total length? News for you, Mr. Bernstein: the total time is fifty-three minutes and fifty-one seconds, which happens to be twenty-three seconds *faster* than a performance you recorded not long ago (available on Deutsche Grammophon) with the pianist Christian Zimerman, on which there is no disclaimer from you or anyone else. True, the first movement (marked maestoso, Mr. B., not allegro) clocks out long (at twenty-six minutes and nine seconds against Zimerman's twenty-four minutes and thirty-six seconds), but the sense of speed is so elusive anyhow that the Gould sounds propulsive in just the spots where any number of shorter-by-the-clock performances seem to disintegrate into unconnected puddles of sound. (Zimerman's reading of the slow movement, two and a half minutes slower than Gould's, loses its shape utterly within the first ten bars and goes downhill from there. The range of overall timings among recordings of this Brahms concerto, by the way, is full of surprises, from Lazar Berman's forty-four-minute sprint, with Erich Leinsdorf conducting, to the fifty-four minutes plus of the Zimerman/Bernstein.) If there are adagissimo passages anywhere in Gould's performance, they must have eluded the microphones.

What we have here, it begins to appear, is not so much an authentic musical legend as a shaggy-dog story compounded of half-remembrances, prejudices before the fact, wishful thinking, and pure hype. In a reasonable world (a concept unrelated to music, of course), so spindly a legend wouldn't have lasted the weekend. Its ultimate denial is right there on that tape, by the way, an ovation that doesn't sound like the dear ladies of any Friday matinee Philharmonic audience in my experience. Such cheering, Ossip! Like you never heard!

[*Keynote* magazine, July 1985]

David Helfgott: Freaks

"Where were all you people when he needed help?" wailed Scott Hicks, director of *Shine*, to a gathering of music critics in Boston before the American debut recital of the subject of that film, David You-Know-Who. You have to wonder where the line can be drawn between the rational and the off-the-wall, as a hitherto little-known film director scolds the press and critics of the world for not having supported a dysfunctional and woefully unpromising pianist in the years before the media turned him into a package. The absurdities pile up; like Helfgott himself, Hicks has drawn upon inner virtuosic resources to achieve his swift and sudden rise from obscurity to spotlight. He has assembled an impressive entourage, including Gillian Helfgott—astrologer turned mothering wife, countering hostile critical barbs with that most damning of epithets, "self-appointed elitist"; and a German piano teacher with the reassuring name of Peter Feuchtwanger—who explained away Helfgott's pianistic lapses at his debut recital by noting that "even Artur Schnabel and Clara Haskil had their bad days." The gall!

Worse yet, the evidence is mounting that the obvious ultimate beneficiary of this lurid charade, the film itself, is falsely based. I had some words of praise in these pages for *Shine* when it opened, as a somewhat more trustworthy depiction of a life in music than certain other blatant examples. Now I need to recant. Witnesses, including members of Helfgott's family, refute the film's romanticized concoction of David's breakdown, absolving both Poppa Helfgott and the Rach 3 and pinning the blame on conflicts in a first marriage that the film never mentions. A friend who played in the Copenhagen orchestra during the sessions tells me of unconscionable amounts of stop-and-go rehearsing (partially due to Helfgott's compulsion to jump up and kiss everyone in sight every few minutes) and other prodigies of doctoring to make the absurdly successful "live-performance" recording (on RCA, No. 1 on the classical charts now for several weeks) even minimally listenable. Instead of all that honest artistic verisimilitude I had once hailed, *Shine* turns out to be no less a crock than *Amadeus* or *Immortal Beloved*. Why, you have to wonder, didn't the sponsors of Helfgott's concert tour go the whole way and hire Geoffrey Rush to do the playing? (After all, he did his own fingerwork in the film.)

In the annals of virtuoso hype at work on less-than-virtuosic artistry, Helfgott's case is hardly unique. There was Margaret Truman, whose modest singing career went into high gear when the presidential pa threatened to punch out a critic for daring to trust his ears. There was Florence Foster Jenkins, a singer so monumentally awful that her Carnegie Hall concerts sold out regularly. There was Liberace, his abject music making artfully camouflaged behind sequins and a candelabra. In Helfgott's case his career wasn't merely helped by the movie; it was created.

But now the invention has been taken out of the inventor's hands. Does anyone dare to ask whether, in his current state, Helfgott can learn enough new repertory to keep his career going past this initial flurry? "Image, image, image...," he is heard repeating to himself; the mind recoils at thoughts of brainwashing, of a zombie programmed to commit mayhem on much-loved music and God knows what else. Other images come to mind: Dostoyevski's Idiot, the "holy fool" in Wagner's *Parsifal*...not to mention *The Manchurian Candidate*.

Like that other bugbear known as liberalism, elitism now ranks high on the tastemakers' enemy lists; Gillian Helfgott wields it like Darth Vader's light saber. Never mind that we are all infected to some degree; elitism is what tells us to drive on the right side of the street—a nicety which, come to think of it, hasn't yet reached Australia—and that it's wrong to rob banks. The elitist in me, the product of a lifetime of trying to learn what makes great music great and how to measure the quality of a performance against my personal vision of the work being performed, leads me to rise up in horror when Beethoven's "Appassionata" Sonata is turned into an inchoate scattering of aimless notes, when the gypsy dancers in a Liszt *Hungarian Rhapsody* are obliged to lie motionless in the mud, abandoned there by a performer evidently programmed to turn the music of Beethoven and Liszt into a freak show.

At the Music Center last Tuesday night, before a cheering crowd (including a galaxy of movieland luminaries probably just on their way home from the Oscar parties the night before) obviously mesmerized as much by the weavings, bobbings, and croonings of the blissed-out mooncalf on stage as by the awesome churnings of the hype industry that created and maintains him, David Helfgott hit a respectable percentage of the right notes without once betraying any awareness of where those notes were supposed to go or what convey. And the real star of the show, Scott Hicks, scourge of the self-appointed elite, Dr. Frankenstein to the dysfunctional, tells the press that this kind of gross and grotesque falsification "has drawn a large, new audience into classical music," the pious pronouncement last heard when the Three Tenors were in town and making no more sense now than then. You don't arrive at the truth by telling lies.

[March 1997]

Life with Lenny

During the entirety of my career as a music critic—briefly in Boston, the dozen Berkeley years, the New York twenty, and back to California—the phenomenon of Leonard Bernstein has never been far from view. For better or for worse he remains the defining force in musical awareness: what it means to love music, to hate it, to create, to accept or reject it. For me as a New York critic—and for every one of my colleagues—he was the perfect antagonist; I've never gotten more fun in my job than in writing pieces like this first one now forty years old—nor in pouring out the love that pops up now and then in the rest of this article.

Bernstein's New Symphony: A Review

Philharmonic Hall, Lincoln Center, April 1964

New York Philharmonic, conducted by Leonard Bernstein. Participating artists: Felicia Montealegre, speaker; Jennie Tourel, mezzo-soprano; Camerata Singers, and Columbus Boychoir

The program:

Tragic Overture	Brahms
Symphony No. 3	Brahms
Symphony No. 3, "Kaddish" (first New York performance)	Bernstein

Having survived his entanglements with Plato, Shakespeare, and Voltaire, Leonard Bernstein has now set his sights higher. In his new symphony, subtitled "Kaddish," he has decided to lock horns with the Almighty. The results were unveiled as the second half of last night's Philharmonic concert.

Naturally, Mr. Bernstein has set his own rules for the contest. In his forty-three-minute score for boys' chorus, mixed chorus, mezzo-soprano, narrator, and an orchestra that includes just about everything short of offstage vacuum cleaners, he sets about the considerable task of stripping God down to size, coddling him with a sweet lullaby and then telling him off in no uncertain terms. "Kaddish" is a reasonable enough name for the piece, but "Chutzpah" would do just as well.

His narrator is, of course, humanity. "Must I reintroduce myself," she asks, with the petulance of an ignored guest at a cocktail party. "Don't shrug me off," she then demands. Later she comes to God with all the solicitude of an elderly relative: "If I could comfort you...rock you to sleep. Shall I tell you a story?" One can almost see the bowl of chicken soup in her hand.

God dreams, and the narrator guides him through his own kingdom "with every immortal cliché in place" (described in twelve-tone music, the avant-garde will kindly observe). He is restless. "I am running this dream," she scolds, "and you must remain until the final scene." Doesn't she know about deadlines, for heaven's sake?

It's all very cozy, you see, and there is a message: it is not we who have lost our faith in God, but God who has lost faith in us. Now it is up to him to learn once again how to believe. The message is valid, but its telling verges upon the offensive. It is one thing to meet Romeo and Juliet on the Upper West Side, but it is quite another to find the Almighty snoozing in a warm kitchen.

For his musical setting Mr. Bernstein has stirred up quite a lot of excitement in not especially novel terms. Huge outbursts for percussion are always surefire, as is a narrator shouting into a public-address system over a torrent of orchestral and choral blooey-blooey. Parts of the score will remind you of Walton's *Belshazzar's Feast*, a fine piece to remember but one hardly in need of a rewrite job this soon. There are many other old friends, as well; "Kaddish," like most of Mr. Bernstein's music, is a season's repertory in itself.

To Mr. Bernstein's credit, it must be noted that his score contains moments that are effective and interesting on their own. What his music lacks in originality it makes up for in pure theatricality. The lullaby has a long and attractive melodic line, and the slow quiet music that begins the final section is quite enchanting. There is also a genuinely thrilling moment right after the dream sequence: the narrator calls out "Believe! Believe!" and the huge chorus comes in on a blazing G-flat-major chord to begin its exultation.

On the whole, however, "Kaddish" will not do. It clothes a noble thought in shoddy language and surrounds it all with music that—for its few expressive passages—is basically coarse, blatant, and derivative. It got a strong and effective performance from an excellent choral aggregation and the orchestra, with Jennie Tourel producing some of her familiar vocal magic in the solo passages and Felicia Montealegre pronouncing her pompous text with dramatic credibility.

There was another novelty at the concert. Mr. Bernstein conducted the first half, the two Brahms works, without a baton—the first time he has done so since 1957. This did not amount to a hands-down victory, however; the orchestral response to its leader's beat was as clear as ever, but the justice to Brahms was less than complete.

The *Tragic Overture* went well enough, in a somewhat sharp-edged but finely energetic performance. The Third Symphony did not go so well, however. The two inner movements were laggardly phrased and quite swollen in sound. The outer movements were better projected until the glowing final bars of the symphony, which were once again slack and unlovely.

[*New York Herald-Tribune*, April 1964]

The Self-Importance of Being Lenny

Sony's new eighteen-disc set of reissues bears *The Bernstein Century* as its oratorical title. It's not the title I would automatically choose to epitomize the last nine-plus decades—which probably explains why I don't spend my hours at handsome recompense grinding out sexy-sleazy ad copy.

Every one of us has a private list of the forces that shaped human thoughts, feelings, and welfare during the century about to enter the past tense. In the musical pantheon I wouldn't propose the notion of a Bernstein century over, say, a Toscanini—who, after all, bullied the entire concept of orchestral playing up several notches. I would argue for an Artur Schnabel Century, or a Maria Callas—for the proof they offered, in widely divergent ways, that music's charms extend beyond the savage breast and invite the participation of the mind as well. I would throw up but faint opposition to the proposition of an Aaron Copland Century, or a Pierre Boulez, to name two of the many motivating figures whose own work obliged the redefinition of their creative art.

All these figures worked within the boundaries of music itself. The cumulative force of Toscanini's performance of the "Eroica" hurls us into Beethoven's maelstrom; we think we know the work, yet the suspense from one moment to the next is unbearable in this performance. We feel at home in the shapely prettiness of a Donizetti tune, yet Callas's singing of that tune affords an insight into musical drama that requires us to rethink our whole concept of opera and, indeed, of the relationship of human voice to melodic line. Amid all the chatter about searching out an honorable American style of musical composition, Copland simply went ahead and achieved it—on his own and for all time. Each of these figures—Boulez and Schnabel no less than the others—reexamined their art, rethought its boundaries, and cajoled us to come along as they crossed those borders.

Bernstein's place, as we draw up the final score sheet on the era drawing to its numerical close, has little to do with music itself and everything to do with the shifting, dangerous relationship between the arts and their public. At no time in his life did it matter that his grasp on the structure of a great work of the past, the cumulative energy in the journey from first note to last, was, let's say, imperfect. The new Sony release is made up mostly of music of Bernstein himself and works of his American near-contemporaries Samuel Barber, William Schuman, Lukas Foss, and Aaron Copland, almost all of it in recordings with the New York Philharmonic previously packaged and reissued many times over. One disc of Beethoven Symphonies (Nos. 4 and 5, recorded in 1962 and 1961), delivers a strong if somewhat crude likeness of those glorious works, but an even stronger demonstration of how little Bernstein's own career drew glory from his roughshod excursions through this kind of music.

Later on, in his "second" recording career (with the Vienna Philharmonic copiously exemplified on Deutsche Grammophon CDs and videos), it apparently occurred to Bernstein that the way to celebrate his accession to elder statesmanhood was to play the repertory pieces more slowly than before, and with greater range of dynamics—turning Beethoven and Brahms into Bruckner, in other words. That didn't work either. The adulation lavished upon Bernstein by the Viennese, as he confronted them with his garish and soulless versions of the music they held most sacred—operas from *Fidelio* to *Der Rosenkavalier*, symphonies from Haydn to Bruckner—remains one of music's prime mysteries. He, of course, knew how to revel in that mystery. "Think of it," he fairly chortles in his pre-performance speech at a Brahms concert taped for PBS, "here's a Jew boy from the United States, conducting a German symphony in the land of Adolf Hitler's birth." (Oh, the wonder of it all! The importance of being me! Gee whiz!)

There is little likelihood that Bernstein's lasting fame will rest on his prowess as a conductor of other people's music past or present—or, for that matter, of his own; think, with inevitable regret, of his ponder-ous "all-star" disc (on DG) of the great *West Side Story* score, hyped like few recording ventures in the history of the human race, but a fiasco nonetheless. The new mid-price Sony series is culled from its previous every-sound-of-Bernstein-short-of-peristalsis series; its performances date from 1959 to 1974, the full span of Bernstein's time as the New York Philharmonic's music director and a few years beyond. Many of the soloists—the mezzo-soprano Adele Addison, for example, or the young baritone Alan Titus, the only reason to endure the blatant ponderosities of the Bernstein *Mass*—are wonderful to encounter once again. The fact that not a single performance, in this or any other Bernstein anthology, seems capable of revealing its conductor's state of mind toward the music, may in this case be only secondary.

His achievement lies in his bridge building, and his structural elements were more often words than music. Winnow out the nonsense in some of his TV stuff that sold the notion of music's greatness to audiences young and old, and you still find the spirit of a man desperately in love with two things—the essence of music itself, and the thrill in being able to put that essence into words and then to shout it from the rooftops. (I won't deny that my own work affords me the same thrill; I cannot, in fact, imagine anyone's going into writing about music for any other reason.)

The nature of his legacy remains to be determined. Good-looking boys from Boston (and perhaps from Chippewa Falls as well) now make their debuts every day in the week; the music that Bernstein "discovered"—Ives alongside Mahler—now figures in the active repertory of most orchestras. The New York Philharmonic had been playing Mahler symphonies since the 1920s; the Bernstein triumph is not that he played them first, but that he made them matter. He lived with one hand on the spotlight switch and had the media chops to determine on his own terms the events worth making significant. The new pile of Bernstein discs, like the previous ones and others sure to come, don't do very much to reconstruct the image of the extraordinary figure on the podium; for that you would have to have been there. But they are a reminder that once he was a presence among us—that he mattered, and still does.

This Much I Owe Lenny

Once, long ago, when I was still covering the New York music scene for one or another moribund newspaper, my parents came down on a visit. At home in Brookline, Massachusetts, my mother worried constantly that my occasional harsh words on the matter of Leonard Bernstein might somehow compromise her status with some of his relatives in her bridge club. Those worries turned to stark terror one night when I took the folks to a concert—and who should come up the aisle at intermission but Bernstein himself. "Shouldn't you get out of here?" she whispered frantically. Instead, Bernstein greeted me with that famous hug, and I introduced him all around. For that whole intermission, my parents stood schmoozing with the fearsome Lenny about Aunt Rosie and Aunt Stella and all the *mischpoche* back at Coolidge Corner. Later that night, his eyes still shining, my father finally forgave me for not going to medical school.

That much I owe Lenny and, of course, a lot more. We all do.

The obits all referred to him as America's greatest-ever musician, which seems a little strong until you think about. If not Lenny, who else? Louis Armstrong? John Cage? George Gershwin? André Previn? Glenn Gould? (Canada is part of America, too.) It has to be Lenny, not because he was the greatest in any of the areas he pushed into, but because of the incredible skill with which he orchestrated those pushes. He had that uncanny knack of turning every battle into a conquest.

No, he was not the greatest conductor of his time. The appealing arrogance that made his early failures so interesting—the wildly erratic performances of the classic meat-and-potatoes repertory, the feverish exaggerations that sold his championing of Mahler to the most resistant nonbeliever, the garish hoopla around most of his new-music interpretations—gave way in his later, "statesmanlike" years to a bland reserve that some critics mistook for an onset of mature eloquence.

Listen to those greatly hyped later performance—the cycles of Beethoven and Brahms symphonies, the Viennese classics performed on their own turf with the Vienna Philharmonic—without the sight of Bernstein himself on the videos, every fiber of his ravaged body an embodiment of the tensions in the music, and most of what you hear is some fairly faceless, provincial time-beating.

Sure, there were sublime moments, flashes of the high-flying Lenny of old. The performance of the Beethoven Ninth on Christmas of 1989, with eight symphony orchestras and nearly that many choruses converged on Berlin to tromp on the ruins of the Wall: no orchestral leader, Bernstein least of all, could resist the chance to give a little extra under such circumstances. That night, at least, Leonard Bernstein stood in as the greatest conductor who ever lived. But that was one night out of a long career.

No, he wasn't the greatest composer of his or anyone else's time. What he brought to composition wasn't all that different from what he brought to everything else about him: the lifestyle, the indiscretions, the public flamboyance, the affectation of omnipotence that was at least partially justified.

Not omnipotence, perhaps, but certainly multipotence; not all, but most. The many things that will always remain important are the boundaries crossed, the distinctions eliminated. Young American boys with names like Bernstein can now become symphony conductors because of what Lenny accomplished—on that October day in 1943 and on the thousands of days since. Young serious composers can bring the best of their style to Broadway, ballet, even the movies, with no sense of compromising their art. Lofty musical personalities can now do television talk shows and use words like "groovy" in public, because Lenny did so first.

Just the look of him portended importance. He'd walk onstage through the ranks of the players, and something in that walk told you that there was nothing in the world he wanted more than to reach that podium and touch hands with the masterpieces on that evening's program. Even later on, when he lost some of the sheer reckless energy of his youthful conducting manner, those onstage arrivals remained a thrilling sight. You watch Zubin Mehta sleepwalking toward his podium or André Previn oozing along, a small cloud of grayness, and then it becomes easy to remember why just the arrival of Bernstein onto a stage gave off sparks. I used to watch it happen in New York's rickety old City Center, when (in 1946 and1947) he had his own orchestra, the New York City Symphony, and walking through the ranks of the players meant rubbing shoulders with veteran players twice his age and more. Even then, you sensed the love feast that was in progress.

Then he'd get to work and, oh my, what a sight that was! Maybe his feelings about the work at hand were way off base; maybe, as in the idiotic "avant-garde festival" he inflicted upon himself, the New York Philharmonic, and his dead-head audience in 1964, he had come to loathe the task he'd set for himself. And maybe all that dancing around, the deep-knee bends, the wild flinging of arms as if to extract the music by sheer physical effort out of the last stand of the violins, the percussion at the back of the stage or the very ghost of the composer, hovering in the wings—was, as more than one critic noted at the time, a little much. But just maybe, also, it was all the outward manifestation of the soul of the genius on the stage wrestling in mortal combat with the soul of the music itself. Showbiz it certainly was, the spectacle of Bernstein on his podium; fraudulent it never was. The only real sin, in that podium manner, was the number of unworthy imitators it spawned. The greatest mistake, overall, would in fact be to think in terms of imitators, of the next Bernstein, of shoes to be filled. Lenny, and he alone, filled those shoes and did it so handsomely that nobody will need to wear them again. It's hard to imagine any area in our vast cultural panorama that hasn't been changed, during our fifty years of Lenny, by Lenny himself. He opened all the doors, and he left a world free to pass through them as the world had not been before his time. That much we owe his memory, and it's a lot.

[November 1997]

David Robertson: Return of the Native

Ask any orchestral manager, anywhere in the world, and you'll get the same answer: there is no better way to pave a pathway to financial ruination than by playing new music. The real money flows in to the tunes of Beethoven and Tchaikovsky; substitute the abstruse patterns of Boulez and Carter, and the money flows toward the exit doors.

Still, the brave souls dot the landscape, and the true nobles in adventureland pull in fair-sized—if not always well-heeled—crowds. Our own EAR Unit draws respectable aggregations to its County Museum concerts; the New York New Music Ensemble holds its torch aloft; in Frankfurt the Ensemble Modern concerts are hot-ticket; so, in Paris, are the programs of extraordinary range by the courageous, much-traveled Ensemble Intercontemporain (henceforth to be noted as EIC), which pays its third visit to the UCLA campus with a concert at Schoenberg Hall on Sunday afternoon.

Out on the podium that afternoon won't be the formidable Pierre Boulez, the ensemble's president and chief image maker and the name most associated with EIC since its founding in 1976. Boulez will be on the program—the pair of pieces collectively known as *Dérive*, along with music by Philippe Hurel, Elliott Carter, and the extraordinary Korean-born Unsuk Chin, who had a knockout piece at a Green Umbrella concert earlier this season—but the music director will be David Robertson, who has held that post since 1992. And if the name "David Robertson" strikes you as rather un-French for someone leading an ensemble from notoriously xenophobic Paris, that's understandable; he was born—some forty years ago—right here in Santa Monica. If your memory goes back to, say, the mid-1970s, you may remember Robertson as a seventeen-year-old wonderkid assistant conductor in the days when Santa Monica High School was first beginning to attract worldwide attention for the excellence of its young orchestra.

Now, however, David Robertson has earned his own worldwide attention and gives phone interviews from his Paris apartment. He starts by explaining why, after his promising start in Santa Monica, he didn't climb the usual American ladder toward stardom. "Sure, I started on the audition route, and I had a few good chances. But I also got the feeling early on that the American way of breeding top musicians had too much to do with marketing and too little to do with music. Some people take quite readily to all this image-building nonsense. I didn't."

Instead, soon after high school, Robertson enrolled at London's Royal Academy of Music. By twenty-one he had already begun a substantial career, with a door-opening win at a modest but important Danish conducting competition. In 1984 he began a two-and-a-half-year stint as conductor of the Jerusalem Symphony. By 1987 he was well established in a circuit of small opera houses and concert halls just below top level. "The value of Europe for me," he remembers, "was the way I could easily get to conduct a lot of different things: concerts, opera, new music, old. Some of this may have been in piddling small towns, but the value for me was far from piddling."

Much of his early European renown came from his work in opera houses, with a particular leaning toward the grandiose virtuosity of the Italian bel canto—Bellini, Donizetti, early Verdi. "Yes, it's a long way from *Norma* to Boulez," he admits,

> but to me the basis of all music is the vocal line, and the way all music moves along some kind of line. I don't believe in trying to fit a performer's musical tastes into compartments: early-music specialist, new-music

specialist, that sort of thing. Every kind of music has to sing. Every piece of music creates its own language.

I don't think in terms of "gear-shifting" in moving from one kind of music to another; I'm more aware of the spaces between the notes, and how each kind of music generates its own dynamic for filling in those spaces. If I conduct early Mozart, I don't let myself get hung up in matters of "authentic" instruments; it's hopeless to try to recreate the way Mozart heard his own music, because an audience today can't listen through Mozart's ears. It's much more important to concentrate on what is in the language of each piece, the incision of its rhythms, the roundness of its triplets—that sort of thing.

Robertson's career fell upon the chance to shift gears almost by accident:

In 1990 I was asked by the French Radio to conduct an opera by Philippe Manoury, an important, upcoming French composer. What I didn't realize at the time was that Manoury was a protégé of Pierre Boulez, and that Boulez was going to be in the studio audience that night. He was, and a few months later there was a call from Boulez's secretary, inviting me to come in for a chat. Well, I figured, perhaps he wanted me to guest-conduct a program sometime. Instead, he asked me to become music director of the Ensemble Intercontemporain, replacing the departing Peter Eötvös, who had held the post since 1979.

The EIC was created by Michel Guy, then France's minister of culture, to fulfill Boulez's vision of an ensemble devoted entirely to performing the music of our own time, the thornier the better. The idea from the start was to create a body of extraordinarily capable soloists who would commit two-thirds of their time to the ensemble without abandoning their solo careers for the other third. (The recent Deutsche Grammophon recording of Luciano Berio's solo *Sequenze*, performed mostly by EIC members, spectacularly illustrates the group's level of performance.)

Robertson himself has put his one-third off-time to good personal use, including Janáček's *Makropoulos Affair* for his Metropolitan Opera debut three seasons ago, the world premiere of Berio's stunning new opera *Outis* at Milan's La Scala in October 1996 and a *Rigoletto* at the San Francisco Opera a year later. The present tour with EIC takes him to six college venues—UCLA, Stanford, Berkeley, Seattle, Buffalo, and MIT at Cambridge—with performances and student workshops at each stop. Robertson himself is due back at the Los Angeles Philharmonic next December in a "hugely difficult" (his own words) program: Ives, Janáček, Lutosławski, and the contemporary Dutch composer Tristan Keuris. Further plans include Robertson's abandonment of the EIC post in August 2000 to take over what amounts to the musical directorship of the entire city of Lyon—head of its National Orchestra and of the municipal arts center as well. [To this he has now added music directorship of the St. Louis Symphony.]

Eight years working in the shadow of Pierre Boulez, beyond doubt music's most influential shaping figure in the second half of the twentieth century: has that left David Robertson scarred, enriched—or both? "Not at all scarred," he claims.

> From the beginning, my relationship with Pierre took the form of a dialogue. I came to the EIC with my own set of ideas, my own set of styles different from his and also different from those of Peter Eötvös, whose job I inherited.
>
> We have come out of a time when music had formed a more or less homogenous language within well-defined social conventions. Now we have to create new priorities. I like to think back to Jackson Pollock, who never got further into an explanation of his own painting than to say "it works." In music, too, we have to experiment, to take chances...and to go with whatever works.

[March 1999]

Ernest Fleischmann: Guardian of the Guard

And so the Los Angeles Philharmonic strides mightily, past its seventy-fifth-anniversary milestone and into its insecure but glitteringly orchestrated future. This weekend we face a "special performance," so called on the handouts, of the Beethoven Ninth Symphony with a "chorus of 200." If you don't think too hard about it, that sounds like an impressive start to the new season. If you do think about it, it might occur to you that a chorus of 200 is at least three times too big to balance against the orchestral forces without sounding like a lot of wet blotting paper. But we mustn't prejudge, not on musical or on marketing grounds.

The news, basically, is as good as it can be in these parlous times. Despite the best efforts of the Messrs. Reagan and Bush, the serious arts have not as yet been outlawed in this country. Something that could someday be a new concert hall has begun to assume shape on the lot just south of the present Music Center. And the hand of Esa-Pekka Salonen, falling upon both the planning and the performance qualities of the Philharmonic, has so far proved benevolent.

Seventy-five years: the Philharmonic has existed entirely within the lifetimes of some of its still-regular concertgoers. Its history is an interesting reflection of the cultural emergence of this whole area. Until recently, that history seems to have been one of unbroken prosperity, simply because the orchestra has been the battleground for several tycoons anxious to outdo one another in the size of their donations. (Where are they now, when we need them?) The roster of come-and-gone conductors is fairly spectacular, what with Otto Klemperer in the 1930s, Eduard van Beinum (briefly, alas) in the 1950s, Georg Solti in 1961 for a half-season that ended in anger and in Zubin Mehta's accession—and, more vivid in the memory, the bittersweet Giulini years from 1978 to 1984. Salonen isn't even the first Finn to hold the job; in the 1920s there was George Schneevoigt.

Symphony orchestras give off two kinds of relevance. They are socially relevant, the week-after-week orgy of enticing resonances on the stage surrounded by the glitter of fund-raising banquets, award plaques, and tour dates to lands even more exotic than our own. They are musically relevant as the storehouse for a repertory of past creativity; if their collective hearts are in the right place, furthermore, they guard the flame of present creativity as well, offering to the world the message that music itself, not merely the people who play it, has a future.

Salonen guards that flame, and he seems to be proving himself a trustworthy custodian. It is Ernest Fleischmann's job, as general manager, to guard Salonen. Fleischmann, too, has an anniversary worth noting; this is his twenty-fifth season, a considerable achievement in a profession that is known to eat its practitioners alive. Closer to being an actual musician than most managers—he had studied conducting with Albert Coates, who also held the Los Angeles podium for a time—Fleischmann's arrival here was fortunately timed. By 1969, five years into the existence of the Music Center and eight into the tenure of Zubin Mehta, it had become apparent in discerning circles that Mehta, having been thrust into his job far too soon in his own career, needed a daddy to help him jump over puddles. This Fleischmann willingly became, taking onto his own shoulders most of the music director's prerogatives that Mehta had inadequately fulfilled.

As manager–*cum*–music director, Fleischmann assumed a control over the Philharmonic's well-being that few orchestra managers anywhere have enjoyed. When Mehta departed it was Fleischmann who, with the blessing of several board members, wooed and won Carlo Maria Giulini away from Chicago, again with the assurance that Giulini would be music director in name only and that Fleischmann would control the moves (including a complex but beneficial tax arrangement that enabled the Italian Giulini to take home American dollars). When André Previn came on the scene, any amateur tea-leaf reader could have foretold the inevitable dustup that came about simply over Previn's trying to regain his rightful prerogatives as music director (responsibility for setting tour dates, recording dates, guest conductors and on and on) and Fleischmann's being too fond of them to give them up.

I don't mean all this as bad news, exactly; the good news is that Fleischmann is good at what he does. His mistakes—a guest soloist or conductor now and then hired not entirely on musical grounds, a bit of footsie playing with the board over lucrative outside job offers that did not entirely exist—are easily outweighed by a remarkable outlay of imagination and resource. He has sniffed out important conductors—Simon Rattle and Kurt Sanderling, to name just two who have made Los Angeles their principal American base, and, of course, Giulini—with the assurance of a hound after truffles. Sure, the story that Fleischmann "just happened" to be in London when Salonen "just happened" to make his famous last-minute debut smacks a little of the tooth fairy. So what? The bottom line is that Salonen is here, and that happens to be the most exciting acquisition by a major symphony orchestra in a very long time.

Orchestras are boiling cauldrons in which leadership qualities are excruciatingly tested. No orchestra—not even the Cleveland, with its touted built-in pride of place—will give more than it is asked for, and asking can take strange forms. Mehta, for all his excellent stick technique, lacked the power to make the orchestra *want* to perform well; Giulini and, later on, the aged Sanderling, lacked any stick technique at all but had an indefinable magnetism that made a player, as one of them put it to me, "want to live inside the music." Previn's failure was similar to Mehta's; "it was though he sent his hands to rehearsals," my informant said, "but left his brain at home."

Salonen has the hands and the brain, and so far he has put them to good use. It will take more than one year, or even five, to return the orchestra to the tonal elegance it had in the great Giulini days (and that only sporadically, during the limited number of weeks when Giulini was actually here). And then, in its new hall (shall we pray?) the orchestra will have to relearn many matters about tone to fit a new acoustical setting. The prospect, however, is exciting.

Fleischmann is aware of this and ostensibly delighted. The finances are rough right now; the orchestral endowment figure ($23 million in the bank, says Fleischmann) is well below the annual budget ($36 million on this year's books), and the sacrifices so far have included the valuable Philharmonic Institute, a resource of incredible value for involving young musicians in music. But the widespread financial gloom right now is not the worst problem. "It's not a bad time for orchestras," Fleischmann told me last week, "as much as it's a bad time for quality. The boring orchestras are in trouble. There are too many of them."

I didn't press him for names, but the biggest bores these days are, surprisingly, the biggest names: Chicago, New York, Philadelphia, Boston. and—despite a legend-sized mountain of marketing hype that archaeologists will someday study with awe—St. Louis. Los Angeles is not of their number; fulfilling the old Chinese saying, we do live in interesting times.

[October 1993]

Giulini Takes the Fifth: Los Angeles's Master Conductor Resolves His Struggle with the Symphony He Has Avoided for Fifteen Years

During the month of October 1982, Carlo Maria Giulini and the Los Angeles Philharmonic rehearsed, and later performed, the Fifth Symphony by Ludwig van Beethoven. Since the Beethoven Fifth is, by some distance, the most popular and most often performed of all classic symphonies, this piece of news should be of little more consequence than the assertion that, say, the sun rose and set thirty-one times during that same month. Strange to relate, however, Giulini had not conducted the Fifth for at least fifteen years, a remarkable act of abstinence on the part of any major symphonic conductor, and even more remarkable in the case of a conductor who, like Giulini, has worked for most of his life within a fairly narrow repertory in which the nine symphonies of Beethoven reign supreme.

Rehearsals, from Tuesday, October 13, through Friday, October 16, were held at the Pasadena Civic Auditorium. (The Philharmonic's usual home at the Music Center had been preempted by the road show of *Fiddler on the Roof*.) On Saturday, the 17th, Giulini and the orchestra gave the entire program in Santa Barbara, followed by performances in Santa Ana and San Diego before their return to the Dorothy Chandler Pavilion. In late November, they recorded the Beethoven Fifth for Deutsche Grammophon in still another venue, Royce Hall on the UCLA campus. By then the after-fifteen-years reunion of Carlo Maria Giulini and Beethoven's Symphony No. 5 in C Minor, Op. 67, was a well-traveled act.

At lunch during rehearsals Giulini had little to say about his last performance of the Fifth. "I only remember that it was terrible," he said. To understand why a failed performance of a symphonic masterwork—or, at least, a performance that failed by his own standards—might have led Giulini to back off from the symphony completely, you have to understand the man. Above all else, he is a serious musical scholar, driven by a concern for the spiritual nature of his art; almost incidentally, he is a spellbinding conductor, supremely able to impart his knowledge to an orchestra. In his passion for the music he truly knows—the classical repertory and a highly specialized selection from the romantic era—he is something of a throwback to an earlier time of music making, before conductors were expected to lead *Star Wars* concerts and function as media heroes.

"The problem I have always had with the Fifth," Giulini went on, "is something you hear right at the beginning":

> How could Beethoven, after that brutal, huge beginning, go immediately into all those fast notes that seem so trivial? To me there were conflicts inside this symphony that were beyond my power to resolve.
>
> But then last year I realized: How can I go on and ignore this symphony? I could understand someone not wanting to cope with one of the early, light symphonies—the first two, or even the fourth. But you cannot step so easily around the Fifth. So I paid a return visit. Actually, I spent most of the time with Beethoven's own manuscript, in the facsimile printing. When you look at a Beethoven manuscript, you know immediately the tremendous struggle he went through to compose. Everything is crossed out, changed. The greatest heroes in music are the copyists who prepared Beethoven's music for publication.
>
> Everything in that manuscript is a battlefield. Look—right at the start Beethoven is in conflict. First, he writes the first motive—da-da-da-DAAH—four notes, the last a half note with a fermata over it so that you hold it a little longer (see below). Then he writes the answering two bars,

four more notes, again a fermata. Then he must have changed his mind. Maybe, in that fantastic mind, even with deafness coming on, he hears that it won't work, that it sounds…well, a little trivial. And so he makes that second long note even longer: a half note tied to another half note. When you see, in the original manuscript, that first he had one note, then he added the second note tied, that tells you how he regarded that opening: not four notes and then four more notes, but eight notes together as a single breath.

So you see, when I return to Beethoven's own manuscript, even when it takes so much effort just to read the notes, I learn from what he wrote, and also from what he changed. I learn about all those fast-note passages that I couldn't reconcile before…that Beethoven was extremely exact about where he marked staccato, with a dot, and where there is no dot. So you cannot play these passages like notes; when you play them exactly, with all these tiny details, then they are no longer trivial. Now I have studied all this, and that's why I now am ready to play the Fifth.

The Beethoven Fifth exists in plenty of modern editions, carefully edited and clearly printed; it is not necessary for a conductor these days to return to the original manuscript. On the other hand, plenty of conductors have taken the trouble to explore those primitive hen scratchings on their own, invariably to their own advantage. But from Giulini I heard more clearly than from anyone in the past what a musician learns from restudying original score material: not only the notes themselves as the composer wrote them but evidence of the creative struggles behind those notes.

"It will be generally admitted that Beethoven's Fifth Symphony is the most sublime noise that has ever penetrated into the ear of man." Chapter 5 of E. M. Forster's sublime novel *Howards End* begins with this sentence, and before Forster has released his assorted characters from an afternoon's music at Queen's Hall in London he has escorted them through the symphony's many moods, up through "the gusts of splendor, the heroism, the youth, the magnificence of life and of death...amid vast roarings of a superhuman joy" of the finale.

Even before it sounded the clarion call of the Allied cause during World War II—the rhythm of those opening four notes being the Morse equivalent of *v* as in "victory"—the Fifth had inspired such writing as Forster's of 1921. In the history of musical style it is a landmark: a symphony made up, for the first time, not of four disconnected movements but unified by a recurring rhythmic motto, by a bridge of sound connecting the third movement and finale, and by the repetition in that finale of a large chunk from the preceding movement. It explodes into time and space with an emotional oneness unencountered hitherto (although foreshadowed in the "Eroica" of three years earlier). Its legend is variously assembled; Beethoven himself did it no harm with his remark, thoroughly authenticated, that the motto represents "fate knocking at the door."

No fancy legend is needed, of course, to explain the hold the Fifth has exerted since its completion in 1808. Yet the music lends itself to many shades of misunderstanding by interpreter or listener. Giulini's own words about those four, and then those eight, opening notes are part of one major controversy. Those first four notes, or the first eight, are commonly spoken of as the "theme" of the first movement, but they are not. The theme is actually a span of twenty-one measures in which the four-note motto is heard in its bare form twice, played off against itself in tense and bristling counterpoint for thirteen ensuing bars, and brought to a suspenseful half cadence. In those twenty-one bars the tensions and ultimate relaxations of the symphony as a whole are enacted in microcosm.

Better than any work I know, the Beethoven Fifth illustrates the supple, indefinable relationship between a piece of music and its listener. It is, as all masterpieces should be, a two-sided mirror. The one side reflects the hearer, the other side reflects the performer. The Fifth is put together out of so many interrelated elements, some of them so trivial on the surface, that we hear it—when we give ourselves to it—as a vise slowly but inexorably tightening around us. That tiny four-note figure, endlessly reiterated throughout the four movements, sometimes clearly heard and sometimes buried in the texture, pounds inside us almost subliminally, so that the coming of those final "gusts of splendor" is like the redemption of the universe. Beethoven clearly saw this progression as the aim of his grand symphonic designs; in his final symphony, the Ninth, unable any longer to define that sense of redemption in purely orchestral terms, he brought in words and singers. In its tensions and the intensity of its structure, I suggest, the Fifth accomplishes an even more overwhelming effect, and in half the time.

The current [1982] Schwann LP catalog lists twenty-nine conductors of stereo versions of the Fifth (some with two or more versions with different orchestras). Glenn Gould has recorded a version for solo piano. Peter Schickele (a.k.a. P. D. Q. Bach) has done a hilarious but accurate play-by-play analysis of the formal features of the first movement of the Fifth in the style of Howard Cosell. There are three mono versions listed in the Schwann supplement. I could also, without effort, list at least another dozen performances that have been issued and withdrawn. The Fifth was the first symphony ever to be recorded complete—by Arthur Nikisch and the Berlin Philharmonic in 1913.

The rampant duplication of effort may strike you as foolish, but it also says something about the Fifth being many things to many conductors. Just for fun, I took about a dozen versions from my own record library and put a stopwatch to just those opening 21 bars—roughly 4 percent of a movement that runs about 500 bars in all. The spread in timing is amazing: Bernard Haitink and the London Philharmonic come in at a breakneck sixteen seconds, Arturo Toscanini and the NBC Symphony at a brisk nineteen and a half, Nikisch at an oratorical twenty-six.

Speed in musical performance is deceptive; it is an illusion made up as much out of emphasis, articulation, louds, and softs as of actual timing of notes. At Giulini's rehearsals the opening passage came off broad, fiery, heaven storming, but not particularly speedy; yet it clocked at eighteen seconds, one and a half fewer than the Toscanini, which sounds as if it rides on the wind. After all, in the Giulini entry in *The New*

Grove Dictionary we read that he "has sometimes been compared with Toscanini...but his tempos are often slower."

After three days of rehearsal Giulini couldn't answer when I asked how fast he thought he was taking that opening theme. When I told him that his pacing was faster than Toscanini's, he was incredulous.

An orchestra rehearsal is, to an observer, an exercise in conjury. You watch and listen enraptured; you are astounded by the welter of detail, seemingly insignificant, that makes up the sound of a piece of music and the force that moves it. As hard as you concentrate on the happenings on stage, the communion between conductor and orchestra and among the members of that orchestra, you invariably miss that moment of pure magic, when those details merge into whole music.

At precisely 10 A.M. on October 13, the first day of rehearsals and Giulini's first time with the orchestra since last August at the Hollywood Bowl, he came onstage in what was to be his rehearsal uniform for the week: gray slacks, a lightweight gray turtleneck, and a white cardigan, which was soon parked on a nearby vacant chair. There were few words of greeting, but soon you could see that Giulini relates to the orchestra through his music making, not through the jokes or affected camaraderie with which other conductors try to buy Brownie points.

No two conductors rehearse the same way. Giulini deals, patiently and methodically, with a skein of small details; Leopold Stokowski, from all reports, underrehearsed his orchestras deliberately to obtain an edgy, nervous spontaneity in performance. Giulini constantly invites cooperation from leaders within the orchestra to resolve specific points of articulation: Serge Koussevitzky, whose Boston Symphony rehearsals I used to attend uninvited during my ushering days at Symphony Hall, handed down orders as the self-appointed avatar of God Almighty. Giulini's podium manner in rehearsals is exceptionally demonstrative as opposed to the serene simplicity of his public appearances: the more renowned podium prancers—Leonard Bernstein, for one—are more restrained when only their colleagues look on.

There is no acting in Giulini's case. At rehearsals he is an extraordinary sight: that long, beautifully formed patrician countenance a continued reflection of the music, the left arm held in a gigantic curve, as if to contain the bigness of the sound, the long legs out at straight angles, like supports tilted and in danger of collapsing. But it is not a show. It is the conducting of a whole man. Sometimes the language fails him and the body takes over. "Please, please," he will say in that tone of quiet supplication that is the way he always speaks to the orchestra, "please. I would like this passage more...." And he cannot finish the sentence: he goes instead into the pose of a string player: the right hand (with or without baton) becomes the bow, the crooked left elbow the instrument. Then perhaps the concertmaster, Sidney Weiss, will explain Giulini's needs to the orchestra in more practical terms. Or perhaps the orchestra itself will sense what is needed.

Giulini started with the last movement, those "gusts of splendor" that invariably bring some hearers to their feet, almost without their knowing. Thirteen bars in and Giulini halted the orchestra to work out a particularity. "I know you've all played this so many times you have the notes in your fingers," he began. "But please, there are things I want to change, not to be different, just to play what's in the score."

You and I and probably everybody we know have listened to the Beethoven Fifth all our lives, and the rest of the repertory as well, without noticing the hundreds of microscopic details in the scoring that establish the fact that composers of great symphonies are more than mere spinners of romantic tunes. The passage that Giulini now worked on with the orchestra, occurring in bar 13 of the finale of the Fifth, is such a detail. There is a passage for the full orchestra in a jagged rhythm, eighth notes and sixteenths for the most part. Beethoven wrote out the rhythm as you might expect: dotted eighth, sixteenth, dotted eighth, sixteenth—daaahm-da-daaahm-da-daaahm.... But for the first violins the notation is different: eighth, sixteenth-note rest, sixteenth note, eighth, sixteenth-note rest, sixteenth note—daaahm-sniff-da-daaahm-sniff-da-daahm...(see below). The whole orchestra plays the same notes at the same time; why should Beethoven go to the trouble of inserting those tiny air holes into the first violins?

Giulini worked with the orchestra, lending each section through that rhythm, insisting that the first violins cut off cleanly so that those tiny silent spaces could be heard. The difference was astounding; when the full orchestra played through the passage a second time, the texture bristled, gave off sparks. Obviously, no conductor can take an orchestra with such care through every subtle nitpick that makes up a score. But Giulini's work with this passage furnished the orchestra with a guidepost for dealing with other details along the way.

Later, I went home to my own collection and listened for that passage in several recordings. Sure enough, there are orchestras that seem to slide through it and others that apparently have had the drilling that Giulini has given. I asked a pal, long with the Philharmonic, whether Zubin Mehta ever rehearsed the detail in this passage, or any passage, as meticulously as Giulini had. "No, never," was the answer. "The only thing I remember Zubin saying was, 'You're not together.' And then it was usually his fault."

Giulini says that he learned about the Beethoven Fifth from what Beethoven wrote and also from what Beethoven crossed out. In somewhat the same manner, I learned about Giulini at these rehearsals from what he stopped to correct and what he left out. It seemed to me, for example, that the string sections weren't in very good tune during these early rehearsals, yet Giulini didn't call them on this. I assumed that he trusts his players' ears enough to allow them to make their own peace with concert pitch as the week progressed, and indeed the results later in the week bore out this assumption. At lunch Giulini talked about details, about his own view of what is important in a rehearsal and what can be left to trust. Apparently his own preference to trust his players in obvious aspects of their playing came from a memory of his own musical past.

"Bernardino Molinari was the first conductor I knew. I was a violist in the Santa Cecilia Orchestra in Rome. Molinari would come to rehearsals, and first he would have every stand, every pair of players in the string sections, play a passage separately—every player, front or back, criticized before the whole orchestra. It was sheer meanness; it meant that we all hated Molinari for shaming us this way; and it also meant that we all hated one another."

"Did it improve the playing of the orchestra?" I asked.

"No, not at all. In fact, I remember once Richard Strauss came to Rome, an honored guest. We had rehearsed a program of his music under Molinari. Strauss came to the last rehearsal. 'You play the notes very well,' he told us. 'But you don't play the music.'"

The bowing of an orchestra's string players is one of those picky details that affects enormously the way the music comes out: whether, in other words, a violinist takes a phrase with the bow going up or down, or with the tip of the bow or the part closer to the fingers, or, when there's a choice, with the G string or one of the higher strings. Giulini is one of the few conductors who mark his own bowings in the orchestral parts; his background as a viola player, situated in the "middle" of the strings, has given him a heightened sense of the value of carefully planned bowing.

Yet I also sensed a democratic process at work. Giulini marks the parts in the abstract, working at his desk with only his superlative ear and musical memory to guide him. In rehearsal a passage may not work as bowed. "What do you think," he asks Sidney Weiss, or the first violist, Jan Hlinka, or the first cellist, Ronald Leonard. "Maybe if we changed...," comes a reply. "Good," says Giulini, "let's try it that way," and the orchestra makes the change. "Better?" asks Giulini, and he asks as if expecting an honest answer.

And in this manner of execution the concertmaster becomes crucially important. It is Sidney Weiss whose major responsibility it is to turn Giulini's poetic vision into practicality. "I want a big sound, a real song," the conductor told the orchestra at a point further into the finale. Weiss came to the podium; there was a consultation. "Keep the passage on the G string," Weiss told the violins.

Observing this constant interplay between Giulini and Weiss, I learned volumes about the real value of a concertmaster, who must be far more than merely a splendid fiddle player. Concertmasters do tend to be popular with the crowd. Weiss now gets a hand from the Music Center audiences when he comes onstage, as did Sidney Harth, his predecessor. Concertmasters also get to play many solo passages during a year of concerts, and sometimes even concerti. This enhances their standing with the crowd, the violin being, after all, an emotional instrument. New conductors, however, almost always fire the incumbent concertmaster or at least make it impossible for him to stay, and that almost always puts the new conductor in dutch with the public and the press. This happened a couple of seasons ago in San Francisco, for example, when the incoming conductor, Edo de Waart, came to a parting of the ways with the orchestra's longtime concertmaster, Stuart Canin. The local press chose to make this a cause célèbre against de Waart, totally ignoring the fact that the two guys merely couldn't work together for simple reasons of artistic chemistry. But after watching the way Sidney Weiss works in rehearsals, constantly turning his conductor's poetic insights into the nuts and bolts of good string playing, I understand why a conductor's right to select his own concertmaster is as personal a matter as the choice of a psychiatrist or a lover.

An intense, shy man, Weiss didn't want to talk about his work, and I respected his right. Instead, backstage I cornered instead Haig Balian, a grizzled veteran of this and other orchestras. "How many times, at a guess, have you played the Beethoven Fifth—not rehearsals, just performances?"

"Oh, maybe 175, maybe 200."

"How can you possibly stay awake for another round of performances? Doesn't your fiddle play itself by now?"

The answer was as good as a press release, but it was from the heart. "No, not with Giulini. He makes it like a brand-new piece."

The Arlington Theatre in Santa Barbara is an honest-to-God horror, precious of its kind: a foolishly long auditorium with a teensy balcony, seating 2015, mostly on one level. Inside, you think you're in the middle of a Spanish town: whole housefronts with tile roofs line both side walls, and overhead a dark-blue ceiling is pierced with electric stars. The building is also an acoustical horror. The orchestra is squeezed against the flat back of the stage so that the sound is sent out front with no resonance. Every thwack on the kettledrums sounds as if that back wall has been hit with an amplified sledgehammer.

But Santa Barbara turns out for its few symphony concerts, and the Arlington was packed. The concert went capitally, and the Fifth got a standing ovation. Santa Barbara had no inkling that it was in on a historic occasion: Giulini's first public performance of the Beethoven Fifth since some nondescript and preferably forgotten foray nearly a score of years ago.

Giulini beamed at the end; I wanted to think that he had heard beyond the poor hall acoustics, that he had even forgotten the moment during the finale when he dropped his baton and had it handed back up to him by the second violist. I liked to think, rather, that he had now brought the Beethoven Fifth back to his own public, his own vision of this sublimely vital score. The performance wasn't all that different from the rehearsal the day before, except that on the podium Giulini's motions were now far more restrained than the expressive, almost pleading movements in rehearsal. He has done his work, he seemed to be telling us; now it is Beethoven's turn.

[*California* magazine, November 1982]

Jeffrey Kahane: Playing the Identity Game

Coming out onto a concert stage, heading toward either the podium or the piano bench, Jeffrey Kahane could pass for somebody's ragamuffin kid brother in borrowed black- or white-tie. Never mind that he turns forty-one this week, or that the reddish-blondish crowning thicket has receded somewhat over the years, or that at home in Santa Rosa—where he conducts the local symphony orchestra—he is husband to Martha and father to Gabriel and Anna. The appealing boyishness remains one of Jeff Kahane's calling cards, along with the splendid music-making that has elevated him to a high place among performers of his generation.

This weekend Kahane takes over as the Los Angeles Chamber Orchestra's music director, the fifth in that ensemble's thirty-year history, the first native Angeleno and, thus, a link to the days in local history when the musical outlook was being shaped by the great Europeans—Kahane's teacher, the late Jakob Gimpel, for one—who had fled here years before. His program—Friday night at Brentwood's Bel Air Presbyterian Church (the usual venue at UCLA's Veterans Wadsworth having been preempted for tap dancers), Saturday night at Glendale's Alex Theater—consists of only three works, but they form a pretty good portrait of Kahane himself, his visions of his personal musical world, and his hopes for an orchestra that, despite its long and valuable service to the community, has never really nailed down its identity. Beethoven's "Eroica" Symphony is the concluding work, itself a brave step into the unknown by a composer still in search of his own identity. Full-sized symphony orchestras have claimed the "Eroica" as their own, and it does make a glorious noise in the hands of the Los Angeles Philharmonic's fifty-six-member string section. But there's much to be said for returning the work to an orchestra the approximate size of Beethoven's original ensemble—LACO's twenty-two strings, say; the balance between the strings and the winds, brass and timpani actually enhances the resonance.

But starting the new regime with the "Eroica" does revive the question of identity, LACO's ongoing bugbear. Neville Marriner (not yet "Sir") founded the orchestra in 1968, drawing on the spectacular riches of the Los Angeles freelance pool, as a mirror of his much-loved Academy of St. Martin in the Fields in London, a small ensemble aimed at returning the proper baroque sound to the Vivaldi–Handel–early Mozart repertory. Ten years later, Gerard Schwarz seemed determined to turn LACO into competition for the Philharmonic; Brahms and Tchaikovsky came onto the programs, and Vivaldi took a back seat. Iona Brown's accession in 1987 moved the balance back to the baroque, although her plan to do some of her conducting from the first violinist's chair—an "authentic" touch, after all—set off a brief who's-in-charge dustup within orchestral ranks. Five years later, Christof Perick's ambitions once again seemed to lean toward the symphonic. Given this back-and-forth struggle out front, it's also not surprising that some of the leading figures on LACO's downtown mural (visible from the northbound Highway 110 at about Seventh Street)—the concertmaster Ralph Morrison, for example, the bearded chap with what looks like a three-string violin—are no longer on the roster.

On the phone from Santa Rosa, a few days after his splendid week with LACO at the Hollywood Bowl, Kahane expressed no doubts about his view of the orchestra's image. "The board has insisted, since we first began to talk, that LACO be recognized for what it is, a chamber orchestra determined to be the best of its kind in the world, and pretty close to that already. Sure, I may want to bring in a couple of trombones and try the Schubert Ninth, or some Schumann. But when I do, it will only be to show how the music can benefit from the chamber-orchestra approach, not as competition with the Philharmonic or any other full-size orchestra." (Actually, there's a fair smattering of Brahms on this season's programs—not the big symphonies, however, but the two youthful serenades, which can work with small orchestras.)

Also on this first LACO program is an interesting test of Kahane's own identity, Mozart's C Minor Piano Concerto (K. 491) with Kahane as both soloist and conductor. Pianists who conduct, or conductors who play the piano, aren't all that rare; Chicago's Daniel Barenboim and Houston's Christoph Eschenbach come immediately to mind, as does everywhere's Leonard Bernstein. Usually, however, it works out that a pianist/conductor will give up the podium for a year or two to concentrate on the piano or vice versa. Kahane sees nothing wrong with maintaining an ongoing dual existence—within certain limits, of course.

"The piano came first," Kahane remembered:

> Jakob Gimpel [the beloved Polish-born pianist who settled in Los Angeles as part of the refugee wave in the 1930s] gave me my first direct contacts, the sense of music as poetry, as narrative. When I got to the San Francisco Conservatory I found that conducting interested me at least as much as piano, but when I was accepted for the Van Cliburn Competition [in 1981] I naturally had to set the baton aside for a while. Then came one thing after another—the Arthur Rubinstein prize, the Avery Fisher Career Grant [both in 1983], Carnegie Hall, chamber music with Yo-Yo—and I didn't really get back to conducting until around 1988. But then I was amazed at how quickly things happened.

"Things" included an official conducting debut at the Oregon Bach Festival in 1988, founding the Gardner Chamber Orchestra in Boston in 1991, an associate conductorship with the San Luis Obispo Mozart Festival (where he also performed—but did not conduct—Rachmaninoff's hardly Mozartian Third Piano Concerto the weekend before the Hollywood Bowl stint) and, since 1995, the Santa Rosa Symphony post:

> They wanted someone who'd be really committed to Santa Rosa, not just the usual fly-in-fly-out conductor. And so we moved up there, bought a house right in town. The area is growing culturally; we give seven or eight

subscription concerts a year and play each program three times—which is unheard of for a regional orchestra—plus the usual family and holiday concerts.

The Santa Rosa is actually one of the oldest orchestras in the state, although most of its seventy years were spent in a fairly amateurish condition. Now we're almost completely professional: a few locals who also have other jobs, and a large group that comes up from San Francisco. When I got here I found that the repertory pretty much ended with Mahler; now I've been easing them into this century, with the Copland Third and the Barber First. We also have a resident composer, Ken Frazelle, who has written a big orchestral piece for Santa Rosa for this season. We're also doing a smaller commissioned piece of his to start the LACO season, *Laconic* (get it?) *Variations*. Frazelle is a really fine composer; I've known him since Juilliard, where he was studying composition with Roger Sessions. But his family roots are in Appalachia, the Blue Ridge Mountains, and that music has had a big influence on his recent development.

As to this so-called double existence, I really think the world has become too obsessed with specialization. You're a baroque conductor or a twentieth-century conductor, a Beethoven pianist or a Schoenberg; I'd like to break away from that attitude. Of course I realize that there are things I can do and things I can't. Conducting Mozart concertos from the piano, or Bach, or the first couple of Beethovens, isn't much of a problem; that's the way those pieces were meant to be performed. But I couldn't do Brahms that way, or Tchaikovsky, or Rachmaninoff; there's too much happening in the orchestra.

Well and good, but as a journalist I need to know what you call yourself: pianist, conductor, whatever?

"Just put me down as musician," said Jeffrey Kahane, "and let it go at that."

[October 1997]

Playing Drumpet with the Kronos

They were all over the place a week or two ago: the Kronos Quartet in a concert at the Irvine Barclay Theater one night, at Glendale's Alex Theater a couple of nights later, then at UCLA for an afternoon kiddie event. Their programs were all over the place, too: big, recent pieces by Steve Reich and Terry Riley alongside exquisite string-quartet reworkings of medieval tidbits by Hildegard von Bingen and Guillaume de Machaut. There's an undercurrent of fierce explorative energy in the Kronos's renowned eclecticism; they love to hurl things together that are actually great distances apart, just to see if they'll cohere. Usually they do. There's nothing else in the world like the Kronos.

All three events were marvelous, but the children's concert at the Wadsworth Theater left me with the warmest afterthoughts. It drew a pretty good audience for a rainy Saturday afternoon. Each of us was given a paper bag on arrival; it contained a small plastic box (the kind you get at a salad bar), a couple of rubber bands, a length of nylon fishline, a paper tube and a soda straw—about a penny's worth of material on today's market. A jovial chap named Craig Woodson, who was billed as an ethnomusicologist and instrument builder, showed us how to put everything together to make a "drumpet." With the soda straw, for example, we could scratch around the crinkles on the plastic box and make a rasping sound. The nylon line went through a hole in the box, which then became a resonator. We could toot through the paper tube, or pound one end of it: not quite the sound spectrum of a full symphony, perhaps, but close.

The Kronos came onstage and played a few short pieces on their own. Then Dr. Woodson set things up so that we could all play along: part of the crowd would do the rasping thing, another part would toot or twang the string, then we would all change off. The Kronos played some more—pieces by Harry Partch and, would you believe, John Cage—and we all joined in. Somewhere along the line, it occurred to me that there's a lot of talk about the public schools' not being able to afford music programs, and here were the sponsors of this concert, spending less than zilch per kid on teaching materials, and sending several hundred kids home with the sense of having participated in the making of music. Sure, it was wonderful to involve the Kronos in this event—I'm told they do it often around the country. But there are local musicians with lower fees who can be made to understand that participating in this kind of music education helps to assure them a continuing audience a few years down the line.

The other Kronos concerts were marvelous as well. In Irvine they played Steve Reich's *Different Trains*, an amazing piece with its echoes of personal nostalgia and heartbreak woven into a surging sound tapestry. At Glendale the big work was Terry Riley's gangling *Cadenza on the Night Plain*, music that maintains the most ingratiating hour's worth of smile you'll ever come across. Both programs included, midway in the first half, a bouquet of tiny, radiant, breath-stopping pieces—Machaut followed by Cage followed by Hildegard or Arvo Pärt. The Irvine audience took all three works in silence, not wanting to break the spell; no such luck in Glendale. Further audience note: at Wadsworth, during the short "formal" concert, whenever parents seemed interested in the music, so did their children. When not, the little darlings simply squirmed. There's a lesson here.

[February 1997]

Salonen: Musician of the Year

Esa-Pekka Salonen strides briskly to the Los Angeles Philharmonic podium, greets the orchestra and the audience, and then picks up a hand microphone. From any spot in the intimate space of the Walt Disney Concert Hall, you'd mistake him for a beaming, appealingly dimpled grad student. It isn't until you're up close that you make out the lines of his forty-seven years, and then not all that clearly. This is the fair, blond, youthful hero of legend in the pages of Finland's *Kalevala*, and that fairly well describes his status in Los Angeles as well.

Salonen has a few words for the audience about *Wing on Wing*, his new twenty-six-minute piece that begins the night's program. In the last year he has taken to chatting up the audience before conducting some of the less familiar music on his programs, and he has found his ease at it. Tonight's music is actually about Disney Hall; it even incorporates the sampled voice of its architect, the celebrated Frank Gehry. "I struggled with this idea," says Salonen. "How in hell do you write music about a hall? Finally I realized, my job is not to describe the hall, but my personal reaction: how happy I am that it's here, and how grateful I am to Frank."

Twenty-six minutes later the applause is perhaps grateful, certainly proud. The love affair between Los Angeles and its golden Musicus is real and ardent, and it has been going on, depending on who's counting, since either the day in late November 1984 when as a total unknown he made his Philharmonic debut in a killer program, or the day eight years later when the Philharmonic management bowed to the inevitable and proclaimed him the orchestra's tenth-ever music director.

But there's more to Esa-Pekka Salonen than just one of the latest splendid knights in armor who just might conduct classical music out of its current dolorous estate. Taken as an artistic entity, without factoring in the wife, Jane, and the three kids of a joyously normal sunlit family, Salonen is some kind of new and wondrous invention. Just take the circumstances of that aforementioned night at Disney Hall. Here was the conductor about to lead his own orchestra in an extended piece of new music, of which he was also the composer and the fabricator of its very plan. The piece, furthermore, celebrates the concert hall in which the performance is taking place; the composer/conductor/planner of the piece has also been deeply involved in the planning of the hall during the entire time of construction. The only fly in the ointment, in fact, is that the economics of the industry have ordained that the piece be recorded not in situ but by an orchestra in Finland.

Life as a musical polymath, Salonen has always claimed, has simply been the product of a series of lucky accidents. "I studied composition and analysis primarily," he told a reporter on his first American visit, "with conducting merely as something useful for a composer to know. Then came the calls, and I simply noticed after a while that I was a full-time conductor." Most important among those calls came from London's Philharmonia in September 1983 to fill an emergency last-minute vacancy to conduct the Mahler Third. The work was at the time unknown to Salonen, and he had a week's time to learn its ninety minutes of vagaries. "I just jumped in," he remembers. The Los Angeles Philharmonic's Ernest Fleischmann "just happened" to be in the audience that day. Fourteen months later Salonen was in Los Angeles for a debut that included the Third Symphony of Witold Lutosławski, the Polish composer with whom Salonen had briefly studied. Los Angeles wasn't used to such challenging fare, especially handed off by an eager, unknown newcomer, but that night the crowd erupted in the first of the aggressively positive ovations that have been regularly accorded Salonen to the present day.

The Los Angeles Philharmonic in 1984 was not the orchestra that might tempt a young musician to cast his lot with the city's musical life. Carlo Maria Giulini's eloquent leadership could elicit loving, moving performances of a narrow repertory, but his absences were frequent and demoralizing, and he would resign the next year. André Previn came on; to nobody's surprise, he and Ernest Fleischmann locked horns almost immediately as to whose orchestra it actually was. "André used to send his hands to rehearsals," an orchestra member recounts, "but leave his brain at home." The orchestra, never an admirable ensemble as such under even Giulini and Zubin Mehta, turned up some weeks in truly wretched state.

Back then the only bright moments came with the guest shots, more and more frequent, from Fleischmann's two young "discoveries," Britain's Simon Rattle and, now, Salonen. Rumors flew; obviously either would have been a glowing choice as successor to redeem the Philharmonic from the somnolence imposed by Previn. But Rattle's heart belonged to Birmingham. In 1990 Fleischmann booked the Philharmonic on an international tour with Salonen as conductor. Exit Previn in a huff. In 1992 Esa-Pekka Salonen became the tenth music director of the Los Angeles Philharmonic. That summer, he and the Philharmonic began a distinguished association with the Salzburg Festival with a production of Olivier Messiaen's *St. Francis* staged by Peter Sellars. For his inaugural concert as music director at the Music Center, however, Salonen's chosen work was the Mahler Third, the symphony that had put him in Los Angeles's line of sight nine years before.

You need some history to realize the extent of Salonen's accomplishment in those first Los Angeles years. He took on a demoralized orchestra in a city that had to be taught all over again to care about its cultural amenities. The boyish good looks helped, but the musical qualities helped even more. Not every orchestra member was immediately pleased. The stick technique took getting used to at first; it has warmed considerably since. When the New York reviews came in after the touring began, and when the recording engineers from Sony came to call, Los Angeles began to get sold on its newly acquired treasure.

Even Sibelius helped; clearly the new guy had new things to say on the subject. Dead though he was, and even deader though some found his music to be, Sibelius accounts for a lot of Salonen's excellence, and the musical excellence of a whole generation of Finns among whom he stands tall. He explained this a couple of years ago:

> For 600 years Finland was under Swedish rule, and the Finnish language was spoken only by peasants. From 1809, under Russian rule, the Finnish identity was even more endangered. In came Sibelius. He spoke Swedish, but he was chasing a girl whose parents were fanatical Finnish speakers, so he learned Finnish. He composed, and the patriotic messages in *Finlandia* and the Second Symphony became symbols of a Finnish identity. The Russians could cross out dangerous lines in political writing, but you can't censor musical phrases. Sibelius became a monument, which killed his creativity but gave birth to his country. Finland's classical music has always been the best way to tell the world we exist.
>
> And so the Finnish government established a system of communal music schools about thirty years ago, and this is now the harvesting time. Every little town has a music school; if a student can't pay tuition or buy an instrument, those are provided free. A capable student moves on from the small music school to a bigger one. The best are taken to the Sibelius Academy in Helsinki. Whatever quality there is, is found; you can't hide talent.

Something else was brewing in Los Angeles that would have sweetened the prospects for an oncoming Philharmonic conductor. In 1987 Lillian B. Disney, widow of the beloved Walt, came out of the blue to inform Ernest Fleischmann and the Philharmonic board of her intention to endow a concert hall in her husband's name, a state-of-the-art building to serve the city and to honor Walt's love of music. A long architectural competition ensued, and the radical, wondrous design by Frank Gehry, another deeply devoted music lover, was chosen. The notion from the beginning was to bypass traditional concert-hall paraphernalia—chandeliers, heavy upholstery, and the elements that made the present Chandler Pavilion a visual and acoustic liability—and build a contemporary hall that would welcome its audience both visually and sonically.

Disney Hall did not happen overnight, and it took many times Lillian Disney's original $50 million before the hall finally welcomed its first paying audiences at a gala on October 23, 2003. By then, however, its impact had spread beyond the artistic to the psychological. In the city long looked upon from beyond the mountains as the archetypal cultural desert, suddenly a structure devoted to the arts had become an anchoring force and even a tourist magnet. A city proverbially lacking a "downtown" had blossomed into a downtown that everybody wanted to see, to visit, to become a part of. And Esa-Pekka Salonen himself, during the long, sometimes frustrating years of building, planning, postponement, and completion, had himself been implanted in this process and had allowed it to govern his own future. "To be completely honest," he told me just the other day, "I worked my butt off trying to get the hall built. Now it is there and I want to enjoy the harvest."

For Salonen, that harvest consists in large measure in a conductor's ability to plan out a season's repertory and actually hear it through; acoustic effects, instrumental blends, the interplay of sounds and silence. Such freedom of choice, impossible to achieve in the former hall—or, for that matter, in most "standard" concert halls worldwide—falls handsomely within the realm of possibility in the embrace of the warm-hued Douglas fir of Frank Gehry's and the acoustician Yasuhisa Toyota's magical room. Salonen's first year at Disney was his year to discover Berlioz: the evanescent delicacies of the "Queen Mab" Scherzo from *Roméo et Juliette* seemingly suspended in space, the blasts of the Requiem's "Dies Irae" shaking a listener's inmost spinal interstices without the slightest distortion. In the second year there was Wagner: Salonen's first-ever interface with *Tristan und Isolde*, surrounded by a Bill Viola video realization and, once again, seemingly transforming the whole space of Disney Hall into a human heart. Upcoming in next season's planning: a Beethoven Festival like none other, setting off the genius of nineteenth-century violence juxtaposed with such latter-day innovators as Dutilleux and Ligeti; and a "Minimalist Jukebox" curated by John Adams, the orchestra's virtual composer in residence. Not without a certain chortling, the Philharmonic's general manager and president, Deborah Borda, points out that when the American Symphony Orchestra League holds its annual convention next year, the place will be Los Angeles, and the theme will be "Innovation." Where better?

Where better, indeed? Salonen came to the Philharmonic, without much of a mark as a conductor but with plenty in upper realms of new music. His portfolio listed a considerable content of music composed during his European wander-years, from his basic studies at Helsinki's Sibelius Academy to base touching with the likes of Lutosławski and Boulez and Franco Donatoni. Early Los Angeles audiences were properly titillated by charming short solo works and a bit of verbal fluff called *Floof.*

There was also a rather sassy if undisciplined Saxophone Concerto, which gives off the sense of a young man's need to get something out of his system this once. All this early reaching-out seemed suddenly shaded, however, in the fall of 1997 by *LA Variations,* a twenty-one-minute orchestral piece written for and performed by the orchestra, a tribute and a mark of respect for a skilled large orchestra playing important music worthy of itself. *LA Variations* marked an extraordinary emergence for Salonen, the unleashing of a steady stream of large-scale orchestral works, a remarkable stylistic turn.

Salonen himself confronts this "turn," but hesitantly. "I guess the main shift in my thinking," he recently wrote, "was a result of culture shock":

> I lost interest in dogma and ideology and decided to write music that would satisfy and bring together both sides of my personality, the performer and the creator. I wanted to be able to luxuriate in the full resonance of an orchestral *tutti*; I wanted to have real pulse and rhythmic drive in my music. I developed a harmonic system that would allow me to create a sense of modulation, something that we completely lost in twelve-tone music. (A big loss! So many of the greatest moments in the repertoire are modulations! Think of the Beethoven "Eroica" or the Brahms Fourth or *Tristan* or...). Also I wanted to be able to do simple things (still working on that...), as well as complex things.

The love affair continues. Salonen's contract at the Philharmonic has been extended through 2008, with an "evergreen" clause allowing for further extensions. It's no secret that other orchestras have played footsie for his services over the years, but that's hard to balance against Brentwood's sunshine. The Hollywood proximity hasn't hurt, either: witness the sensational success some years back of Salonen's disc of Bernard Herrmann's film music, which he might not have discovered as easily if he had taken the job in Cleveland. He and the Philharmonic have worked out an amicable time-sharing: twenty-six weeks a year for conducting, twenty-six for "composing and the so-called life."

"I have been very happy both professionally and personally in L.A.," he continues:

> I cannot imagine any other major city that would give its probably most important cultural institution into the hands of some Finnish guy in his early thirties and—even more amazingly—support him wholeheartedly along the way. This kind of openness and lack of prejudice is rare if not unique. Okay, people did not necessarily read Schopenhauer a lot in L.A., nor were they interested in the pseudo-intellectual dogma of post-Darmstadt post-serialism. The mental and physical distance between myself in L.A. and Europe had a liberating effect on me. (There are some people in Europe who would replace "liberating" with some other, considerably nastier sounding/smelling attribute, but I don't care anymore. I'm a middle-aged guy with three children and not some young thing who worries about one's identity and how it is perceived.)

"To keep classical music alive," Esa-Pekka Salonen has said, "is a complex issue":

> It's making sure that it's not seen as something that has reached its peak long ago and now is in decline. It's making sure that we are developing something, we are developing a tradition, we are questioning certain conventions, we are presenting old works in new light, new works in new contexts, basically taking care of the tradition, but also taking care of the talent of today. My sympathies lie very much in the music that is composed today because it interests me and it excites me, and for me it's

the most natural way of communicating with the rest of the world, to deal with composers who reflect the world in their music now.

Those were his words to a gathering of music lovers in 1994. Ten years later, their glow abides.

[*Musical America*, December 2005]

Slonimsky at 100: Birthday Boy

I dropped in on Nicolas Slonimsky a few days ago. The small West Los Angeles cottage was all bustle, as usual: secretaries and assistants straightening out papers, bundling books, coping with endless telephone calls. "Now that The Birthday is upon us," sighed an assistant, "everybody wants to come by, even people who don't even know him. Something about being 100 years old makes you into a kind of guru, I guess. They all need his handclasp."

Slonimsky himself wasn't participating in the bustle. He has had his good and bad health days lately. Tucked into a small bedroom, he wondered jokingly if perhaps he ought to switch to the old Russian calendar, which would have moved The Birthday up a few days, to April 15 or 16 instead of the 27th. No, he decided with something of a twinkle; he'll stay with the rest of the world, which is poised to honor Nicolas Slonimsky's centennial on the due date. National Public Radio and the local cultural stations have celebrations on tap for that date; the *New Yorker* has sent over its high-prestige photographer Richard Avedon; there will be concerts here and there; somebody is bound to sing one of Slonimsky's "Advertising Songs" in which, long ago, he set some of the more blatant ad slogans to his own caterwauling music. "Children cry for CASTORIA!!!" runs one of the texts.

Very old people are often endowed with crystal-clear memories of distant actions. We spoke that afternoon about the times sixty years ago, when America's young composers were carving out a native musical language—Charles Ives, Henry Cowell, Edgard Varèse, Carl Ruggles—in the face of almost total public apathy. It was Slonimsky who led the fight for acceptance, as critic for the belligerent magazine *Modern Music* and as conductor of his own ensemble, giving the world premieres of such major works as Ives's *Three Places in New England* and Varèse's *Ionisation.* Does anyone carry on that fight today? Nicolas and I wondered together.

If new music gets by today without the kind of activist advocacy that Slonimsky and his colleagues found necessary in 1930, it's probably because they did their work so well. In 1933 Slonimsky was, for reasons nobody has ever been able to fathom, offered the conductorship of the entire Hollywood Bowl summer season. He showed up with programs of the new music he had so vigorously championed: Roy Harris, Aaron Copland, Ives, and Ruggles. After a week of this kind of buffeting, the shocked Bowl board bought up his contract.

"But that music is all repertory now," said Nicolas with a participatory, satisfied smile. "You don't shock people any more." It's interesting, actually, to trace the gradual process of assimilation whereby names like Copland and Ives acquired household status. The other side of Slonimsky's contribution, his work as historian, scholar, and lexicographer, lights our path. *Music since 1900* is a phenomenon like none other, a chronicle of major musical events throughout the world, practically day by day, crammed into over 2000 densely packed pages; an eighth edition is due out next month. His other heavyweight tome, *Baker's Biographical Dictionary,* begun by a man named Baker but run almost single-handedly by Slonimsky since 1958, ran to 2111 pages in its latest edition; it's the authoritative source for looking up anyone from Jackson, Michael, to Josquin Desprez.

Memories began to drift, like clouds on a bright sky; it was time to go. Between quick naps, Nicolas talked on about his wife, the art critic Dorothy Adlow, thirty years dead; about other beloved personages now departed; about his nephew Sergei Slonimsky, now one of Russia's foremost young composers. The house itself inspired my own memories, of Slonimsky at a healthier time, demonstrating in his big easy chair how to conduct five with one hand and two with the other; ramming his way through Chopin's "Black Key" Etude at his obscenely out-of-tune piano while holding an orange in his hand; gleefully quoting from his favorite of all his articles, "Sex and the Music Librarian."

Our friendship over the years has been made up of fragments. In his prime Nicolas could be terrifying; our love of cats helped bridge the gap. Our private joke was that he had let me write my own entry in Baker's; I did it so well ("music critic of an uncommonly bellicose disposition") that it lost me at least one job. I've known Nicolas well enough to know this: nobody has ever taken so much into his own life in the sheer joy of creative energy. And nobody worked harder, over longer time, to repay that joy in so many ways.

[April 1994]

Carlos Kleiber: The Catalyst

Carlos Kleiber's passing last month left no noticeable tremors on the musical landscape. He had suffered, the obituary notices read, from a "long-term illness," but the world had suffered from his even longer-term absence; his last performances of any consequence were in 1994, although there were scattered appearances (and scattered cancellations as well) in ensuing years. I saw him once, in September 1990, conducting *Der Rosenkavalier* at the Met in his last American engagement.

Even so, I have always spent a lot of time with Kleiber and have stepped up the pace in the last few weeks. My laser disc treasures include Mozart, Beethoven, and Brahms symphonies; a Johann Strauss "New Year's Concert" with the Vienna Philharmonic in its gold-encrusted Musikvereinsaal; and two versions of *Der Rosenkavalier* along with one of *Die Fledermaus*. Some of these have also appeared on DVD and all of them should. I also cherish an *Otello* from La Scala on videotape, many times dubbed but with the sound still clear.

A performance of Mozart's "Linz" Symphony from Vienna is a particular prize. What passes between Kleiber and the orchestra is not so much a matter of master and commander—a Lenny B. or a Herbie von K. handing down the tablets from on high. It is more a matter of sharing, of a communion between players and conductor, with an audience invited to look on. Perhaps other matters have passed between Kleiber and the players beforehand—his rehearsals were famously inaccessible—but what

I see in these extraordinary performances, and love to watch time and again, is this extraordinary oneness of the musicality and the seeming lack of self-serving personal furor in the process of making it happen. There are times when he sets his baton at rest and simply lets his gentle smile do the job.

The furor is there, all right. The blurred images on my precious tapes of the La Scala *Otello* show a musical storm seething through the house that could send anyone for cover—with an occasional fleeting view of Kleiber himself, his young (fortyish) face lit with a beatific smile, mouthing the words of the "Fuoco di gioia" chorus as a privileged participant. On compact disc there is a Beethoven Fifth Symphony from Vienna, on a bargain-priced Deutsche Grammophon, that will knock your socks off. No matter how many times that surge to the end of the first movement has picked you up by the scruff of the neck and shaken you helpless, this one will do it again, with the electricity turned up to eleven. There is a Schubert "Unfinished," also on DG, whose celestial dying out will leave you shorn of access to words.

Seldom heard, even more rarely seen, Kleiber among us was some kind of catalytic force. His performance repertory was small, fatally so for anyone attempting to build a "normal" conducting career in this or the past century. That was obviously not his purpose; his limited range of public activity and the quality of his performance values stand as a touchstone, a reminder of times when a sublime performance of the Beethoven Fifth could make people stop and think about the music's greatness and how to get it into the bloodstream. Nowadays, with anywhere up to 100 Beethoven Fifths competing for your dollar at the local megastore—and with the classical department often moved over behind pop so that you have to leave your brain outside anyhow—you have to ask whether Kleiber died for the cause, and whether the cause soon will die with him. In his time he was a small but clear beacon light; the job now is to keep it aglow.

[August 2004]

John Cage: The Great Enabler

                inadequate Judgment, merely
                        tO regard
                        Him as some
                        kiNd of
                        Malcontent
                revolutIonary, because
        the whoLeness of his
                spiriT embraced the
                        wOrld as if it were all
                        eNdless musical
        resourCe; his
                stAked-out territory
        stretched Gloriously
                        bEyond music's familiar bounds,
                and Jostled
                        ouR wildest expectations

                                                —A. R.

We begin with a paradox. The above is my own attempt at a mesostic, a
poetic and typographical form invented by John Cage at an indeterminate
moment in his lifespan (1971 will do). Cage's friend Norman O. Brown,
the psychoanalytic historian, suggested the title; if an acrostic is built on a
vertical string of letters at the start of each line, a mesostic runs the string
down through the middle of the lines. Cage devised a whole complex

of rules, of which the most famous is this: the "pure" mesostic may not repeat either the previous or the next capitalized letter in between those two capitals. Between the capital J of the first line and the capital O of the second line, in other words, you are not allowed to use the letters J and O.

There, in the full range of his complexity, is the man whose work spreads across our consciousness for three months starting this weekend: a panorama of creativity winding its way through the galleries and theaters of the Museum of Contemporary Art, finding its echo in the activities of museums, performing spaces, even an opera company throughout Southern California. More than a memorial, it becomes a celebration of the joy and the imponderability of creativity, not just music but all the arts conjoined. It has been heading our way for several years, with Cage himself very much in on the planning and insisting always that the word "circus"—not exhibition, not concert, certainly not tribute—be the operative term. "It never occurred to either of us," says MOCA's curator, Julie Lazar, "that we wouldn't always both be here."

If nothing else, "Rolywholyover a Circus" and the concomitant "Citycircus" will compound the paradox. On one hand there is Cage the freedom fighter, operating from a command of artistic anarchy that could push the process of expression beyond all thinkable limits; on the other hand, Cage the uptight typographical grammarian, devising this willful straitjacket to confine the language within unthinkable restrictions. On one hand, a creator who demanded for his art the right to define itself on the basis of its mere existence—"music is whatever a musician says it is"; on the other, this linguistic martinet, a paradox indeed. When Cage came to Harvard in 1988 to deliver the hallowed Norton Lectures, from the platform whose laurels Stravinsky, T. S. Eliot, and Leonard Bernstein once bore, he spoke them all, six ninety-minute exercises of alternating self-definition and self-obfuscation, as mesostics.

Not easily defined, this imp-eyed, soft-spoken elderly child who left us a year ago but lingers still—lingering in full view, as it happens, while MOCA reveals the awesomely widespread panorama of the world as touched by John Cage. Yet the thinking that imposed the need for redefinition across that panorama (and beyond, onto the backs of those who deplored his existence no less than adored its fruits) forms Cage's clearest legacy.

Redefining: the term is deceptive. It isn't as if music, say, or any of the expressive arts, for that matter, comes to rest on a certain definable evolutionary level and then awaits the next liberator to discard all traditional definitions in a single swipe and install new ones in their place. Generically defined, music is the art that exists in a time continuum demarcated by a sequence of sounds determined by a composer. Direct the focus to a specific musical object, and you add density to the list of definitions. A Mozart symphony uses an orchestra of strings, winds, brass, and percussion as its noise-making apparatus; the composer works with musical materials (melodies with symmetrical phrase lengths, regular rhythmic patterns, harmonies, and tone color) simple enough that a hearer can grasp the outlines of a plan, recognize tunes when they recur, and glean an awareness of contrast, climax, and overall structural logic. Shift the focus to, say, Stravinsky's *Rite of Spring*, and you encounter new definitions: orchestral sonorities rethought so that the string section, traditionally the bearer of melody, may also serve as a percussive force; complex rhythms; and irregular phrase lengths. Move on to our own time, when composers use computers and synthesizers to expand the range of possible sonorities; now we must rethink accepted

What would such a project be called? He quickly replied, "A circus," but not one named after him. "Rolywholyover," an onomatopoeic concoction from James Joyce's Finnegans Wake (a source for many earlier compositions), appears toward the end of the book following the tenth thunderclap ("the thunderclaps . . . are a history of civilization's technology") and implies revolution and dynamic movement.

—Julie Lazar, talking to John Cage

Soe? Lamfader's arm it has cocoincidences. You mean to see we have been hadding a sound night's sleep? You may so. It is just. It is just about to. It is just about to rolywholyover. Svapnasvap. Of all the stranger things that ever not even in the hundrund and badst pageans of unthowsent and wonst nice or in eddas and oddes bokes of tomb, dyke and hollow to have happened!

—James Joyce, Finnegans Wake

definitions of intervals (the distance on the sound spectrum between, say, C and C-sharp) and sonority (a Steinway piano, a symphony orchestra). Every redefinition implies reexamining an old definition and expanding its implications: silence, for example, as the logical extension of sound. The process goes on in all the arts. The formulation of perspective in the fifteenth century didn't eliminate all previous art, but it added greatly to art's realm of possibilities; an all-black or all-white painting of Robert Rauschenberg suggested to John Cage the musical potential inherent in noise and silence.

Music critics, professional or self-proclaimed, subsist through the process of asking "why?" Leaf through Nicolas Slonimsky's cautionary *Lexicon of Musical Invective*; his landscape is littered with the whisperings. Why does Beethoven shock us with those discords? Why must Rachmaninoff inflict that plague of insects? Why that Wagnerian clash-bang-clatter? Cage lives on in the bravery of his "why not?"

> He thinks of himself as music's corrective, as a prophet denouncing the whole of Renaissance and post-Renaissance Europe, with its incorrigible respect for beauty and distinction, and dissolving all that in an ocean of electronic availabilities.... It is not the first time that an artist has fancied himself as destroying the past, and then found himself using it.... Destroying the past is a losing game. The past cannot be destroyed; it merely wears out.... He is also a major musical force and a leader among us.
>
> —Virgil Thomson, 1971

Another paradox: Despite the list of cultural agencies participating in the three months of citywide Cage, our most illustrious musical organization has little to contribute: a Halloween event called "Cage: Indoors and Out," not at the Music Center but indoors and outdoors in MOCA's small auditorium and in the California Plaza nearby. At that, that modest event will swell the Philharmonic's Cage statistics. Since 1972 there have been exactly four Cage performances produced under Philharmonic auspices: three at campus runouts and one of an early work for percussion ensemble at a Green Umbrella concert at the Japan-America Theater. As far as anyone can discover, nary a note of Cage's music has ever resounded inside the Dorothy Chandler Pavilion.

> Zen is profoundly serious, but full of humor; Zen demands being rather than representing, yet has inspired many different kinds of art. Zen teaches us not merely to hear, but to listen; not just to look, but to see; not only to think, but to experience; and above all not to cling to what we know, but to accept and rejoice in as much of the world as we may encounter.
>
> —Stephen Addiss, *The Art of Zen*

Julie Lazar chose that passage to head her contribution to the fanciful toy box that serves as catalog to her MOCA exhibition, and it is, indeed, a fair stand-in for Cage himself.

MOCA first approached Cage in 1990 with the idea of creating a project that would be, in Cageian terms, no more a museum creation than an actual composition. "He insisted from the beginning on thinking of it as a circus," Lazar told me, "but not with him as the center. He really believed in art as a group process. It isn't someone saying something, but people doing things."

"The same as *4'33"* isn't just someone sitting at the piano in a room," I suggested, "but the whole world of sounds and silences and actions and nonactions within that room."

"Exactly," Lazar said.

And so the space of "Rolywholyover" at MOCA will be filled with a non-thematic non-exhibit. "We want it to be like some big living room—like John's apartment, you know, you've been there. We want a clutter: plants, books, pots, maybe some scores strewn about. There'll be tables where people can actually play chess, as John would be doing. There'll be a main exhibit area, with maybe 200 objects. John spoke of the idea of putting any two objects side by side that didn't really go together. 'It'll give people a new way of looking at both objects,' he'd say."

From the start, the exhibition has been planned as a continuously changing phenomenon, a constant gathering of artworks, artifacts, performances, screenings, readings, and dramatic events; you have to plan several visits, or it'll be like approaching a smorgasbord without a plate. Each day's actual content will be determined by chance operations, the computerized *I Ching* that has served Cage as compositional collaborator for the past several years. It was also Cage's idea that the day-to-day changes should happen while the public is in attendance. "He explained to the staff," says Lazar, "that if their work could be done when the public is there, you get to see all that happens in the museum. So if we go to a museum, and it doesn't look like a museum but it has things we can see, we can learn to look with interest at the parts that don't have anything showing." *4'33"* again? You betcha!

Cage Cooks!

Dinner at Cage's was an experience of which food was, literally, the least. Present were John, Merce Cunningham, Betty Freeman (the Los Angeles patron and new-music supporter who'd been sending Cage his monthly rent money for longer than they either could remember), and me. The view across Sixth Avenue (at Eighteenth Street), through John's veritable jungle of potted tropical plants, took in a glorious hulk of a one-time great building, the Ladies' Block, dating back to when this area comprised New York's fashion center (now moved twenty blocks uptown). John's fearsome activity in the kitchen produced an endless supply of brown rice, a couple of plain slabs of white fish for Betty and me, and, as the main dish, fronds of parboiled kale to be dipped into warm soy sauce. A desperate craving for a hamburger, which I usually loathe, took hold.

Betty reminded me recently of the way John, while preparing dinner, would wipe off the kitchen counter dozens, hundreds of times, always with intense concentration. "That night taught me about paying attention," she said.

John Cage's Gruel Bread: Go through the refrigerator, collecting food you no longer wish to eat: rice, beans, cooked vegetables or raw (parsley that's turned yellow, etc.). Include any liquids you may have saved (such as water from parboiling string beans). Put through Cuisinart and measure. Add more than an equal amount of whole wheat flour. Mix and then knead (adding dried dill weed if desired) for about forty-five minutes or an hour, until it is all of a piece. Then put in oiled bread pans. I use corn oil. After putting it in, take it out and put it in upside down. (This oils the pan.) Take a wide knife and make a deep indentation down the middle of the loaf. Cover the loaf and leave in warm place overnight. In the morning bake at 375° for one hour and 15–20 minutes.

—John Cage

The length was predetermined by Cage to be seventy-two minutes, because he wrote it to fill a compact disc.... He wanted to come to grips with a new recording medium. Cage himself didn't like recordings; he liked his music live; he liked it to be different every time, and he liked active listeners. "Remove the records from Texas," as Cage once put it, "and someone will learn to sing."

—Mark Swed, in the "Rolywholyover" catalog

By that standard, *4'33"* ought to be the work of Cage best suited for recording, since the ambient sounds are bound to change around every playing. As it happens, there is a recording (in stereo), on Hungaroton, by the Hungarian percussion group Amadinda; sounds fine to me.

Common practice is to accord Cage the full value of his iconoclastic pronouncements and to downgrade the music itself as somehow of less importance. There are precedents; the first operas, back at the start of the baroque era, didn't amount to much, nor the earliest classical symphonies. Then came Monteverdi, then came Haydn and Mozart, and matters were set straight once again. Do we now pray for the advent of the Cage disciple who will turn some of these compositional precepts into a new generation of masterpieces? Or is it time, perhaps, to revisit some of these works whose listing takes up three columns of six-point type in *The New Grove Dictionary of American Music* and find what we missed the first time around?

I suspect the latter and offer a discography of sorts to back it up. The order is chronological, not according to preference; these are six discs for the open-minded to cherish.

1. *Second and Third Constructions for Percussion Quartet*, 1940–41 (New World). Under the tutelage of the archetypal musical iconoclast Henry Cowell (he of the fist-clobbered piano keyboards) Cage and his colleague Lou Harrison began raiding Bay Area junkyards, retrieving a range of noise-making apparatus including trolley-car springs, brake drums, and metal sheets: a sound resource for a whole new musical language, divorced from traditional timbre and harmony, surging with new sounds and rhythms. A half-century later, Cage's *Constructions*

(and *Double Music*, a collaborative effort with Harrison, also included on this disc) have a freshness and vitality that comes from the energy of young creators rediscovering the world. New York's New Music Consort recaptures this vitality in its playing.

2. *Sonatas and Interludes for Prepared Piano*, 1942 (Newport Classic). The story is well-known of how Cage, needing something percussive and yet melodic for a dance performance, hit upon the idea of inflicting bits of hardware on piano strings. Beyond their elegant, exotic sounds, the dozens of pieces he wrote for tampered-with (or "prepared") piano capture a side of Cage's own musical outlook that didn't show up often in later works: the simple, open, hypnotic antiqueness of the melodies, a clear descendant of Erik Satie's music (which Cage adored). These remain Cage's most popular pieces (next to 4′33″, of course, which people are wont to hear in self-defense), and recordings abound. I like this disc, which includes nineteen separate, small pieces, performed by Joshua Pierce (who has also recorded the whole caboodle on a five-CD Wergo set), playing at a live concert in Greenwich Village, and also some delightfully oddball music by another American original, Charles Ives: his Three Pieces for pianos tuned a quarter-tone apart.

3. *String Quartet in Four Parts*, 1949–50; *Four*, 1989 (Mode). Both works, composed four decades apart, disarm the listener with their intense, simple quiet. The earlier work instructs the players to perform without vibrato; this gives the music a kind of otherworldly character that matches the exotic effects from the prepared piano. The message here seems to be that even as traditional an ensemble as a string quartet can, with the right kind of urging, create a vocabulary of new sonorities, ravishing the ear and arousing the imagination. *Four*, the later of the two works, is, simply put, the most beautiful chamber-music composition of our time. The four quartet members distribute their parts in any way and play the work through. Then they swap parts with one another and play the piece through again—with the music, of course, transposed from, say, violin to cello. The result is a kind of tapestry, an unmodulated surface in muted tones, and the confluences among the

instruments occur largely by that favorite Cage word: change. Hearing this performance by Britain's extraordinary Arditti Quartet (which has recorded all of Cage's quartets), you have to imagine that there is something more than sheer chance at work here, a performing intuition that brings the music to juncture after juncture of harmonies so rich as to stop the breath. I would choose this music, in this performance, as the ultimate refutation of the old bromide that Cage's importance lies elsewhere than in his music.

4. *Concert for Piano and Orchestra*, 1957–58; *Atlas Eclipticalis*, 1961–62 (Wergo). Here is Cage for the strong of heart: tense, explosive, tough pieces whose ultimate shape is arrived at through nontraditional means. The *Concert* has no overall score; it exists as a series of single scores for the pianist (who could, actually, go it alone) and for a group of solo instruments that overlay the piano part without actually interlocking. *Atlas Eclipticalis* is what its name means: star map, a work whose notes are derived from laying transparencies of star maps over lined music paper and, thus, changing with the day. This was the work of Cage introduced by Leonard Bernstein, back in 1964, as part of an avant-garde festival imposed by the New York Philharmonic on a subscription audience, a tactical boo-boo rewarded at the end of the piece by a panorama of vacated seats (except for mine). The music survives, as it deserves, on the strength of its punching energy and sheer nerve; it survives very well under the direction of Petr Kotik on the enterprising Wergo label.

5. *Indeterminacy*, 1958 (Smithsonian-Folkways). John Cage reads, in his seductively buttery, if slightly twee delivery manner, ninety tiny anecdotes or mood pieces, each lasting exactly a minute, while—as if in the next room with the door ajar—the pianist David Tudor provides discreet punctuation. You might wonder whether the idea of turning ninety minutes of impressionistic storytelling into a piece of music, by just proclaiming it so, has any ancestral relationship to contemporary rap performance. In the sense that the work is a transfiguration of vernacular, maybe so. But rap carries its own rhythmic and rhyming

baggage; the Cage imagery floats free. If you were at the complete performance at Ojai some summers ago, read by Charles Shere with "punctuation" by Amy Knoles, you might remember that it floats quite enchantingly.

6. *Quartets*, 1976; *Music for Fourteen*, 1985 (Newport Classic). Beautiful, airy works, superbly played by San Francisco's Contemporary Chamber Players. Never one to turn his back on his American-iconoclast heritage, Cage has taken eight hymns by Revolutionary-era New England composers, fragmented them, and woven them into a new musical fabric. A large orchestra is used, but only four players perform at any one time. The sound is like a nocturnal landscape, with several church suppers and a lot of singing heard off in the distance, and you in the foreground taking in the enchanting blend. If this sounds more like Charles Ives, maybe it is, and beautiful of its kind.

Again, there is no written-down score for *Music for Fourteen*, only a set of parts for flute, clarinet, trombone, three percussion, piano, violin, and cello. Each part is marked off in time segments, within which the player can decide when to begin and end. (Each musician must carry a stopwatch.) Like almost everything of Cage's since his emergence as a resolute innovator and questioner, it is compounded of an exquisite balance of prescriptions and freedoms. He encourages individual autonomies among the players. "Each player," he wrote, "should

The most important piece is my silent piece. No day goes by without my making use of it in my life and work. I always think of it before I write the next piece.

—John Cage

Doing nothing is clearly distinct from expressing nothing. Silence means the whole world of sound, Life; and its entrance into the world of music means the end of that exclusive activity called Art whereby the composer makes a separate act meant to "illumine the darkness" of the chaos of everyday life.

—Jill Johnston,
Village Voice, *1962*

I have nothing to say, and I am saying it.... All we have to do is pay attention to anything, it seems to me. Thoreau had this view; he said about music that music is continuous, only listening is intermittent.

—John Cage

prepare his part by himself.... There should be no joint rehearsal until all parts have been carefully prepared. They are then to be played as if from six centers in space."

And what of us listeners, marooned out there in one or another block of Cageian space? Hearing this music on a recording, the same every time repeated, defeats some part of Cage's notion of constant change, constant autonomy. Yet, it seems to me that Cage's most fervent admirers, as well as his most outspoken detractors, miss one most important aspect in even his most loose-limbed, indeterminate music: its beauty. In its thirty or so minutes, I hear the workings of a delighted, industrious creative spirit, pouring forth the hard-edged fragments out of which the fourteen players create a web of enchantment. Bright, irregular splotches of color rush by; think of a rush of butterflies, a Calder mobile, a Pollock canvas; why not? Cage was a master of all the arts, all the senses, and in these last two extended works of our brief discography they are all happily placed on display.

> I use the I Ching when it is useful, just as I turn on the water faucet when I need a drink. I generally say, "What do you have to say about this?" and then I just listen to what it says and see if some bells ring or not.
>
> —John Cage

Cage first mentions recourse to the *I Ching* in 1951, when he found a substantial concordance between its oracular charts and hexagrams and some particular compositional problems he faced at the time. Previously he had often consulted tarot cards to deal with some specific nexus, but found their answers vague and often useless. The *I Ching* served his purpose far better. Initially he activated the oracle through coins. "You must realize that I spend a great deal of time tossing coins," he wrote to Pierre Boulez, "and the emptiness of head that that induces begins to penetrate the rest of my time itself."

More recently his colloquies with the oracle have been facilitated by computer programs set up by his longtime disciple Andrew Culver, who will stage the Cage *Europeras 3 & 4* at Long Beach as one of the events in

CityCircus on November 13 and 14. The *Europeras* are the *I Ching's* lyrical masterpieces. With the oracle close at hand, Cage raided the vastness of the operatic repertory, assembling familiar scenes, arias, and plot gimmicks according to ascertained oracular advice and recreating them along newly devised plotlines. *Europeras 1 & 2* were first given at the Frankfurt Opera in 1987 (miraculously so, since the house had been torched during the last rehearsals) and brought to the Pepsico Summerfare in New York State the following year: exhilarating, agonizing, thrilling, for reasons somewhat beyond rational explanation. At Long Beach there will be live singers, but records instead of orchestra and chorus: a whole 'nother dimension.

[April 1992, April 1994]

A John Cage Obituary (August 1992)

John Cage left us a few days ago, a couple of weeks short of his eightieth birthday. That's already sad news. Cage loved his big birthdays; when I last talked with him, just a few months ago, he was still celebrating No. 75, while also letting on that No. 80 would be an event of even more earth-shaking importance, with himself on hand to do much of the shaking.

It's hard to imagine how his memory can best be celebrated. He left a voluminous legacy of music, to be sure, but with Cage himself no longer on the scene, with his infectious, boyish grin and his wonderfully quixotic gift for self-definition through the inspired manipulation of language, the music itself suddenly seems less important in and of itself. It's hard to claim important-masterpiece stature for some of Cage's most famous works: *4'33"*, the piece for silent performer (on whatever instrument happens to be at hand), the *Imaginary Landscapes* for ensembles of variously tuned radios, the theater pieces involving electric blenders and grand pianos tied up in rope, the *Europeras* that consist of famous excerpts from other people's operas, chosen and strung together on the advice of the *I Ching*. Beyond anyone's questioning, however, Cage *was* important; no

American composer in this century has had a greater impact on the course of music throughout the world.

His importance lay in his steadfast refusal to accept anything in the arts that smacked of perceived wisdom. Henry David Thoreau was his role model above any other. He read his Thoreau backward and forward and based whole long compositions on the words of Walden Pond's loner. And from Thoreau Cage absorbed the continued obsession to question, to challenge, to propose outrageous creations and then to assume the right to create them. Normal artistic boundaries—as, for example, the separation between "serious" and "popular" music, or between music and the visual arts—didn't interest Cage in the least. He created the notorious silent *4'33"* on the inspiration of an all-white painting by Robert Rauschenberg.

The very definition of music became his battleground; he demanded, and eventually gained, the right to insist that a piece of music can be anything its creator says it is, from a Beethoven symphony to a four-and-a-half-minute silence to a taping of random jabberwock at a Beverly Hills art gallery opening. "Everything we do," he repeatedly declared, "is music." Detractors (and there have been many, not surprisingly) have detected a madman's hand in his music and his writings. Cage has always had an answer. "Let us say 'yes,'" he once wrote (in a piece called *Where Are We Going?*), "to our presence in Chaos."

His arrival on the musical scene, first on the West Coast and later in New York, was nicely timed. Modern music was in something of the creative doldrums in the late 1930s, when the young Cage, alongside his fellow idol smasher Lou Harrison, both inspired by the teachings of the elder revolutionist Henry Cowell, put together "orchestras" made up of found objects from Bay Area junkyards—old brake drums, trolley-car springs, metal plates—and first proposed the tearing down of the barrier between music and noise. In "preparing" a piano by dropping nuts and bolts onto the strings, Cage invented the American equivalent of the gamelan. His father had been an inventor, his idol Thoreau had been an inventor (who devised a method for manufacturing lead pencils that is still in use), and Cage himself aspired to be of their number. His inventor's spirit enabled him to keep pace with the world of invention; his door was always open to the latest gadgetry coming down the pike. Tape recording, sounds electronically produced, and, late in his life, the computer found ready welcome into the Cage cosmos.

Pioneers in the arts are not always the creative masters. The first operas, early in the baroque era, were pretty pokey pieces; so were the first symphonies a century later. The geniuses who transfigured these art forms usually arrived a few years later: Monteverdi and Mozart. Cage's musical legacy takes up three columns of fine print in *The New Grove Dictionary of American Music*, and a dry reading of some of those items ("*Variations III*, any number of people performing any actions") doesn't hold out much promise as an addition to the permanent repertory. Yet they form the enabling force for much music that was to come. Such latter-day works as Terry Riley's *In C* and the exquisite, close-to-silence legacy of Morton Feldman rest on the foundations laid by Cage.

And there are works in that huge Cageian bequeathal that do, of themselves, seem vested with a real sense of imagination, beauty, and an unmistakable overlay of genius—the *Thirty Pieces*, spectacularly performed by the Arditti Quartet on a Mode release, or the song-and-dance piece *Four Walls*, enchantingly sung by Joan La Barbara on New Albion, or *Quartets for Twenty-Four Players*, forthcoming on Newport Classic. But these seem strangely "normal" in both structure and scoring, not the stuff on which Cage's public image has been based. Eclipsed for the time being by the more sensation-building side of Cage's art, this music will emerge some day as the more enduring, and endearing, measure of his artistic stature. (His fame in Italy, by the way, rests on another foundation entirely: his big win on a TV quiz show on the subject of edible mushrooms. Thoreau would have been proud.)

It was that willingness to expand his artistic view, to move across boundaries, to seek companionship and collaborators in all the arts— the dancer Merce Cunningham, the painters Rauschenberg and Marcel Duchamp, the archetypal iconoclast Thoreau—that made John Cage so important a role model to generations of composers after his time. His shadow fell across creative spirits as dissimilar as Laurie Anderson, Frank Zappa, and John Adams. Adams once told me that a reading of Cage's *Silence*, an essential set of essays, rescued him forever from the clutches of the academy. But Adams was only one of many whose lives—and, more to the point, whose artistic outlooks—were touched by this smiling, soft-spoken, yet obsessed idol smasher on whose lips there rested the perpetual question: why not? John Cage is gone, but that question remains, to demand constant reply. It always should.

WRITERS

These are some of the people who have guided my pen—toward greater understanding, or away from greater foolishness—over the many, many years.

Sir Donald Tovey and the Ideal Listener

Sir Donald Francis Tovey changed my life—for the better, I like to think.

I was twenty, as hapless a pre-med as ever walked along ivied walls. Somebody in physics lab showed me a slim volume he'd just acquired: *Essays in Musical Analysis* by Sir Donald Francis Tovey. The title was forbidding; the prose was warm, welcoming, and congenial. They weren't "musical analyses" as I understood the term—first movement in the tonic, modulating to the dominant via enharmonic bridge, etc. They were, instead, program notes about specific pieces that Sir Donald would conduct with his Reid Orchestra in Edinburgh. "This is what I plan to conduct," they told his good Scots readers, "and these are my thoughts to take the music closer." In my friend's book (one volume of a set of six) I read about Antonín Dvořák's particular kind of sublimity "which trails clouds of glory not only with the outlook of the child but with the solemnity of the kitten running after its tail." I read about one of the crabby tunes in the César Franck Symphony "striding grandly, in its white confirmation dress." I read, spellbound, though forty-five pages of glowing, adoring prose about why Beethoven's Ninth Symphony is what it is. This, I decided, is what I want to do, and to hell with "my son the doctor."

What Tovey wrote about was not only the structure of a piece of music; his focus was on the aura that forms in and around a piece of music after it leaves the printed page and makes contact with the listener out front. His ideal listener, he proclaimed time and again, was the person not necessarily trained in music, but endowed with a willing ear to accept a musical experience and examine the results. He enlisted the dangerous allies of simile and metaphor to make and to illustrate his points, but he used them as convincingly as any writer about music before or since his time, including—dare I say it?—our own Lenny. To my dying day, perhaps beyond, I will not get past a certain spot in the Beethoven Ninth without hearing Tovey's "flashes of red light" from the trumpets. They're there.

And now, sixty-two years after Tovey's death, he is with us again in astonishing plenitude, *The Classics of Music*, a volume huge in girth (864 pages) and in price ($95), a treasury of never-before-published Tovey: more essays in musical analysis, formal lectures, radio talks, reviews, even an account of a newfangled piano that could play quarter-tones. An editor at Oxford University Press, Michael Tilmouth, persuaded the Tovey archive at the University of Edinburgh to make its contents available for publication; after Tilmouth's death his work was completed by David Kimbell and Roger Savage. The result is a compendium so wise, so friendly, so *essential* as to heap further disgrace on the sorry pile that has in recent years come to clutter the far corner of my worktable—ghastly small tomes with titles like *Who's Afraid of Classical Music?* or *Getting Opera*. On every page, amid essays on Haydn quartets, Mozart arias, and Tovey's own piano concerto, amid a set of Beethoven lectures, another set with the prickly title "Music in Being," and a broadcast talk called "Music and the Ordinary Listener," Tovey's greatness lies in his wise love of his art and his uncanny skill at sharing it.

Tovey (1875–1940) composed, and enjoyed a fair career as pianist. His A Major Piano Concerto (available on Hyperion) isn't a bad academic exercise, and there's a clarinet sonata that's even prettier. By 1905 his writing career had taken hold, and he was asked to contribute major articles—including one extraordinary piece called "Music"—to the great eleventh edition of the *Encyclopedia Britannica*. These have been published by Oxford from time to time but are probably no longer easy to find. (The good news here is that the entire eleventh Britannica is now available for download: http://www.1911encyclopedia.org.)

From Tovey I learned to bear blatant prejudices as a badge of honor. The violinist Joseph Joachim was a close friend and certainly shaped Tovey's strong bias toward the music of Brahms and, consequently, away from the Wagnerian camp. On a single page among the *Essays*, Tovey manages to demolish the whole line—Wagner to Bruckner to Mahler—with a couple of pen strokes. There follow eight pages of kindly encomium vested upon two orchestral "poems"—*The Riders of the Sidhe* and *Springtime on Tweed*—by a certain William Beatton Moonie, on whom obscurity has cast its pall. Then come some thirty pages of exquisite insights into the inner workings of a sheaf of Mozart works in which at least two—the last piano concerto and the Violin and Viola Concertante—are dealt with briefly but with heartwarming insight; "galloping at his laziest," we read, "Mozart never allows his square rhythms to fall into monotony."

Tovey the critic fought the same battles that we fight today, with only the names changed. Before the legendary Arthur Nikisch, the glam conductor of his time, Tovey stands forth in mingled admiration and horror: "a splendid interpreter of all that is obviously dramatic, his mind is almost a blank on matters of quiet poetic intensity of feeling." He wrestles mightily with the looming specter of the upstart Richard Strauss. "There is nothing unusual," he grieves upon the advent of *Ein Heldenleben*, "in the spectacle of a man of genius associating his own finest art with all that is pretentious and undignified."

As befalls every observer of the cultural scene, Tovey witnessed an occasional cloud across his crystal ball. Visiting the inventor Emanuel Moór to observe the "duplex-coupler" piano that could switch between tunings, Tovey ventured the prophecy that "the ordinary pianoforte will be extinct as the Dodo in ten years." On the other hand, an essay on the problems of maintaining a symphony orchestra (his own Edinburgh ensemble)—funding, adequate rehearsal time, the livelihood of the players—might have appeared in yesterday's headlines.

So, for that matter, could the very spirit that infuses this remarkable, indispensable, unaffordable musical "witness for the defense" (his words). The introduction to the first volume of Tovey's *Essays*, the book that caused my pathway to swerve nearly six decades ago, ends with a statement of faith: "While the listener must not expect to hear the whole contents of a piece of music at once, nothing concerns him that will not ultimately reach his ear either as a directly audible fact or as a cumulative satisfaction in things of which the hidden foundations are well and truly laid." Funny, but I still believe that.

[June 2002]

The Gadfly in the *Grove*

Precious words abide. In 1986 I turned up in one of the *Grove* dictionaries as "an unpredictable gadfly"; now, in the latest *Grove*, I still am. At least they spelled my name right, both times.

The latest arrival is the second edition of *The New Grove Dictionary of Music and Musicians* (hereafter *NewGrove II*). In the twenty-one years since *NewGrove I* the noble and time-honored lexicon has proliferated; the family now includes *AmeriGrove, OperaGrove, JazzGrove,* and *SheGrove* (women composers). In its print version, *NewGrove II* consists of twenty-nine volumes (up from the twenty of *NewGrove I*); there's an index volume, for the first time since 1890; there are 29,000 articles running to 25 million words (their count, not mine); nearly 9000 of the articles are newly commissioned; 2000 articles are on world music, compared to a mere 1000 in *NewGrove I*. There is also an online edition, with promises of updates four times a year. The asking price is $4850 for the print edition and $295 a year for the online version. You could always wait for the movie.

Perhaps I shouldn't strike so light-headed a note about this most prestigious publication in any field of the arts, for this latest *Grove*, like every one of its predecessors, is exactly that. Few publications in any language challenge its awesome inclusiveness. Take an overview of the way the *Grove* editors have defined "inclusiveness" in every succeeding edition and you end up with a fascinating map with consistently expanding borders, a study in the evolution of musical taste. Take just one example, comparing the content of *NewGrove I* and *NewGrove II*: in the 1980 edition the alphabetical sequence went from "Raoux" to "Rapeguero"; in the *NewGrove II* the sequence is "Raoux" to "Rap" to "Rapeguero," with David Toop's piece on Rap decked out with an impressive bibliography.

George Grove (1820–1900) was the kind of dedicated connoisseur that the English have always been particularly good at breeding. His father was a fishmonger at Charing Cross; young George studied engineering and built cast-iron lighthouses in Jamaica and Bermuda. Somehow he got from there to a secretaryship at London's Crystal Palace, where he wrote program notes for concerts. An admiring George Bernard Shaw noted that Grove "fed on Beethoven's symphonies as the Gods in *Das Rheingold* fed on Freia's apples." With his friend Arthur Sullivan (of "Gilbert-and-" fame) he played a huge role in unearthing Schubert manuscripts that had been scattered among collections all over Europe. In 1873 he joined the publishing firm of Macmillan to edit their new *Dictionary of Music and Musicians*; the first of four volumes appeared in 1879. His own articles on Beethoven, Schubert, and Mendelssohn were included in the first three editions, although their built-in passion extended them far out of proportion to other articles—fifty-seven pages for Mendelssohn against twelve for Bach. (Those three articles were eventually dropped and published in a separate volume in 1951—worth the search.)

Bach and Mendelssohn had regained their proper size long before *NewGrove II*, but something of Grove himself persists. Along with such later avatars as England's Donald Tovey and our own Nicolas Slonimsky, Grove was a special breed of compiler, clearly descended from the archetypal Samuel Johnson, with his own *Dictionary* of 100 years before. Unlike the straight-arrow collaborators on Germany's *Musik in Geschichte und Gegenwart*—the only effort comparable in size and splendor—Grove's people always seem to emulate the master in dispensing incontestable information with one hand and an unmistakable passion for their subjects with the other. Whether you land at Toop's splendidly documented pieces on rap, gangsta, and hip-hop, or Joseph Kerman's exhaustive and exhausting Beethoven study, the old sense I've always gotten from Grove—the strange but lovable mix of deep research and deep feeling—remains in place in this new edition. (I did find it disheartening, though, to discover in Robert Winter's Schubert article two song titles misspelled on the same line: "Liebesbotschat" for "Liebesbotschaft" and "Ständcher" for "Ständchen.")

There are, of course, other nits to pick, as in any 25-million-word undertaking. We are reminded once again that our overseas colleagues still haven't accepted the notion of cultural possibilities this far from Big Ben; this shows up in an ongoing tendency to allot Los Angeles—and everything else west of the Alleghenies—only the shortest of shrift. The basic Los Angeles article first appeared in 1980, returned in the 1986 *AmeriGrove*, was expanded ever so slightly for the 1989 *OperaGrove*, and now has shrunk back for its current incarnation. It is the work of the venerable UCLA scholar Robert Stevenson. It takes the Los Angeles Opera up to its 1986 opening night and no further, ignores entirely any new-music developments, and, in short, writes off as unimportant the nearly two decades of growth that have defined this area.

Okay, it's a small matter—if not as small as Dr. Stevenson and his editors would have the world believe. Here is something of greater concern. In considering with awe and admiration this new blockbuster compilation of everything in music worth knowing, you may stop to wonder where it all fits in the currently troubled world of serious musical thinking. Will all that knowledge—about Schubert, or hip-hop, or Duke Ellington (with André Hodeir's original article eloquently expanded by Gunther Schuller)—create a new generation of music consumer adept in the use of ears and in processing the information they harvest?

A few weeks ago one of our serious-music radio stations, one without commercials and therefore, you want to believe, free to explore interesting cultural byways, cancelled a popular weekly program devoted to music before Bach. When confronted with complaints, an executive explained that the station preferred to concentrate on "significant" composers—thus relegating to "insignificance" such nonentities as Purcell, Monteverdi, Palestrina, Dufay, Machaut, and Hildegard von Bingen. I don't know what musical treatises grace the bookshelves of KUSC's Brenda Barnes, if any, but if you had to guess between the twenty-nine volumes of *NewGrove II* and one of the dozens of current sleazeball tomes with names like *Mozart for Idiots* and *Who's Afraid of Classical Music?* you wouldn't need my help. Whatever its undeniable greatness, the indispensable new *Grove* just might become, against today's cultural realities, an insignificant other.

[June 2001]

The Oxford History: You Could Look It Up

Having completed, in his own write, the 3825 pages (1.25 million words, twenty-one pounds) of *The Oxford History of Western Music*, Richard Taruskin now merits entry into the niche of honor besides such figures as Bill Wambsganss (first unassisted triple play in a World Series game, 1920) and Charles Lindbergh (you know what, 1927). There have been Oxford music histories before; the last was completed as recently as 1990 by a consortium that drew copiously from the panoply of musical scholarship. Their multitude was explained in the introduction: "To attempt a detailed survey of the whole history of music is no longer within the power of a single writer."

Fearless and unstoppable, Professor Taruskin (Musicology, University of California, Berkeley since 1987; Columbia before that) is hardly your garden-variety single writer. Words pour forth; a two-volume study on Stravinsky requires 1757 pages to get us up to 1921, leaving fifty years still to go. He also wields a critic's sword, terrible and swift, and it serves to stir hot cauldrons; a renowned *New York Times* article from December 9, 2001, takes the side of the Boston Symphony Orchestra, against general outcry, for having canceled music from John Adams's *Death of Klinghoffer* out of fear of post–9/11 sensitivity. Not stopping there, he goes on to rake old coals, condoning the long-standing, if unstated, anti-Wagner boycott by Israeli audiences. "Why should we want to hear this music now?" he asks, a curious question in a critical context.

Anyhow, the first thing to know about Professor Taruskin's huge new solo flight is that he has not left his critical hat behind. He affects an ingratiating tone, downright chummy and certainly rare among authors of multivolume histories. More than once you get the feeling that he's walking alongside, his arm firmly on your shoulder, carefully steering you past some composer he's decided isn't worth your while—England's sturdy old Sir Ralph Vaughan Williams, say, who is vouchsafed nary a word in the text, save for a note in the intro ordaining his banishment—and into the arms of some nonentity whose importance he's decided to fabricate: four pages for the absurdly insignificant Nikolai Medtner, say. He spares us footnotes, relying instead upon endnotes keyed to words within the text. (In one instance, at least, the keying goes haywire, and his own quoted comment on the *Klinghoffer* matter is linked to an exactly opposing view by the San Francisco critic Bob Commanday. Whatever happened to careful editing?)

A question needs asking: is not the bundle of critical predilections on which Taruskin has climbed to fame in recent years an impediment per se to an encyclopedic history such as the Oxford banner proclaims? Questions of selection infect this work; they are more than mere judgmental quirks. Where, for example, is there mention of the enormous richness that has come into Western—yes, *Western*—music from the awareness of Far Eastern music? A decisive date, 1889—when the young Debussy hears raga and gamelan in Paris, absorbs their sounds into his own music, and passes his enthusiasms on to European generations—goes ignored. Where is Lou Harrison and the awareness of the vast cultural panorama of the Pacific Rim that he has spread to young Americans on both coasts? What about Toru Takemitsu? The influx of brilliant young talent that slipped out of China's clutches to give the West some of its best new music? (Tan Dun earns a mention not much longer than his name, and an erroneous reference; it is the *St. Matthew Passion*, not the *St. Luke*, that he has set to music.) Where, amid page after page of homage to the Beatles and Laurie Anderson and Bob Dylan and the other manifestations of with-it culture, is notice taken of Stephen Sondheim? And what of today's great Finns, who do their nation proud?

Priorities

Of the ten volumes in the previous *Oxford History*, seven were filled before Beethoven (i.e., 1800) was reached. In his five volumes (plus a slender volume for references and index), Taruskin covers that ground in two. A third volume encompasses the entire nineteenth century, while the twentieth century, padded out with its ain't-I-the-cool-one excursions into cultural hinterlands that would have frazzled the chin whiskers of musicologists in my day, demands two volumes on its own. Priorities, in other words, aren't what they used to be. Supplementing and illustrating the previous edition were albums of recorded excerpts, two LPs per text volume (at extra cost, of course). In their place the new volumes offer rather a lot of printed excerpts, usually considerably simplified and in modern notation. The intent, I suppose, is that the books can be read at the piano, and up to a historic point—the point of finger-friendly Mozart piano sonatas, say—the device works fairly well. What can be gleaned, however, from a printout of the last few measures of orchestral blooey-blooey from the Shostakovich Fifth Symphony, however, is open to discussion.

Music demands a central literature to ally the inscrutabilities of the art itself to the society it serves. Paul Henry Lang's *Music in Western Civilization*, now sixty years old, a single volume but, at 1107 pages, a fat one, is part of Taruskin's ancestry along with the previous Oxford histories. They have served their purpose well; the graduate student, the musicologist, and the serious enthusiast leave them shelf space, or make sure to live near a library that stocks a copy. It isn't likely that anyone, any time soon, will challenge or replace this huge effort of Taruskin's; it stands as *the* Oxford music history for the next few decades. As such it is a staggering accomplishment. Its faults are exactly what was foreshadowed in the preface to the previous series: the inevitable critical bias of any single observer, especially one as famously bristling with passions as Taruskin is known to be.

Those passions rumble through the project, and the eruptions are wonderful: a brilliant discussion of the constructive principles within one of Josquin Desprez's early Renaissance motets; a fine-tuned side-by-side evaluation (in a chapter called "Class of 1685") of the great choral works of Handel and Bach; a chilling twenty-page account of the musical drama in Berg's *Wozzeck*; a deep penetration into the astonishing, newly invented harmonic usage that Schubert lavished on his "Unfinished" Symphony. At one point in the Schubert chapter the author misidentifies 1828—the composer's last year—as the time of the "Great" C Major Symphony; several pages later he sets it back, correctly, to 1825. (Poor Schubert, how he suffers at the hands of the encyclopedists: first Robert Winter's error-studded article in the *New Grove Dictionary*, and now this!)

Oh, and did I mention...asking price for *The Oxford History of Western Music* at this moment is $500, which works out to $23.80 a pound. After January 31 the price jumps to $699.99. Be warned.

[January 2005]

New York Times Critics: Home of the Brave

"Now that's *music*," whispered the man behind me to his companion, as Esa-Pekka Salonen and the Los Angeles Philharmonic launched into the merry A-major opening bars of Mendelssohn's "Italian" Symphony. After a stiff dose of forward-marching works from his own century to start off last week's program, my neighbor had finally achieved heartsease in this music from the listener-friendly distant past. Never mind that neither of the two preceding works—Dmitri Shostakovich's Second Piano Concerto and Hollywood's Jerry Goldsmith's *Music for Orchestra*—ranked particularly high as standard-bearers for twentieth-century innovation. The lightweight Shostakovich concerto, written as an adult toy for the composer's pianist son, Maxim, and masterfully toyed with last week by Yefim Bronfman, burbles along in a crystalline F major, throws in some quirky rhythmic changes to recognize its own time and place, but tells us little we couldn't learn from a scampering virtuoso exercise from a century before. Goldsmith's eight-minute sequence of agreeable noises, composed in 1972 but only now achieving its West Coast premiere—so much for Southern California and its close-knit arts community—is the same kind of loose compilation of favorite moments from here and there (Stravinsky, Ravel, Rach, you name it) that light up the soundtrack creations by some of Hollywood's more literate music spinners.

The music page of the March 22 [1998] *New York Times* carried a couple of articles that explored the queasy relationship between the music of this century and what should be (but seldom is) a receptive audience, scattering blame over the fallow landscape as a farmer might manure. The lively, controversial Paul Griffiths takes to task a pronouncement by Julian Lloyd Webber (brother of Andrew and a cellist on his own), that the blame for the decline of admiration and support for new music rests on the composers themselves of the last forty or so years, who have failed to provide the public with music they could like. New music terrifies people or makes them angry, says Lloyd Webber; they then seek revenge by boycotting the classical masters as well. Not only Carter and Babbitt, but also Beethoven and Haydn, wither away, and record producers go belly-up. Balderdash, retorts Griffiths. Fear stalks the land, he agrees, but the blame doesn't fall only on the composers. "Exposure to the best new music," he claims, "remains woefully inadequate," and the entire industry—from music's failure to take root in schools to the timidity of managements to risk brave programming—shares the blame.

Further down the page is Peter Gelb's message of comfort and joy. Yes, says the president of Sony Classical (and newly anointed Metropolitan Opera honcho), composers of new music have egregiously misbehaved in the last four or five decades. "A major record label," he states, "has an obligation to make records that are relevant.... It is neither commercially rewarding nor artistically relevant to make recordings that sell only a few thousand copies.... For far too long classical music audiences have suffered through an almost exclusive diet of music that was atonal and difficult to enjoy." Accessible new music, claims Gelb, has until now been "blocked by a cabal of atonal composers, academics and (!) classical-music critics"; now—thanks to the emergence of a new breed of "relevant" composers (all under contract to Sony, as it happens), typified by the slushmastery of John Corigliano and the slick opportunism of Tan Dun—the millennium is at hand, the atonal beast has been slain. (I love the way Gelb employs the epithet "atonal" as a synonym for "bogeyman.") As for the notion of ascribing blame for music's problems to the musical press—beheading the messenger for the message, in other words—would that we made that much difference in the health of new music or old!

What saddens me the most in Gelb's article is the realization that he is, in his workplace, the direct descendant of one of classical music's unchallenged heroes, the late Goddard Lieberson. Long before the Sony takeover, when the label bore the revered name of Columbia, Lieberson built a stupendous catalog of the new and important music of his time: a vast American repertory, including songs by Copland and chamber music by Schuman; the first recordings of Boulez and Stockhausen; the first samples of the emerging electronic music; and even a big and disturbing piece of minimalism, Steve Reich's *Come Out*. These records never sold more than Gelb's "only a few thousand copies"; Lieberson liked to 'fess up that the losses were covered by sales of Columbia's André Kostelanetz and Broadway original cast discs. His legacy—which also included extensive surveys of such giants as Stravinsky and Schoenberg—added up to one of the most glowing testimonials to the relevance of serious-music record-ing. There was word a couple of years ago that Sony was planning a major reissue of the Lieberson repertory; then there was word that the people hired to pursue that project had all been sacked. Sony's one current new-music project of great value, but of uncertain future, is its György Ligeti series under Esa-Pekka Salonen—financed not by Sony but by a private individual who happens to worship Ligeti's music. Now word is out that that project, too, has now been dropped.

[March 1998]

My Weekly Reader Strikes Again

Here's a letter, one of many. Its writer—whom I'll identify only by noting that we have the same initials—has been rendered morose by my words that suggest a negative reaction to music closer to his heart than to mine.

"There is no composition of any era...that deserves the words 'trash' or 'abomination,'" the writer claims. Ah, if only it were true; the post of music critic could then be abolished, and we professional listeners could spend our days eating lotos and wallowing in the trashy abominations of the Scharwenka Fourth Piano Concerto and the Rach 3—whose self-appointed protector Mr. R. has become. He invokes the name of Eduard Hanslick, the well-known scourge of Wagner and Tchaikovsky, the defending angel of Brahms and Verdi, the role model of any God-fearing music critic who dreams of getting turned into a big operatic role, as Wagner transformed Hanslick into *Die Meistersinger*'s Beckmesser. "Hanslick tried to dispose of Tchaikovsky's Violin Concerto...as 'odiously Russian,'" my correspondent goes on, "but aside from academics who remembers Hanslick?" Gotcha that time, Mr. R.; *everybody* remembers Hanslick, who also wrote of Tchaikovsky's concerto that "it stinks in the ear."

"Music is the most abstract of the arts," proclaims Mr. R.; no problem there. "So writing about it must be painful," he continues, on shakier ground. Sure there are pains of the standard variety: long hours, meager pay, I-405 to Costa Mesa in a rush-hour cloudburst, or letters like this one. Mr. R. has only to check out his Freud to realize how close pleasure and pain can sometimes be. ("Sometimes," I said.) I have the feeling that after Hanslick relieved himself on the matter of the Tchaikovsky Violin Concerto, he tumbled into bed purged, proud, and happy.

It's the very abstractness of music that warms the backsides of letter writers. Whether you listen for pleasure or pain, or for both plus a paycheck, music cuts you adrift to think and react for yourself. It comes with a few user's manuals, of course; Aaron Copland's *What to Listen For in Music*, first published in 1939, is (despite its grammatically clumsy title) an infallible guide for directing your ears toward the music itself, its chain of events and the composer's skill in inserting a few surprising and thrilling links into that chain. What it tells you eventually, however, cannot be more than "this is the music, this is what happens in it, and this is how I react": not a brainwasher, in other words, but a role model.

To Mr. R.—and his co-complainers by the hundreds—being cut loose to form your own musical opinions is frightening; finding differing opinions from your own in the exalted state of printed permanence is all the more terrifying. At the supermarket you find packages labeled with everything you need—calories, carbs, protein—to identify the quality of the product. If each of those package also bore a label with dissenting facts and numbers, you might become confused and start writing hostile letters. That phenomenon, however, doesn't exist in supermarkets; it does in concert halls and record stores.

With deference to Aaron Copland—the hem of whose toga I am unworthy to touch—I gladly admit that role modeling is the most important aspect of writing in the first person about the experience of music, even more so (despite colleagues' howls of protest) than writing about film and theater. "This is what I heard, where and by whom," the rubrics of journalism ordain at the start. "This is what the music was like"—continuing our trek toward the heart of the matter—"what the performance was like, how does it match up with my personal vision of the music (in the case of a familiar work), or (in the case of a new work, and quoting the eternally crucial line of the worldly-wise composer/critic/curmudgeon Virgil

Thomson) "is it merely a piece of clockwork or does it actually tell time?" And finally, "this is what I heard, this is what I thought about it, and these are the reasons I arrived at this opinion and the processes that got me there. Now go do it for yourself."

Mr. R. does get into deep water at times. He has nursed a canker since last summer, when I objected to incongruous cadenzas inserted into Gershwin's *Rhapsody in Blue*. "A cadenza," he reveals from his own podium, "is a tribute to the work performed," and an opinion to the contrary is "a stupid insult to the performer." Fine and dandy, provided the improv sounds as if it belongs to the piece itself, as last summer's pianist's did not. About the recent performance of John Williams's Violin Concerto, he is miffed that I should be miffed that Williams hasn't yet conquered the classical field as well as other fields. "That's called creative growth, Mr. Rich," he glowers; so would it be if I took up bricklaying along with my modest talent as an answerer of letters. I know better, and tried to express the wistful wish that John Williams knew better as well.

Writers of letters to music critics have their own repertory of clichés. "I wonder if you and I heard the same concert" is one of the most familiar. "You need a hearing aid, and I enclose a catalog," is another. Mr. R. falls back on one of the hoariest, the fact that such-and-such a performance drew a standing ovation and, therefore, how dare I, etc. "Mr. Rich probably would react by thinking 'so what?'" True enough. It would take only a few concerts to convince Mr. R. of the particularities of the Los Angeles standing ovation, which you can get just by showing up onstage in matching socks, and which has become the Music Center equivalent of the seventh-inning stretch.

The critic has the responsibility to develop a writing style—throbbing with passion and including such value-judgment words as trash and abomination—horny enough to attract potential converts. "Hey," I like to think of myself as saying, "there's something going on out there, and I'm excited about it, and here's why, and maybe you should check it out, too." The worst that can happen to a musical community is to be drained of curiosity about anything beyond the Top Fifty Masterworks. Los Angeles at the moment is well served symphonically, less well operatically, and terrifically well within the thorny stalks of new music. I'm enough of an egotist to believe that the critical press—the improvements at the *Los Angeles Times* above all—has something to do with this.

"There will be 'wrong' critics only as long as there are lazy listeners," wrote Virgil Thomson. "The critic cannot stop at merely handing out grades...but [needs] also to nag, wheedle, cajole and—if the occasion calls for it—pontificate. It is not the 'yes' or 'no' of a judgment that is valuable to other people. What other people profit from following is the activity itself, the spectacle of a mind at work.... A musical judgment is of value to others less for conclusions reached than for the methods [by which] they have been, not even arrived at, but elaborated, defended and expressed."

Fifty and more years old, Thomson's brave new words say it all.

[February 1993]

B. H. Haggin: A Voice from the Past

Mr. B. H. Haggin has been writing music criticism for as long as any of us can or care to remember: in the old Brooklyn *Eagle*, in the *Nation*, and more recently in a large number of intellectual weekly and quarterly publications. He is a man of distinctive taste and standards and an unmistakable writing style that resembles somewhat a spiral staircase. You could not confuse his thinking or style with those of anyone else in the profession.

Mr. Haggin has always been fortunate in having publishers eager to put his thoughts between book covers, a good fortune we all dream about, and his latest anthology, *Music Observed* (Oxford University Press, $6.50), has just come our way. Like every other Haggin book, it is stimulating, difficult to read, and even more difficult to stop reading. Those familiar with his earlier collections can rest assured that the familiar Haggin household gods are still on their pedestals: Berlioz, Mozart, Toscanini, Stravinsky (but only as rescued by Balanchine). The demons are also still in place: almost everything by Bach after the initial statement of the theme, other writers about music in general, and music critics in particular.

From the beginning of his career, Mr. Haggin has clung to the admirable premise that music criticism is a legitimate and integral part of the total musical scene. We could not agree more. But he has carried the premise onto somewhat shakier ground by extending it to assume that as such, music criticism and its practitioners should be subject to continuing evaluation by the profession itself, that a legitimate review of a concert or a retrospective Sunday article by any one critic should also include analysis and opinion on how the event was viewed by one's colleagues.

Mr. Haggin supports his thesis with considerable documentation: the facts that George Bernard Shaw (one critic generally exempt from his scorn) took pleasure in doing just that, and that historians, anthropologists, and philosophers constantly evaluate each other's writings. Actually, if Mr. Haggin could overcome his dread of musical scholarship enough to investigate the current specialized literature in the field (the *Journal of the American Musicological Society*, for example, or *Perspectives of New Music*) he would find enough high-potency backbiting to content him for years to come. I am unaware of any popular medium like a newspaper or weekly magazine where historians or philosophers are given space to bicker, except in book reviews, where music critics review each other's books all the time. As for Shaw, yes, he did indulge in this pastime, and delightfully.

Actually, there is no hard-and-fast reason why critics of the arts in the areas of popular journalism decline to tee off on each other except for a purely practical one, the question of space. It has been a long time since Mr. Haggin has had to work against a nightly deadline, and he's probably forgotten the continuing struggle we all have just to get enough space to keep up with the pianists, the composers, the playwrights, and the movie stars. Something has to give, and what has to give in most of these cases is our friend across the aisle. Certainly there cannot be a question of professional ethics involved. If there were, the current advertising naming battle between those car-rental agencies could serve as an object less on how such matters could be sidestepped.

Suppose that the space problem could be overcome and that, say, the *New York Herald-Tribune* worked out an agreement with Brand X that in odd-numbered weeks we would hold our reviews one extra day so that we could include a lambasting of its critics for disagreeing with us, and on even-numbered weeks Brand X would have the last word. Let's look at Mr. Haggin's own writing for an example of how this can work.

Here is a typical Haggin situation, from a *Nation* article dated February 26, 1955. It seems that Wilhelm Backhaus had given a piano recital in Carnegie Hall the previous March, which Haggin did not attend. Nevertheless, he had found "difficult to believe" the statement by one critic that the concert "must be ranked as one of the greatest evenings of the interpretations of Beethoven piano music heard here in [twenty-eight years, since Backhaus's last concert]," and from another that "he played Beethoven as he hasn't been played here in twenty-eight years."

A year later Mr. Haggin gets hold of the live-concert recording of that recital and joyously discovers that the results justify his skepticism. He then proceeds not merely to offer his own conflicting opinion (insofar as that is even possible from an imperfect recording), but to lay down prerogatives; not to say that Backhaus's Beethoven does not represent *his* ideal (as it did his colleagues' a year back), but to find in one reviewer an "insensitiveness" that he claims was apparently acquired by listening not to Beethoven at all but to the thinking of yet another pianist (Horowitz) who is a friend of the critic in question. "It is appalling," he concludes, "to think of a reviewer in Mr. Downes's position and with his influence on the public not having the musical understanding that would enable him to perform his function—which is to rebuke Horowitz's ignorance and arrogance, not to be taken in by them."

This is intramural warfare with a vengeance, but it is not being carried out according to the rules of the game. Aside from the obvious facts that Mr. Haggin is willing to admit freely having prejudged the case and to drag in some unsupportable presumptions, the problem here is that the function of the critic, his relation both to event and to reader, has been seriously misunderstood. It is almost as though the author were saying something like this: "In the evaluation of music, or of performance, there is a single truth and many falsities. My colleague Mr. Downes has not told you the truth, so I must proceed to do so myself."

Yet elsewhere in the book Mr. Haggin establishes a premise for criticism that denies the above philosophy in favor of something a little more realistic. "The critic," he writes in a *Nation* article the year before he didn't go to the Backhaus concert, "...writes not what is true, but what is true for him, and what becomes true for other people who find it to be so when they listen."

This is a statement both clear-headed and wise, which makes it all the sadder that it contradicts so much else in Mr. Haggin's methodology. It is a statement that also contradicts, of course, the stated need for critics in music, or in the other arts, to devote time and space to public bickering. The fact of simultaneous disagreement among critics at the time of their initial reviews takes care of the matter quite satisfactorily; when any of us feel that it doesn't, we have our Sunday pieces in which to go over the ground in greater detail.

And if Mr. Haggin is correct, as I believe he is, in defining musical truth as a flexible and personal matter, then there cannot be a single right or wrong in criticism. Once we assume the basic competence of the critic (*ahem!*) by virtue of the previous careful training—scholarly training, if you will—in the materials of the musical language, we must allow him the leeway of formulating his own reaction to the expanse of the repertory. His own precepts, his intellectual makeup, his emotions, his personality govern this reaction and shape the nature of his personal truth. He then employs it in his evaluation of the specific musical event, the performance or the music itself: not to lead his readers by the nose into blindly accepting *his* truths, but to stimulate them, delight them, even irritate them into formulating truths that are completely their own.

[*New York Herald-Tribune*, October 1964]

OPERA

The operatic scene when I arrived in Los Angeles was an amusing mass of false hopes and false starts. The "season" consisted of a four-week visit by the New York City Opera with its then-waning stars Beverly Sills and Norman Treigle and its waning audiences to match. A couple of misguided would-be high rollers proclaimed the rebirth of opera with the formation of new companies that wasted a lot of money and time and got nowhere. A struggling company down in Long Beach tried out some standard repertory with cast-off, aging Metropolitan Opera not-quite stars. A troupe from Berlin came over for a couple of interesting weeks; Britain's Royal Opera did the same. Both companies had the indefatigable Plácido Domingo as their up-front attraction. The companies departed, but Domingo hung around.

On October 7, 1986, the curtain rose on Los Angeles's own opera company. The opera was Verdi's *Otello*, with Domingo as its star, and actually the curtain didn't quite rise. It stuck about a quarter of the way up, then dropped, then rose, then dropped, then rose finally. If you know the way *Otello* begins—*BAM!!!*—you know what a disaster, or at least an omen, that must have been. But it's almost twenty years later, and the company flourishes still. Long Beach flourishes, too—no longer with *Butterfly* and *Traviata*, but with adventurous stagings of adventurous stuff. Los Angeles's operatic life still has its squishy side; its guiding spirits still don't seem to know what to do about Wagner, and there has never been a truly magnificent staging of anything by Verdi. Domingo still sings, but he also has a wife who imagines herself something of a creative stage director, and that's a big "but." On the other hand, after all these years there begins to be an interesting relationship between operatic activities and the film industry, and the only question there is why it has taken so long.

Hemmings Farewell: Family Picnic

It was billed as a "gala"; the ticket prices bespoke "gala" and so, I'm told, did the fancy sit-down dinner upstairs after the music ran out. The farewell entertainment concocted by the Los Angeles Opera last week to wish Godspeed to its founder/honcho Peter Hemmings turned out to be, to its credit, less of a gala in the sense of the typical all-star international assemblage of entertainment tidbits that run on and on until the wee hours, and more of a modest and serious family celebration, short and snappy, relatively free of verifiable trash. Above all, it added up to a remarkably accurate portrait of the company that Hemmings has created here in his fourteen years—strengths, weaknesses, warts 'n' all.

One of his major accomplishments goes beyond the company itself, in the creation of a heightened operatic consciousness throughout Southern California. When I came here in 1979 there was, to be sure, the beginning of an awareness. Tito Capobianco's San Diego Opera had launched a project to do all the Verdi operas, but that stopped short when Tito was lured away to darkest Pittsburgh. (Mrs. Capobianco, a.k.a. Gigi Denda, trod upon a few toes in San Diego with her ambitions as designer/director, in a manner not uncommon among wives of opera impresarios.) The Long Beach Opera in its early days ground out a few repertory chestnuts with minor-league casts. The opera "season" in Los Angeles consisted of a month of the New York City Opera squeezed into the Philharmonic season at the Dorothy Chandler Pavilion, a situation detested quite publicly by the Music Center management and that ended precipitously not much later with a short sharp shock from executive hatchet man Tom Wachtell, the limits of whose operatic wisdom were broadcast with his famous put-down of Plácido Domingo: "Well, after all, he's no Pavarotti."

Even without Pavarotti (whose career in staged opera hereabouts consists of one *La Bohème* at the Hollywood Bowl), the Hemmings years have seen the area's emergence as an operatic beehive. Costa Mesa's Opera Pacific, the same age as the Los Angeles Opera, started off as a farm club for David Di Chiera's companies in Detroit, went off-key for a time, and is now admirably resurrected on its own. Michael Milenski's Long Beach Opera, dangling at the end of a shoestring for as long as anyone remembers, miraculously pulls itself together year after year with fringe repertory chosen and staged with resource and sheer gall. San Diego seems in good shape; I don't get down there often enough, but the sound of Renée Fleming's Rusalka is still in my ears.

The operatic underbrush flourishes; I write these words a few hours after a lively, imaginative *Magic Flute*, the inaugural offering of Opera Nova, with young voices, a surprisingly capable orchestra, and a make-do but adequate staging in a dowdy school auditorium in Santa Monica. You can't write off their ambition. Ambition, in fact, blossoms all over town. I'll be sorry to miss *La Gioconda* at the deliciously unreal Casa Italiana this weekend, where full-scale opera comes with a full-course dinner, but Ojai beckons. USC's opera workshop has become a local necessity; UCLA's *Susannah* this season, for a school with a drastically understaffed voice program, gave the opera better than it deserved. You can't hang all this activity on Hemmings, yet the presence of his company, and the particular scope of its activity, has to be some kind of catalyst. The example of Rodney Gilfry, Richard Bernstein, Suzanna Guzman, and Greg Fedderly, all of them distinguished alumni of Hemmings's resident artist program and now active worldwide, looms large on the horizons of the young singers in that *Magic Flute*, The Tamino and Sarastro, in fact, already have their toehold, via membership in the Los Angeles Opera's permanent chorus. You gotta start somewhere,

As much as anything, the Hemmings gala honored the high level attained by those "graduates," with Guzman blatantly stealing the show. It also bore sadder testimony to the company's real failing over the years: its inability—or unwillingness, if you prefer—to build a major operatic production around the musical leadership it deserved. Sure, there were exceptions: Simon Rattle's *Wozzeck*, Zubin Mehta's (yes, Mehta's) *Tristan*, Charles Dutoit's *Les Troyens*, Esa-Pekka Salonen's *Pelléas*, Julius Rudel's *Seraglio*. For every new conductor of genuine merit turned up during the Hemmings administration—Evelino Pidò comes first, and perhaps only, to mind—there was the sad string of time beaters, many of who figured in last week's celebration. How do you honor the head of an opera company who entrusted *Die Frau ohne Schatten* to a Randall Behr? A *Tristan* revival to a Richard Armstrong? Or, for that matter, the company's inaugural *Otello* to a Lawrence Foster?

Edgar Baitzel summoned me to lunch a few weeks ago, shortly after I had expressed terminal displeasure at the company's *Rigoletto* and *La rondine*. Baitzel is the company's new artistic administrator, a post newly created as, perhaps, an admission of the limits of Plácido Domingo's horizons; in Europe he'd be known as a dramaturg. He has held that post with several European companies and worked for a time with the late, great (if greatly controversial) Jean-Pierre Ponnelle. He's a man of consummate charm, with the impeccable talent for handing out tidbits of information that any arts consumer surely wants to be true. Among the hors-d'oeuvres was a recitation of Marta Domingo's considerable achievements as an opera director, spiced with frequent references to Plácido's long-standing friendship with superconductor Valery Gergiev. Dessert consisted of pie in the sky: a complete *Ring* in the spring and summer of 2003, *Moses und Aron*. There might have been more, but I'm dieting.

I'll miss the other lunches. Back in the days of open warfare, Hemmings used to summon me to lunch once or twice each season to hand me my latest report card. He had graded Martin Bernheimer's and my reviews according to an intricate numerical system. Sometimes Martin would win, sometimes I would. I never cared that much about the figures;

what stayed with me was the knowledge that a mover in the musical world took my writings (yes, and Martin's too, if you insist) seriously enough to concoct that kind of numbers game. Without my ever once singing a note on his (or anyone else's) opera stage or standing on a podium, Peter Hemmings regarded me as important. May his tribe increase.

[May 2000]

Pelléas: Twilight in Malibu

Cheers mingled with boos in equal proportion at the Music Center on Saturday night. Considering that Debussy's *Pelléas et Mélisande*—exquisite, subtle, and quiet—seldom arouses that much emotional response on either side, the Los Angeles Opera production must be reckoned a stunning success. There are other reasons, as well.

On musical grounds, there should be no cause for argument. Esa-Pekka Salonen, in his first stint at conducting opera in the United States, has shaped a performance rich in its control of color, responsive to the fleeting moods of the piece and the steady building toward the shattering cataclysm. There is none of Debussy's twilit sky, with its scudding, menacing clouds, in Peter Sellars's deliberately claustrophobic production; they are there, in full measure, in Salonen's music making.

In its grand plan, the strength of its conception, the iconoclastic visuals created by Sellars and his designers make their points. There seems to be a deliberate and ongoing attempt to devise a contradiction between the work itself and its realization, and this is often to the good. James Ingalls's high-contrast lighting, with its clean, fluorescent colors in direct conflict with Debussy's half-tones, helps immeasurably to define the progress of the drama and distracts agreeably from the interminable nattering of its characters. Sellars has also invented a few diversions of his own to speed the pace: the dying and then recovering father of Pelléas (mentioned in

Maurice Maeterlinck's text but not enacted), and a squad of cops, guns at the ready, hassling the homeless beach bums. Some of his inventions work, some add needless fuss and biz. One inexplicable stunt near the end—the brutish Golaud tossing the dying Mélisande out of bed and taking her place—drew guffaws, not to mention shudders; the tearful testimony of Denise Brown [at the O. J. Simpson trial] in a downtown Los Angeles courtroom the day before seemed to hang in the air at that moment.

All this happens, as you surely know by now, in a setting far removed from Maeterlinck's misty medieval forests and palaces—possibly identifiable as a Malibu beachfront (or, for that matter, Easthampton or Biarritz or Tahoe). George Tzypin's single set—a labyrinth of interlocking spaces, some with hospital equipment others bare—hangs suspended from a cliffside; its several rooms light up or go dark as action moves through them. Underneath, the beach is a floor of fluorescent tubes: bright blue for waves down front (flickering rather distractingly), multicolored for distant drive-ins or nightclubs upstage.

There is a superb cast—more than just a gathering of good singers, an ensemble marvelously responsive to the quality of mind in the whole undertaking, Salonen's musical integrity, and Sellars's inventive resource. Monica Groop is an earthy, unusually self-reliant Mélisande, not the vaporous sprite of some past productions. François Le Roux is a curious but convincing Pelléas, confused and diffident at first and strengthened by his love for Mélisande. Willard White (a terrific Porgy on the Glyndebourne recording, by the way) creates a Golaud both terrifying and vulnerable.

Updating operas, at which Sellars is by now a practiced hand, is always a risky business. Even though the mists around the original work make *Pelléas et Mélisande* an opera of no particular place and time, it's not always easy to conceive of a wronged husband in 1995 Malibu going after his rival with the family sword. Perhaps too much has been made of those mists, however—of *Pelléas* as an opera you have to take on faith and forbearance, like *Parsifal*. Take it, simply, as the story of a withdrawn girl marrying an elderly widower and becoming involved with his boyish half-brother, and the mists fall away easily. Sellars and his fluorescents reveal Debussy's opera in a vivid new light, and it glows.

[February 1995]

Florencia: Ship of Foolishness

Under the propitious circumstances—the local premiere of a new opera by a Mexican composer; the first-ever Spanish-language opera commissioned by a U.S. opera company (three, in fact, Houston, Los Angeles and Seattle) and the first new opera produced by the Los Angeles Opera since whenever—it probably never occurred to anyone to question whether Daniel Catán's *Florencia en el Amazonas* might be worth the effort (including enough press releases to paper several walls). The sad news this morning: it isn't. Perhaps its language is Spanish; perhaps its inspiration comes—at considerable remove—from the writings of the distinguished Colombian novelist Gabriel García Márquez; at the bottom line, however, and despite some snazzy values in the production now at the Music Center (through October 18), *Florencia* turns out to be just one more threadbare attempt to rekindle the operatic manner of Puccini and his lesser followers, a *Turandot* without the tunes. In a season that has already offered one inferior Puccini ripoff (or have you already forgotten the forgettable *Fedora*?), Catán's mournful epic is, among its other sins, redundant.

The Florencia of Marcela Fuentes-Berain's libretto is an aging diva, returning to her native Brazil after an illustrious career, driven—even after twenty years—by memories of a bygone love affair (with a butterfly collector, but never mind), "an apparition," she describes herself, "in the vulgar jungle of illusion." She is also one of several passengers on a river boat heading down the Amazon from Colombia to the famous opera house at Manaos—yes, Fitzcarraldo's joint—and her big arias are all about memories and losing her heart to butterflies. "The light gives me wings," she wants us to know.

Well and good; I can quote worse lines from worse operas. What I find particularly bothersome about *Florencia*—well, one of the things, anyhow— is the evidence it gives out that composers still look upon writing musical drama in models dating from 1900. In 1961 the Ford Foundation put up jillions of dollars to commission and perform new American operas; with one exception (an opera in the form of a minstrel show), every one of the resultant operas was rooted in the Puccini methodology—the surging orchestration, the irresistibly gooey harmonies—but without the Puccini tunes. Thirty-six years later, the crowd that cheered and yelled and stood after the *Florencia* premiere last Sunday night seemed anxious to believe that there's still gold to be mined in that exhausted vein; they're wrong.

Peter Hemmings is wrong, too. It's understandable that a Hispanic addition to the repertory would enhance community diversity; I hope he's also looking at the operas of Tan Dun or Bright Sheng. This would have been the time to go after something with a spark of originality, of challenge: Alberto Ginastera's *Don Rodrigo*, for one, whose New York premiere starred a certain Domingo, or—if caution remain the watchword—something of Carlos Gomes, whose old-fashionedness is justified by age.

Quality aside, *Florencia* is a good show—no worse than, say, *Ragtime*. Francesca Zambello's trick-laden staging has an Amazon fog brought on by flying dancers bearing gauze; a sun disc mounted on a pendulum gives an uncanny impression of a ship underway through the gorgeous colors of Robert Israel's make-believe jungle. Sheri Greenwald, the Florencia, hit most of her notes head-on, but not all; the rest of the cast—Rodney Gilfry, Greg Fedderly, Suzanna Guzman, all members of the Hemmings repertory troupe—did what was demanded of them, as did conductor Roderick Brydon. No blame to any of the above; *Florencia* is beyond salvation. Pretty, though.

[October 1997]

Later Words

My words for *Florencia en el Amazonas*—the opera by Daniel Catán that the Los Angeles Opera sprang on its supporters in October 1997—were not particularly kind: "one more threadbare attempt to rekindle the operatic manner of Puccini and his lesser followers," etc. Time has been kinder, either to Mr. Catan's opera or to my wavering pen, or possibly to both; a semi-staged, cut-down version of *Florencia*, up at the John Anson Ford Amphitheatre a few nights ago, turned out not bad at all—rather better than that, in fact.

Florencia, drawn from an episode in the writings of García Márquez, belongs to the well-populated aging-diva-and-her-memories genre, set on an Amazonian riverboat. It suffers, as do all memoir operas of my acquaintance, from a tendency to devolve into rather long arias. Furthermore, like most operas of the breed, there needs to be a second, younger singer with a second set of memories—or, at least, prospects—and this, in turn, leads to other long arias. *Florencia* falls into both traps, but does so rather prettily; at the Ford there was the further decided advantage of the excellent soprano Shana Blake Hill to sing Florencia's sad songs and the radiant mezzo Suzanna Guzman to light fires under the music of the young Paula.

All this turned out as stronger, shapelier music than I had remembered from 1997. Yes, the arias did run on somewhat. But the staging at the Ford also included some lively, attractive choral pieces and even, considering the limitations of the outdoor space, some clever shenanigans to suggest jungle and fog and the rest of the make-believe setting. The one real problem—throughout the evening, in fact—was the obviously slapped-together orchestra under the somewhat wobbly leadership of one Sean Bradley—"former army ranger, presidential escort, automobile repossessor and public school teacher." The program was presented under the aegis of Opera Nova and was further burdened by a master of ceremonies, Michael Riggins, who managed to mispronounce nearly every name.

[July 2004]

Carmen: The $135 Question

Two French operas back-to-back: *mon dieu*! Does this spell the end of the Puccini hegemony at the Los Angeles Opera? Not quite, I fear; despite a substantial sop to kick off the company's thirteenth season—and the ominous rumblings of a threatened *Samson et Dalila* not far down the road—there is some ground to cover before the considerable and precious French repertory can assume a rightful place against the murky torrent of *Butterflys* and *Toscas* at the Music Center.

One forward step would be to deal with the best known work in that repertory in a manner mindful of its stature. Last week's *Carmen* was the company's second stab, but no step forward. The 1992 production, staged by Nuria Espert—with the promising (and, since then, acclaimed) Denyce Graves in the title role—was all high-concept revisionism, starting off with a death dance for Carmen during the overture. The new staging by Ann-Margaret Pettersson is a *Carmen* by the book, but the book itself shows its tatters. Both productions dropped the spoken dialogue of Bizet's superior original score in favor of the sung recitatives by Ernest Guiraud added after Bizet's death that slow and muddy the pace and undermine the drama at the opera's climactic moments. Customary and wise practice these days is to revert to Bizet's pristine plan, which has been newly edited and published. The Los Angeles Opera apparently sees *Carmen* as a museum piece and last week performed it as such.

Jennifer Larmore's Carmen has been eagerly anticipated, and I still have hope. Lovely of voice and of stage bearing, she is currently by just those attributes a failed Carmen, gorgeously engraved in the wrong colors. She lets you know, in the most exquisite, ladylike terms, that she would no more let loose with a dusky chest tone or a seductive portamento than sing the role in chain mail. This was her first stage Carmen, after last year's concert performance at the Hollywood Bowl; she may grow into the role. Considering the marvels in her Handel and Rossini bel canto performances, I almost wish she wouldn't, but *Carmen*, of course, is where the money lies.

Plácido Domingo was the Don José in 1992 and sang it again last week, only slightly the worse for wear. He sings the role not as José but as Domingo, which, I guess, is what some people want for their $135 top ticket. Never mind, then, Domingo's unequal struggle with Bizet's prescribed pianissimo ending to the "Flower Song" in act 2. Never mind, also, that the spectacle of the, let's say, portly Domingo, coping with a ladder on Lennart Mörk's two-level set—on his way to murder his sweetie in what is supposed to look like a jealous rage—is not one of opera's more endearing sights. Some day the company may unearth a Don José possessed of a pianissimo B-flat and the looks to suggest a nice mama's boy love-smitten and driven to murder; meanwhile, there's Domingo. Local boy Richard Bernstein's rafter-rattling Escamillo was just fine; Carla Maria Izzo's wan, edgy-voiced Micaëla, in something surely not French, somewhat less so. (She was well-along pregnant, which is a legitimate excuse for her vocal problems, but not for a company asking $135 for this level of work.)

There was nothing wrong (or radiantly right) with Bertrand de Billy's well-routined conducting, except for his acquiescence to using the wrong score. Pettersson's staging consisted of people, people, people, clutter, clutter, clutter. The cigarette girls in the act 1 chorus looked as if holding their cigs for the first time ever. The act 2 set, a name-the-picture ripoff of Sargent's *El Jaleo*, stole the show.

The next night there was *Werther*, the company's long-overdue first dip into the Massenet legacy and, in its modest way, a thoroughly respectable piece of work. In an attempt to drive copy editors off their rockers, the performance enlists the services of the conductor Emmanuel Joel and the director Nicolas Joël; they are half-brothers, but only Nicolas spells his name with the dieresis. Both they and the production itself are from the opera house at Toulouse, which, from this evidence, must be a fine place to visit. The simple, generic sets, by Hubert Monloup, look as if they could serve a company's entire repertory; anything more elaborate, however, would probably clash with this opera's modest proportions.

Nothing much happens in *Werther*, and it does so very prettily. Massenet's melancholy vapors form a fragrant fog around Johann Goethe's 1774 archetypal romantic weeper, which in its time lured generations of adolescents into a suicidal frame of mind. The tenor in the title role learns in act 1 that his beloved Charlotte is otherwise betrothed and wails, wails a little more in the next two acts, and, to nobody's surprise, shoots himself at the end and expires in Charlotte's arms as she, also unsurprisingly, confesses that she has loved him all along. Even the couple of hit arias along the way are patchwork affairs compared, say, to *Carmen's* outpourings or, for that matter, the tunes in Massenet's better-known *Manon*. The characters here are not bullfighters or philanderers, but well-off provincials; in today's world they would own lava lamps and dine at Benihana. Massenet's modest, bourgeois music captures their essence.

Excellent as it is in most respects, this first-ever venture by local forces into the dolorous languors of Massenet makes friends slowly; the opening-night crowd thinned noticeably after intermission. Compared to the one-two punches delivered by *Carmen* the night before, *Werther* moves at a placid pace. Even so, the beauties in the score are deep and genuine, and at the Music Center they are nicely probed. The Los Angeles Opera has peopled its stage with a mostly young cast welded into a fine-tuned musical and dramatic ensemble: maybe not $135 worth of all-star talent or spectacular scenery, but at least that much worth of lyric intelligence. The Charlotte, Paula Rasmussen, is one of the company's homegrown stars, an intelligent and handsome young singer who began in small roles and now has an international career. The Werther, Mexican tenor Ramón

Vargas, has exactly the light-textured, sleek vocal manner to mirror the monotone sadness of his music—and to steer the attention away from his somewhat clunky stage presence. Reminiscences of Italy's Tito Schipa would not be out of place.

The Joël/Joel contingent does itself proud. Director Nicolas controls his cast with no false moves. Conductor Emmanuel draws from the local orchestral forces the properly gossamer, wispy sounds, Chanel No. 5 made audible. It's all very, very French and, as they say over there, *splendide*.

[September 1998]

La rondine: Momma Domingo Gets It Wrong

I have seen the operatic future—part of it, anyhow—and it makes me nervous. I see the Los Angeles Opera under the Domingo dynasty as a grandiose mom-'n'-pop operation. Poppa Plácido nurses his aging voice, transposing the arias downward when necessary, and keeps his right arm in shape with a little stick-waving that might pass for conducting if you don't listen too carefully. Momma Marta, whose career as a professional stage director doesn't go back very far, makes up for lost time by rewriting and then restaging the repertory classics, tacking happy endings onto the tragedies and death scenes onto the comedies.

We have had ample chance to sample the perfectly adequate ordinariness of Plácido's conducting over the years; it fits into the pattern of podium mediocrity that has haunted the company from the start. (His announced *Aïda* next fall looks from here like more of the same.) Right now it's the diminutive Marta who looms large, in the colossally misguided version of Puccini's three-legged puppy of an almost-operetta, *La rondine*, currently sullying the air at the Dorothy Chandler Pavilion, which she not only directs but has also extensively revised in the name of correcting faults that she and she alone has detected in the standard version.

Puccini himself had his troubles with *La rondine*. In one early version, never performed and later disowned, the reformed prostitute Magda, denounced by tenor Ruggero as he learns The Truth, faces the wreckage of her one true love "alone and abandoned" at the final curtain. It's not hard to understand why the final version, with the parting of the mismatched lovers both wistful and inevitable—as in *Der Rosenkavalier*, which Puccini admired—harmonizes far better with the rest of the work. Marta Domingo, however, has chosen to impose her own gloss onto the rejected version; her Magda, more Joan Crawford than Strauss's Marschallin, walks out into a handy nearby ocean and sinks out of sight. Designer Michael Scott has provided a terrific tidal wave.

Marta's editorial hand falls elsewhere as well. Like a fond momma scattering tchotchkes, she has littered Puccini's perfectly respectable score with useless bits: a scrap of text from Godknowswhere stuck onto an orchestral passage here, a newly contrived add-on to a duet for Magda and her sugar daddy there. From another Puccini reject she has exhumed a first-act tenor aria, with a gut-busting high some-note-or-other at the end on which tenor Marcus Haddock foundered most ignobly. One should be polite about people unfortunately named, but Mr. Haddock's Ruggero is decidedly cold fish. And so is the Magda of Carol Vaness—wreathed in whore-frost, you might say—as a soprano still admirable in the classic repertory tries once again (as in her previous Violetta and Tosca here) to remake herself as an Italian romantic. Greg Fedderly and Sari Gruber manage the juvenile roles with charm and ease; the newcomer conductor, Emmanuel Villaume, does some furious arm-waving, fun to watch without significantly mitigating the overall gloom. The unshakable sense is that none of this should really be allowed to happen—least of all at a $146 top ticket.

[April 2000. The top ticket is now up to $205.]

Britten: Rage, *Rage* against the Dying

Only sixteen years (1945–61) separate Benjamin Britten's *Peter Grimes* from his *War Requiem*; they are alike in many ways but different in many more. Hearing them both on the same day, last Saturday at the Dorothy Chandler Pavilion, underlined both their common bond and their differences.

Both are the works of an intensely reactive man with his own nerves rubbed raw from society-imposed frictions: Britten the pacifist, Britten the homosexual, Britten the artist defining a distinctive personality within an area of style which he was obliged to invent work by work. In his magnificent legacy, these two works stand together as the ones motivated by concerns deepest within his own personality. They are the two, out of all the splendor of Britten's legacy, in whose presence it is the most difficult to remain unmoved.

They are works drenched in rage. The misanthropic Grimes is rendered catatonic by the narrow-minded misjudgments of his villagers. The rage in the *War Requiem* is on a far broader scale, as the bitter cynicism of Wilfred Owen's poetry, interspersed among the texts of the Latin requiem, snarls at those classic verses and mocks them into meaninglessness. Both scores become curdling experiences, because their composer is close behind each of them, revealing his own pangs in the only way society would permit, by indirection through these intensely personal, magnificent analogies.

Within their century, they are also terminal works. The genre of the grand, romantic opera, set into a time and place remote from our own, whose populace turns its realities into artifice by forming itself into a chorus, with characters etched by their own music and by goings-on in a large orchestra, came to its end with *Peter Grimes*. Britten himself later worked with smaller models marvelous in different ways; I can't name a later opera comparable to *Grimes* in size and shape that belongs on the same shelf. Not *Gatsby*; not *The Ghosts of Versailles*; possibly *Dialogues des Carmélites*; what else? In the same way, there are no large-scale choral works after the *War Requiem* aimed at reaching out to a hearer's conscience; this work ends the cycle that began with Handel, was variously nourished for the next two centuries, and, after Britten, fizzled ignominiously with the *Liverpool Oratorio* and its unworthy clones.

Not everybody looks to Britten as one of his century's prime innovators. Some things, to be sure, he did better than anyone else before or since, most of all his marvelous insight into the shape of English words, their rhythms and their resonances. Dig into his music anywhere, into my own favorites—which include the Tennyson moment ("The splendor falls") in the *Serenade*, Grimes's "Now the Great Bear and Pleiades," or almost any line in *The Rape of Lucretia*—or any hundred thousand other choices, and you are in thrall to one of the greatest intelligences ever to transmute English language into high art.

It is this, of course, that lends a special thread to any group of performers once they have mastered the pitfalls and potholes of English words, and one of the amazements in this splendid glut of Britten these past few days was the consistent high level of declamation—from the Brits (Philip Langridge's Grimes and the sounding brass of Owen's defiant words as sung by the amazing Ian Bostridge), but from the non-Brits as well (Richard Stilwell's sturdy Balstrode and Suzanna Guzman's delicious Sedley in *Peter Grimes*, the excellent German baritone Thomas Mohr in the *War Requiem*).

One other Brit, the film director John Schlesinger, staged a violent, edgy *Grimes* on Luciana Arrighi's adequate but rather stodgy sets. Richard Armstrong's conducting committed no egregious errors but contributed no egregious momentum either. The Los Angeles Opera has more than held its own in its adventures into the Britten repertory over the years, and this latest—co-produced with the Washington Opera and La Scala—counts as a distinguished addition. Antonio Pappano, who takes over the Royal Opera's podium season after next and who has visited the Los Angeles Philharmonic before with variable results, did everything needed to turn the *War Requiem* into a memorable occasion, with strong work from a huge Master Chorale contingent and, as one miscalculation, the children's choir placed somewhere offstage almost to the point of inaudibility.

[October 2000]

Odd Couple Oddly Coupled

The on-again, off-again romance between the Los Angeles Opera and the other local industry—which sagged a while back as Hollywood's Bruce Beresford turned *Rigoletto* into a lumpy hash—has now moved forward a couple of notches. William Friedkin's take on the double bill of one-acters currently at the Dorothy Chandler Pavilion may contain a trick or two too many, but the entertainment value overall is high. I had a good time there, and so should you.

It's a strange pairing, Bartók's dark, restless psychodrama about the tormented Bluebeard and his latest wife and Puccini's delirious fleshing-out of Dante's mendacious rogue of a Gianni Schicchi. Friedkin has devised a hilarious sight gag to link the two. One of the ectoplasms of Bluebeard's former wives—airborne nighties right out of Disneyland's Haunted House—stays on past intermission as the dying Buoso Donati gives up the ghost at the start of Puccini's opera. To end the Bartók Friedkin devised another marvelous device: as the bride Judith takes her place among the ghosts of the past, Bluebeard comes on the scene one more time with yet another bride. Life goes on, and so does death.

Gottfried Pilz's set for *Duke Bluebeard's Castle*—a handsome spiral staircase and a collapsed chandelier that resembles a tarantula about to strike—serves *Gianni Schicchi* as well, with the staircase framing a view of Dante's Florence (with Giotto's campanile still a-building even though the costuming is more up to date) and the chandelier now properly hung and handsome. (Another built-in coincidence: the Bartók begins, and the Puccini ends, with spoken exhortations meant by each composer to be delivered in the language of the audience.)

Samuel Ramey's performances in the title roles of both operas greatly strengthens the coupling, as does Kent Nagano's splendid musical leadership. Bartók's score has gradually made its way into the repertory, with recent performances hereabouts by the Long Beach Opera (set in a seedy urban tenement) and by Pierre Boulez and the Philharmonic in concert form. It is full of gorgeous musical events, even when its elements do not entirely fuse. By 1911 Bartók had come to share in the widespread (if not unanimous) adoration of Debussy's *Pelléas et Mélisande*; the declamation in his own opera—particularly the way the very shape of vocal lines defines the conflicting personalities of its two characters—confirms his debt to the nine-years-older work. There is Debussy, too, in the surging orchestration, mingled with Bartók's own growing mastery over the harsh, bright colors of his own background. Ramey and Nagano, each in his own way, seemed at home in both the verbal and musical language of this extraordinary work; less so Denyce Graves, who made beautiful sounds as the doomed Judith but had a way of making the language itself both flat and harsh.

The *Gianni Schicchi*—Puccini for people who don't like Puccini—might have done with fewer pratfalls. Against the overexuberant, cavorting Rinuccio of Rolando Villazón—hardly worthy of the Lauretta (Danielle de Niese), who had sung "O mio babbino caro" so prettily—there was Ramey's truly comic, beautifully modulated Schicchi. The excessive biz aside, Friedkin did a fine job in welding together a delightful unit. Among them, as the dowager Zita, there was of all people the veteran Rosalind Elias, fifty-plus years into her singing career, and no less lively now than when I heard her at the Met in the 1950s. Life, indeed, goes on.

[June 2002]

Butterfly: Winged Victory

In Orange County last November the *Madama Butterfly* opened on a stageful of bustle: a consular office in old Nagasaki with secretaries at typewriters, young Japanese clerks pushing papers around, girls singing "Quanti fiori!" with nary a flower in sight, Lieutenant Pinkerton and the marriage broker Goro hot and heavy in negotiations—all in coordination with Puccini's busy, contrapuntal music. At the Dorothy Chandler Pavilion last week the Los Angeles Opera's *Madama Butterfly* began on an empty stage, the figures of Pinkerton and Goro picked out in strong lighting against an equally strong background of color, further identified by the contrast in the way each man held his hands. and with nothing else onstage except a flat landscape punctuated in the distance by a small bridge over a stream. The Orange County *Butterfly* was Francesca Zambello's five-year-old production from Houston, restaged for Opera Pacific by Garnett Bruce; the Los Angeles Opera's was Robert Wilson's 1993 creation for the Paris Opéra de Bastille, rebuilt here for its North American premiere. Having seen both productions within three months and been bowled over both times, I find myself obliged to retract a lifetime's worth of negative estimates of the value of Puccini's exquisite tragedy.

Wilson's *Butterfly* soars, of course, as much in coordination to its own inner music as to Puccini's; yet, the remarkable effect is to leave you closer to its personalities than you might have believed possible. Unlike current and recent smart-ass directors who must reinvent story lines to accord with their advanced visions of an opera's "true meanings" (names on request), Wilson's way seems in general to be one of subtraction rather than addition. His one *Butterfly* addition has been to create an enhanced stage presence for the boy cast as "Trouble," the leftover son of Butterfly and Pinkerton's romance, but this has been so artfully done—and enacted so charmingly by ten-year-old James Prival—as to disarm complaint.

Verónica Villarroel was the opening-night Butterfly, not her first time here as a "sweet and sad" heroine, if you remember 1994's ill-fated *El gato Montès*; the voice is now a little less sweet, perhaps, but she stood well on opening night and captured Wilson's lighting. John Matz was the nicely lyrical Pinkerton; Susanna Poretsky the rich-voiced Suzuki. Greg Fedderly, as Goro, mastered best of all the traditional Japanese walk; I could swear he was on wheels. Kent Nagano's musical leadership, in fact, put the whole evening on wheels, smooth and well on track.

The "inner music" is most aptly defined though Wilson's vocabulary of body movement, a quantity always cherishable in musical theater, but something intrinsic and unique in his language. Memorable moments abound; just to observe this one quality—how it works even on a stage a large as ours, and how it interlocks with constant color changes in light-ing—would be worth a return visit. Take one small but crucial moment: the meeting near the end between Butterfly and Kate Pinkerton, the innocent cause of her ruination. Just the contrast in the two women's holding of their arms—Butterfly stiff out and stylized, Kate beckoning and natural—spells out the culture barrier, the uncrossable bridge so clearly defined at that moment. Take that further, as Wilson implicitly demands, and recognize what that bridge will symbolize: the future tragedy when that beautiful Japanese boy of Butterfly and Pinkerton's loving is force-fully carried into the American life his philandering father and his insig-nificant new wife have come to represent. You don't get that from any dime-a-dozen *Butterfly* production; I did, from Bob Wilson.

Wilson's operatic repertory is small, because his choices fall upon works that generate that kind of resonance. I ache to see *Einstein on the Beach* once—or ten times—again. His technique is famous, and sometimes ridiculed by nonbelievers, for the rehearsal time he spends on the kind of detail I've tried to describe; I watched him once, in Rome for *The Civil Wars*, a piece that Los Angeles never got, working for three hours on the lighting on a hand. I worry, therefore, at the news that the Los Angeles Opera will revive this *Madama Butterfly* in three or four years, but that Wilson will not be here to supervise its preparation.

[February 2004]

The Indian Queen: Nudity, Gunshots, Sex, and Feathers

They've done it again, that weird and wonderful Long Beach Opera. What looked on paper like a couple of time-wasting, doom-destined ventures in operatic futility have turned out—in the time-honored Long Beach tradition—fascinating, irritating, provocative and more than somewhat worthwhile. And even though the two works offered over recent weekends in the Carpenter Center at Cal State Long Beach seem to have journeyed toward that friendly space from different planets—Henry Purcell's not-quite-dramatic setting of John Dryden's *The Indian Queen* and Manfred Gurlitt's not-quite-successful setting of Georg Büchner's *Woyzeck*—they both told welcome tales of horizons beyond the familiar limits honored by other grander but more cautious local purveyors of operatic entertainment.

Of the two, the Purcell/Dryden concoction was by some distance the more curious and rewarding; the Long Beach production stirred up by far the greater range of joy and anger in the gratifyingly large audience. Dryden's play was written in 1664; Purcell's score, left unfinished at his death and probably rounded off by his brother Daniel, was created for a 1695 London revival, not as an operatic setting but as a set of incidental songs, ensembles, instrumental interludes, and dances inserted during the course of the play. Public taste in Dryden's world was held spellbound by exploration. Painters and writers filled the empty stages of the recently discovered Americas with invented, richly colored civilizations that never existed; the craze continued for decades and gave rise to such later exotica as Rameau's *Les Indes galantes* and the novels of Chateaubriand, with their glorification of the "noble savage."

Dryden's play applied a light exotic gloss to the time-honored conflicts of love, loyalty, honor, and deceit that has nourished playwrights since Euripides; his rival queens and their lovers and villains are only casually located in a never-never Mexico of the writer's imagining. Purcell's music sounds like—well, like Purcell's music: a wonderfully rich jewel of the English baroque, astonishing in its flights of dissonant adventure. Neither play nor music is any more "Mexican," however, than *A Midsummer Night's Dream* is Greek.

At the entrance a warning was prominently posted: "the performance will include nudity, simulated sex, gunshots and feathers"; a further warning against hifalutin carrying-on might well have been added. The Long Beach perpetrators—David Schweizer, who directed; Guillermo Gomez-Peña and Elaine Katzenberger, who fashioned a drastically updated script into which tiny dribs and drabs of Dryden's play were occasionally woven—moved the dramatic accents some distance from the original text, thereby widening even further the gap between the original sense and contemporary stage biz. Staggering indeed was the informational overload; the text, much of it delivered as rap, nipped at artifacts Hispanic from *I Love Lucy* to *West Side Story*; a video screen overhead showed quick images of Mexico's struggles pro and con over the centuries: Wallace Beery as Pancho Villa, Pete Wilson as, alas, Pete Wilson. An Inca chieftain, in shades and with an uncontrollable left arm, rode around in a *Dr. Strangelove* wheelchair. A couple of swingin' American tourists scarfed a few margaritas and mixed into the action. You get the picture?

Purcell's iridescent music, however, was left largely intact. A young Austrian conductor, Andreas Mitisek in his American debut, shaped a performance both lively and lovely with the splendid Musica Angelica Baroque Orchestra; in the title role the soprano Sharon Barr sang her one well-known tune, "I Attempt from Love's Sickness to Fly," prettily indeed. Scholarly instincts should, of course, lead me to rise up in horror at all the visual vandalism. But ponder the alternative; consider, that is, any possible contemporary value in a scrupulous, scholarly rendition of Dryden's high-flown imagery in its prissy Restoration prose, broken off now and then by a few shafts of Purcellian light, and then slogging back through the web of Drydenesque metaphor. For all its anachronistic absurdity and monstrous self-indulgence, I had a fine time at the Long Beach *Indian Queen*, and spent my time at the *Woyzeck/Wozzeck* wondering why anyone would bother.

[June 1998. Andreas Mitisek is now the
Long Beach Opera's general director.]

Hopper's Wife: Good Clean Porn

So much talky-talk had circulated before the Long Beach Opera's *Hopper's Wife*—its bizarre scenario, which has Josephine, the put-upon wife of painter Edward Hopper, transmogrified into Hedda, whore of Hollywood Babylon; reports of frontal nudity and porno film clips as part of Christopher Alden's staging; the dossiers of the composer Stewart Wallace and the librettist Michael Korie, perpetrators two years ago of another music drama about, of all people, Harvey Milk—that it never occurred to many of us to wonder if the opera itself might be any good. The greater the surprise, then, at its world premiere last weekend—inaugurating the LBO's new affiliation with California State, Long Beach's Carpenter Center—when it turned out to be very good indeed: somewhat short of great, perhaps, but a nicely accomplished drama, spread across ninety minutes, not one of them too long.

Unlike *Harvey Milk*, a proficient foray into the newfangled genre known as "CNN opera" (alongside *Nixon in China*, say), *Hopper's Wife* is pure fantasy, although built out of characters who bear the names of, and some resemblance to, real-life personages. Did someone named Ava (as in Gardner) actually move in with Edward and Jo Hopper in their Cape Cod cottage and take Jo's place as Edward's nude model? Did the enraged Jo then emigrate to Hollywood, buy a lot of hats, and become the voracious Hedda? Did the widowed Jo celebrate her ultimate triumph over Ava by shooting her dead on the beach? Probably none of the above; the one verifiable moment in the new work comes near the beginning, where Ava, in a blue peignoir open down the front, poses in the doorway of the Hopper house, a tableau vivant of Hopper's *High Noon* (except that she is a brunette, unlike the blonde in the painting, and that the house, in Allen Moyer's tricky stage design, sits at a weird angle).

What we have here is a pastiche text, with music to match. There's nothing much to take home, except for a slinky waltz number called "Here's to the Movies" for Jo/Hedda's fadeout, but enough to keep you awake in Wallace's proficient but faceless music, whose principal ingredients seem to be early Mahler and early razzmatazz. His scoring, for ten-piece jazz band in the wings, suggests an homage to the *Three-Penny Opera* of Kurt Weill, which makes you miss all the more the savage thrust of that archetypal masterpiece. Korie's text is at all times clever, and it zips right along; there are, however, weaknesses, scenes of transformation that seem to be pasted on rather than rationally approached. Perhaps "rational" isn't the right word in the wacko context of the plot; I still got the sense of an occasional unnecessary jolt, where another minute or so of exposition might have smoothed the ride.

But there is the staging, the vintage Christopher Alden transmutation of absurdity into high art that has been an ongoing glory of the Long Beach Opera since its founding: a marvelous sense of light and movement plus a stageful of gorgeously atrocious hats for Hedda. Of the three-member cast I most admired Lucy Schaufer's Ava, both clothed and in the altogether, the conflation of saint and hooker that brought to mind the real Gardner in her best roles. Chris Pedro Trakas's Hopper was beyond reproach, above all in an extended wet-dream aria (with, yes, some projected cinematic hanky-panky, shadowy and fuzzy almost beyond deciphering, history's first G-rated porn). As Jo/Hedda, Juliana Gondek managed the contrasting personas with high skill but seemed to have some problems with getting the words out; I suspect that the orchestration, which set many of her lines to heavy woodwind tone, may have been partially at fault.

The faults are minor; the work attains something respectably close to excellence. Here's an American opera that does not stand as the latest feeble rewrite of either Puccini or Alban Berg, by creators who respect (as did Mozart, Verdi, and even Wagner) the notion that great opera is as beholden to the gods of entertainment as to high art, and have invented their own musical language and grammar to prove their point. May their tribe increase.

Leoš Janáček's *From the House of the Dead*, based on the Dostoyevsky novel, rounded out the Long Beach operatic bash (plus several ancillary events, chamber-music programs and a reading of some of Hedda Hopper's juicier items by the formidable Rachel Rosenthal). This, too, was a new discovery for most of us; the opera—Janáček's final work in the form—has received only one professional American staging up to now. Sure, the title is off-putting, and so is the drama in its bare outline: long recitations by several inmates in a Siberian prison as to how they got there, set into the day-to-day routine of brutal beatings, wretched conditions, wrenching friendships, and bursts of desperate humor. The dark, harrowing beauty of Janáček's music carries the work; its most eloquent moments are poignant beyond retelling. The opera, again barely ninety minutes of music, gets under your skin. At Long Beach it was given with one intermission, badly needed; a straight-through performance might have made zombies of us all.

Triumph again. In Carpenter's main theater, seating 1050, the acoustics have not yet been vanquished; either there was too much sound from Neal Stulberg's valiant, large orchestra in the pit or not enough from the stage. But the work was brilliantly staged by Julian Webber, much of it in "letterbox" format with the window expanding at times to reveal a stage full of menace from huge fragments of abandoned machines and wall units leading to nowhere, and with Anthony MacIlwaine's set and the dark shadows of Adam Silverman's lighting design a mirror of the sound of the work. What was luminously audible, moreover, was the work of a remarkable singing cast, welded under Stulberg's direction into a superb unit. The opera has no fewer than twenty-four roles, almost all for men's voices, most of them only a few lines, four of them extended self-revelatory monologues (magnificently dispatched by John Duykers, Michael Myers, John Daniecki, and Peter Strummer).

Fears for the Long Beach Opera's demise have, thus, been proven groundless. Michael Milenski and his dauntless company are once again in business, doing what they have always done best: serving the area not as an antidote to other kinds of opera, but as a guidepost toward broader, if more perilous, horizons.

[June 1997]

Long Beach: Opera's Alternative

Here are two kinds of opera. One consists of Offenbach's *Tales of Hoffmann*, that seedy old romantic warhorse, produced on the stage of the Los Angeles Music Center's 3000-seat Dorothy Chandler Pavilion, with expensive scenery and costumes, a huge orchestra in the pit, and the superstar Plácido Domingo to sing the title role. The other is the same opera, done on a thrust stage in the Long Beach Convention Center's 800-seat Center Theater, with a set consisting of a couple of functional furniture pieces out of somebody's garage, the costumes mostly torn T-shirts and jeans, nobody you had ever heard of in the cast, and a tiny orchestra tucked onto a platform along the back wall.

Both productions—the Long Beach Opera's in 1986, the Music Center Opera's two years later—succeeded wonderfully well, but when anyone who really cares about opera talks about *The Tales of Hoffmann*, it's always about the Long Beach production, sparse and functional on the stage, vivid in the memory. Grand opera may rank in most books as establishment caviar, but the Long Beach Opera's antiestablishment approach has, over the last decade, earned label acceptance. Even when the company does wrong (as it has, now and then), the perceived wisdom is that it can do no wrong. The city tore down beautiful old theaters along the downtown shoreline to make room for its bland and ugly Convention Center, its two theaters (the smaller Center and the 3000-seat Terrace) decorated in High Ramada. When the Long Beach Opera performs in one or another of those spaces, you could forget where you are.

Michael Milenski founded the company in 1978 and shepherded it through the financial crises that are the lot of innovative programming in all the arts. Now fifty-one, soft-spoken, lightly bearded in the Don Johnson manner, he speaks confidently of another fifteen years, and then another. Undaunted, he shows off sketches of his next production (opening February 11 for a three-performance run in the cavernous Terrace Theater): a double bill of two pieces you've probably never heard. One is Arnold Schoenberg's early, unfinished *Jacob's Ladder*, a work for humongous performing forces (120-piece orchestra divided into groups stationed in several spots in the hall, 100-voice chorus, and 12 soloists) based on biblical verses dealing with Jacob and his visions; the other is Bernd Alois Zimmermann's *Turning, I Saw Great Injustice*, based on the "Grand Inquisitor" chapter in Dostoyevsky's The *Brothers Karamazov* and completed by the tormented, visionary German composer only five days before his suicide, scored for two narrators, one singer, and an assemblage of brass and percussion players. A large company, orchestra and all, is coming over from the German cities of Bochum and Düsseldorf (home of great mustard); the director is the visionary Werner Schroeter in his North American debut.

Neither work, by the way, is an opera as such; the Schoenberg is an oratorio, the Zimmermann, in the composer's words, an "ecclesiastical action." That is hardly likely to shake Milenski's superb and justified confidence, that of an impresario who has, in his time, produced the druggy *Hoffmann*, countenanced a palace uprising and assassination to be tacked onto the end of Mozart's *Abduction from the Seraglio*, and oversaw the transfer of Monteverdi's *Coronation of Poppea* from Nero's Rome to the Rome of Benito Mussolini. He produces a sketch of the upcoming production: the Terrace Theater jam-packed with ladders, pointing every which way and creating within that faceless auditorium an exhilarating counterpoint of design elements. If the Long Beach Opera is famous for nothing else (and believe me, it is), the company has always known how to employ space in a way that could make NASA jealous.

To these adventurous heights the Long Beach Opera has ascended in slow and easy stages. Milenski staged his first opera, *Madama Butterfly*, at thirteen, back home in Cortez, Colorado, and "knew from then on that that was what I wanted to do. Even my high school yearbook predicted that I would end up directing the fleas in a circus." He almost fulfilled that prophecy, in fact, landing a job after college as part of the apprenticeship network backstage at the San Francisco Opera "driving a truck, typing, and helping to put opera performances onto a stage." From San Francisco Milenski moved southward, where he collaborated with the San Jose Symphony on several operatic stagings.

Long Beach beckoned; a few civic leaders had, by the mid-1970s, sensed the value in some home-grown culture. Milenski recognized the importance of careful entrances into a basically conservative venue. The company's first seasons were given over to reheating already-roasted chestnuts, familiar Verdi and Puccini with singers bearing the Metropolitan Opera cachet. "I realized that we had to start slowly," Milenski remembers. "After all, to most people, the idea of opera was, and still somewhat remains, glued to the Met image."

Caution paid off. After a few seasons of square opera for the folks in Squaresville, however, it was time to regard more distant horizons. In San Jose Milenski had worked with a pair of iconoclastic stage directors who also happened to be twin brothers: Christopher and David Alden. By 1981 the Long Beach company was well established, and Christopher Alden came aboard as director of production. The association bore its first fruit two years later. Alden's production of Benjamin Britten's *Death in Venice*, done in the small Center Theater with almost no scenery but copious imagination, counts as the rebirth of the Long Beach Opera, not as a boonie company hawking tired repertory with singers to match, but as a newborn venture in the adventurous mold of Santa Fe, the New York City Opera, or the sadly departed Spring Opera of San Francisco: threadbare resources balanced against infinite resourcefulness. Word of mouth about the *Death in Venice* brought capacity audiences down from Los Angeles and obliged Milenski to add extra performances. Opera in Long Beach had found its distinctive voice and was under way.

All this happened, bear in mind, at a time when operatic pickings for the rest of the Los Angeles Basin were slim, to say the least. The annual Music Center visits from the New York City Opera had lost some of their appeal after Beverly Sills retired as a singer; they ground to a halt in 1983. A misguided impresaria named Joanna Dordick had started an independent company at the Wilshire Ebell Theater, managed a couple of almost-good productions and more that were laughably bad, and killed the venture with her own inane casting and repertory choices. Not until 1986, with the start of the Music Center Opera, was there any trustworthy local alternative to Milenski's struggling operation in Long Beach.

Now, of course, there is—and, again, there isn't. The Music Center Opera—Now just the Los Angeles Opera—has its place. They produce repertory opera, *Tosca*, *La Traviata*, and the like, and they often do it pretty well. Once in a while they come up with something out-of-the way, some Janáček or *Wozzeck*, and they do that pretty well too. Long Beach serves as alternative opera, the way the New York City Opera relates to the Met or the way Spring Opera used to relate to the San Francisco Opera. Repertory opera is now, for Milenski's troupe, the exception and, if truth be told, doesn't underline the company's greatest strength, last season's *Cavalleria rusticana* being a case in point.

Milenski freely admits that productions like that *Cav*, produced in the larger Terrace Theater with its space for 3000 ticket buyers, are necessary now and then for financial reasons. At least, when the company ventures into the chestnut repertory, they do so interestingly; the *Cav* was paired not with the usual *I pagliacci* but with a relative rarity, Massenet's *La Navarraise*. Like all opera companies small and large (and like its neighboring Long Beach Symphony) the company constantly feels the crunch and now and then must bow to expediency (as when this year's scheduled *Carmen* had to be postponed until next summer). It didn't help, for that matter, that the final performance of last season's *Bluebeard*, sold out days in advance but scheduled for the Saturday of the riot weekend, had to be canceled.

When opera buffs think of Long Beach, they usually invoke such out-of-the-way triumphs as *Lucio Silla*, the most valuable contribution to the 1991 Mozart bicentennial from any performing group in the region, with no scenery but with the neophyte stage director Roy Rallo's plan of lighting and movement on the small Center Theater stage, which brought this long and old-fashioned score to brimming life. They talk about Christopher Alden's Monteverdi productions, especially the 1988 *Return of Ulysses*, where the stage seemed to turn into the Aegean Sea as the hero made his way homeward, and where the lamenting of Cynthia Clarey's Penelope resounded across that expanse like the summoning of distant sirens. They talk of David Alden's *Tales of Hoffmann* or the two brothers working together on a *Don Carlo* in which you could almost smell the heretics being burned.

They think shoestring, and daring verging on bravado. Who would have thought, for example, to produce that most indigenously French of French operas, Debussy's *Pelléas et Mélisande*, in an English translation, and with all its scenic implications cut down to fit into the Center Theater? Milenski did, and the result two seasons ago was, in this writer's words, "challenging and memorable." Who would have thought to stage Molière's Le *bourgeois gentilhomme* with the Richard Strauss *Ariadne auf Naxos* inserted into its proper place within the action—and then to produce the whole shebang in twentieth-century comedian costumes in a setting seemingly inspired by one of California's most luxuriant architectural wet dreams, the Madonna Inn? Thus did Milenski in 1987, with the result (in his words) like "the end of civilization as we know it."

Milenski has moved comfortably into his current relationship with the company, as mastermind behind the masterminds, with no seeming ambition to dirty his hands once again in backstage production but obsessively watchful of promising new talent as it comes into view. He singles out the director Roy Rallo, who did the 1991 *Lucio Silla*, as a possible force in the company's future. "He came here as someone good at bringing in coffee and driving the truck, as I once did for Mr. Adler in San Francisco. Now he's a director with ideas of his own. That's the way it goes."

Milenski sits in his office in a shopping mall at the far end of Long Beach, an arm of the marina out a window behind, a garish bit of Madonna Inn wall from the *Ariadne* set out front. It's an out-of-the-way location except for a huge available rehearsal space behind the Trader Joe's next door. Milenski finds his words slowly, but he seems to glow, quietly, as he ticks off future projects: Bizet's *Carmen* next summer at the outdoor John Anson Ford Theater, Verdi's *Falstaff* in the small theater with a cut-down orchestration somebody in England has produced.

He tries out an idea: "What would you think of our doing a *West Side Story*?" I make a face, but we part friends, anyhow.

[January 1993]

Dead Man Walking: The Substitute Soundtrack

The perpetrators of *Dead Man Walking*—the opera inflicted upon the stage of Costa Mesa's Segerstrom Hall these past few nights—have gone to some lengths to distance themselves from Tim Robbins's 1995 film of similar name and derivation. Their source, or so they would have us believe, has been Sister Helen Prejean's original book, her harrowing death-row memoir—even though its central character has undergone a change of name from "Matt" to the more singable "Joe." It was Sister Helen, not Tim Robbins or any of his commendable collaborators on that film, who joined the Opera Pacific cast in the curtain calls at Segerstrom. You can assume, therefore, that this strong and compassionate woman has acquiesced in the turning of her brave words into the unfocused, stumbling, blurred product that has earned the unfathomable cheers of misguided multitudes—two seasons ago at the San Francisco Opera, now here, then onward and upward to a date with destiny at the New York City Opera next September.

Go back and see the film, its outpouring of moral outrage—against capital punishment and against those who wrongly set their minds against the powers of salvation—so memorably caught in the haunted, troubled eyes of Susan Sarandon's Sister Helen and the insidious cynicism of Sean Penn's Matt Poncelet, and echoed in the composite track of Nusrat Fateh Ali Khan's songs twined around the slash of Eddie Vedder's and Ry Cooder's music and even the dull ache of Bruce Springsteen's version of the title song under the final credits. Set this consummate workmanship against the stick figures of Terrence McNally's sudsy libretto set to Jake Heggie's appallingly second-rate assemblage of musical gestures. The only positive note I could extract from this long, excruciating evening was that *Dead Man Walking* in its reality has turned out as abject a disaster as it first appeared on paper.

Opera Pacific's production was actually the work's second; those unlucky souls who have seen both tell me that the San Francisco version, larger and trickier, was even more of a mess. The new one, with Michael McGarty's skeletal sets—its up-and-down panels suggesting a chorus of unmanned guillotines—is slimmed down for travel. John DeMain conducted, as he also will in New York; although I am disinclined to delve deeply into differences between his version and that of San Francisco's Patrick Summers—now available on Erato discs, if you care—I am sure that it was strong and good. Kristine Jepson sang the Sister Helen, richly and caringly, although Susan Graham's singing nun on disc has superior frazzle. Frederica von Stade, for whom Jake Heggie has become house composer, was once again the killer's mother, as in San Francisco, a killer role that deserved killer music but got none.

[April 2002]

Powder Her Face: Going to Bed Early and Often

The big guys had their Verdi last week: the Music Center's *La Traviata* ending its run (not a moment too soon!) at one end of I-405; Opera Pacific's *Rigoletto* starting its shorter run (in happier estate) at the other. Midway there was the little opera company that could (and did): Michael Milenski's undauntable Long Beach Opera, fearlessly striding through the kitsch and commotion of Thomas Adès's *Powder Her Face*, emerging triumphant beyond all hopes and expectations. I urge you to beg, borrow, or steal your way in.

Powder Her Face is pure brat—Brit brat at that: music and drama that could only cascade from the creative mind of the preternaturally gifted twenty-four-year-old that its composer was at the time. In one sense its central character belongs to the great operatic-monster tradition, from Mozart's Queen of the Night to Strauss's Elektra and Berg's Lulu. Unlike them, however, the owner of this powdered face, memorably captured in Philip Hensher's libretto, is a creature out of yesterday's headlines. Unlike them, too, both librettist and composer have filled out this monstrosity with something you could almost mistake for human dimensions.

Scotland's Margaret Whigham (1912–1993) became Margaret Sweeny (the Mrs. Sweeny catalogued in Cole Porter's "You're the Top") in her first marriage and the Duchess of Argyle in her second. As such, she passed a colorful lifetime fornicating her way upward through London's nobility and downward through its working classes into eventual penniless ignominy. (Apparently the Duke succeeded in matching her trick for trick.) With a command of musical coloration that borders on the awesome, Adès shakes this tragic, horrendous sacred monster into violent, brimming life. His music has a captivating insolent slanginess; it captures her vile, poisoned breath and blends it into a range of perfumes both ethereal and stinkpot.

Neal Stulberg's expert small orchestra—winds and percussion mostly, with occasional strings just for a touch of the slinky—worms its way in and out of the fetid atmosphere around its central character. Much of the score is beholden to the language of tango at its rudest and down-and-dirtiest. Four singers—impersonating many more characters—carry the action breathlessly forward: hotel bellhops eagerly available, chambermaids, hangers-on giggling with the latest gossip, all servicing the Duchess's amorous needs and occasionally being serviced in return. As the Duchess Irena Sylya's management of Hensher's fleet, intricate declamation is only approximate, but the venom is horrendously apparent even so. The opera's two hours race by like the wind.

Some of my happiest Long Beach Opera memories concern the way its several stage directors have employed empty space: a flat stage floor ringed with TV monitors for Britten's *Death in Venice*; more empty space for the Mediterranean that Monteverdi's Ulysses must cross. Long Beach's *Powder Her Face*—in its first American professional staging, by the way, after concert-style performances in Brooklyn and Berkeley—is ingeniously (if not exactly comfortably) set on a blocked-off area on the Carpenter stage, with the audience on bleachers on one side. Director David Schweizer fills the empty spaces with spooky dancing shadows. A mobile, glass-enclosed booth stands in the middle of nowhere, pushed here and there, a jeweled, cluttered museum showcase, perhaps, with the Duchess inside, possibly dead but also poisonously alive. One bellhop (James Schaffner) catches her eye and proves a considerable mouthful. High above the action, perched atop a towering ladder up near God, a judge (the stentorian Donald Sherrill) sends down thunderbolts of condemnation. A journalist (Catherine Ireland in one of her five roles) pries into secrets and confessions. "I go to bed early," the Duchess informs her, "and often."

[November 2001]

The Out-of-Town *Tristan*

Times were when a big Broadway-bound show would spend a couple of weeks working out the kinks in an out-of-town tryout run, in Boston, perhaps, or New Haven. Something like that, if not exactly, is happening with the Philharmonic's *The Tristan Project*, which ends its two-weekend run at Disney Hall as you read these words. It will then pack up and, sooner or later, head for Paris, where it begins a seven-performance run at that city's Opéra Bastille on April 12. As here, Esa-Pekka Salonen will conduct, Peter Sellars will direct, and video magician Bill Viola will create the visuals. Unlike here, Richard Wagner's *Tristan und Isolde* will be presented in one lump instead of three, one ticket at a 150-euro top ($210 or thereabouts) instead of three at $125 per. You won't get the Los Angeles Philharmonic as the pit band or the sound of Disney Hall, but you'll get Ben Heppner as Tristan, Waltraud Meier as Isolde, and April in Paris. Go figure.

It hasn't taken very long for the Philharmonic to find a way around the notion that Disney Hall was to be a concerts-only edifice, with opera relegated to that other place up the street. Whether the many important aspects of Bill Viola's video mastery have anything all-embracing to say about the future of operatic production, it is at least true that his artistic insights mesh quite gorgeously with the interweave of symbolism that have kept Wagner's inscrutable masterpiece alive and well for its 140 years of turbulent life. It hasn't required much in the way of onstage gadgetry, merely a projection of Viola's gorgeous conceptualization onto a large (thirty-five feet by twenty feet) suspended screen (with another small screen up back for the folks in the "orchestra view" seats) to realize the magic in actual performance. This is already a step back—permanent, I hope—from the multi-screen and multi-mess creation that management imposed on the Berlioz *Symphonie fantastique* last season.

Three pairs of lovers are involved. One pair, on the stage or, at times, at various vantage points elsewhere in the hall, copes with the notes of Wagner's score, with reasonable if not spectacular success: Christine Brewer, an imposing soprano with a considerable gift for making herself heard, and Clifton Forbis, whose darkish tenor takes on an unpleasant spread at times. (The Danish basso Stephen Milling, in the dishwater-dull role of King Marke, is the only singer really worth staying awake for.) Two other pairs are the personages of Bill Viola's screen, the embodiments of the various levels of ecstasy that he and Peter Sellars have mined from the dark reaches of Wagner's score. The "earthly" pair (Jeff Mills and Lisa Rhoden) are the embodiment of literal lovemaking, making their way through a barrier in most of act 1 and then going at it hot 'n' heavy in act 2. The "heavenly" pair (John Hay and Sarah Steben), aerialists and trapeze artists by trade, epitomize all this with marvelous swoops though air, fire, and water—the water so pure and seductively bubbly as to create an art form of its own.

It's easy enough to dismiss some of this as unnecessary monkeying with the classics, especially with the economics of the one-in-three presentation; you also can't help wondering at the fate of this production with a contemporary Paris audience. On the other hand, this is a *Tristan* of extraordinary beauty; the responses to what lies deep within this extraordinary work of art, the visual beauty of the material chosen to symbolize those responses, and the insight with which that material is used—the changing light on the tree at sunrise in act 2, to note one image I cannot get out of my head. And then there's the matter of just the sound of *Tristan und Isolde* as performed by Esa-Pekka Salonen and the Philharmonic in Disney Hall. That's something else you don't easily get out of your head.

Bushwa

Someone should find a way to set Peter Sellars to music. It would take a full complement of oratorical Wagnerian brass, plus a gaggle of Mendelssohnian woodwinds playing so quickly as not to remember what they've just performed, plus a few other instruments to giggle and go "hee-haw" at times. At one of the *Tristan Project* pre-concert talks the matter came up of why the opera was being spooned out piecemeal, one act at a time, to Los Angeles audiences. This launched a Sellars verbal rocket of breathtaking trajectory, touching upon matters in *Tristan und Isolde* such as epic dimension, inner gravity, and the marvel of Wagner's multilayered orchestration and plot management.

There is just too much in the whole of the opera, Sellars proclaimed in so many words, to cram into a single evening. That may come as a surprise to a couple of people I know. Many of Sellars's points rank as high-class music-appreciation stuff, and you can find them in some of the very best textbooks as part of the respect paid to the whole of *Tristan und Isolde* as the three-act entity that has gladdened operagoers around the world for well over a century—including a few here in Los Angeles, where the Philharmonic, as it happens, participated in a pretty good *Tristan*, with sets by David Hockney, back in 1987.

As partial recompense for the bit-by-bit treatment of *Tristan* itself, Salonen and the orchestra preceded each of the single acts with music whose composers owed much of their own outlooks to the upheavals Wagner's masterpiece had created. First came Alban Berg's *Lyric Suite*—not the entire work, just the three (of six) movements that Berg himself had expanded for full string orchestra—thus, however, omitting the one movement that actually includes a quote from *Tristan*. On the second night there was the orchestral suite, pretty but aimless, that Erich Leinsdorf had cobbled together from Debussy's *Pelléas et Mélisande*. Finally came a suite from the most recent *Tristan*-inspired masterpiece, Kaija Saariaho's *L'amour de loin*, with Heidi Grant Murphy and Kyle Ketelsen as medieval romancers thwarted by destiny. Hugely successful at its 2000 Salzburg premiere and at Santa Fe a year later, Saariaho's opera fairly throbs with music of almost painful beauty, worthy in both plotline and sound to flourish in the Wagnerian shadow. After the final music in this suite, a latter-day *Liebestod* gorgeously sung by Grant Murphy, I would have willingly gone home. Only the prospect of those dark, dark strings at the start of *Tristan*'s final act kept me in the hall.

[December 2004]

MUSIC AT THE TURN

January 1999: A year begins; a century ends. The Los Angeles Philharmonic's last 1998 concert included music by Olivier Messiaen, a significant creator and inspirational force of recent decades; it starts this year with music by Toru Takemitsu, another. Last month the Los Angeles Opera premiered a new American score; later this month UCLA will put on a concert of ages-old but very new music for drums, only drums. Ends of years—or of centuries or millennia—are the listmakers' glory days, the time for summing up in tabular form. And so, like Gilbert and Sullivan's Lord High Executioner—exalted archetype of paid criticism—I've got a little list.

A Memoir and a Personal Selection of 100 Works from the Twentieth Century That Define Their Time

I was sixteen when music first attacked me. My friend Normy and I were in the twenty-five-cent rush seats, upstairs in Symphony Hall, on a Friday afternoon in 1940; Serge Koussevitzky and the Boston Symphony had begun the concert with Gluck and Mozart, full of comforting tunes and harmonies in a familiar language. After intermission, however, I was hurled across a boundary onto a strange and terrifying landscape. Midway in the first movement of a brand-new symphony (the Fifth) by a composer with a barely pronounceable name (Shostakovich), the man on kettle-drums started up a huge bim-bam-boom. A xylophone joined in, maximum hysteria. The piano, for God's sake—whoever heard of a piano in a symphony?—banged away. All around us elderly matrons pushed their way quickly to the exit doors. (The *Boston Herald*'s great satirical cartoonist Francis Dahl noted that one of Boston's indigenous sounds was the rustle of Grandma Saltoncabot's black bombazine in the Symphony Hall corridors, beating a hasty exodus from Dr. Koussevitzky's Shostakovich.)

The first thing I learned about new music, therefore, was that it survived on a battlefield. The critics—including the *Herald*'s Rudolph Elie, who would later hire me as a stringer, my first writing job, at $3 a review—

greeted the Shostakovich Fifth with howls of protest. The dissonances and the banging were bad enough, the sentiment ran; what was worse was that the music, to those apprehensive 1940 ears, contained clear evidence of Soviet conspiracies against the American government. Koussevitzky, ever the warrior, immediately rescheduled the Fifth Symphony for a repeat performance later that season. (There are now close to fifty recordings of the Fifth. It is easily the best-known symphony composed in the twentieth century; people whistle its subversive tunes in the streets.)

To me that afternoon's first encounter with the music of my own time brought a sense of astonishment that I can still feel in remembrance; I simply had no idea that people could take the orchestra of Beethoven and Brahms, throw in a few more instruments, and create sounds like this. A few months later came Walt Disney's *Fantasia* with its *Rite of Spring* sequence (hacked to pieces, I learned only later, from Stravinsky's original score, but thrilling even so): more exhilaration, up to the edge of terror. I've never been much for horror movies or roller-coaster rides; the passion for new music I acquired on those two Boston afternoons, and have tried to nurture on the thousands since, satisfies whatever craving along those lines I might otherwise entertain.

Of all the arts, music inspires the greatest fear of the unknown. If a painting or a sculpture offends, you can walk away. Music attacks, grabs hold, and imposes its own time frame; try to escape from a live performance of some act of blatant musical innovation, and you risk stepping on toes both literally and figuratively. A piece of new music sounds new because it does battle with expectations we've amassed from listening to other music not as new; therein lies its power. Stravinsky's *Rite of Spring* aggressed upon its first audience—in Paris, 1913—with its very first notes; a solo bassoon isn't supposed to wail like that in its highest register. Beethoven's "Eroica" Symphony got in wrong with its first audience right at the start—in Vienna, 1805—because the C-sharp in the eighth bar doesn't belong in the key of E-flat. In the early 1700s, Bach was constantly in hot water with his employers because of his wild and dissonant organ improvisations.

In Florence around 1600, Claudio Monteverdi enraged a critic named G. M. Artusi with passionate harmonies that no composer had dared to use before. In all those cases, and thousands more, the passage of time has smoothed the feathers of those first offended audiences; Stravinsky also gets whistled in the streets.

These offenses all seem to have taken place in the early years of their centuries—by coincidence, or because the chronological upheaval at a century's turn inspires a certain state of mind. Now we're there again, and while the computer guys try to figure out how to cope with the digital problems of double-zero dating, the culture guys are having a fine old time with compiling lists: the best, the most favored, the greatest, or just the most.

My list is different: 100—that figure seems to be the standard—pieces of serious musical artwork, arranged in no order other than chronological, that seem to me to define where composers of serious music have tried to take their art in the century now slouching toward the history books; perhaps also to suggest whence and how these creative urges arose back around 1900, and to intimate, ever so quietly, where music might—repeat, *might*—be headed in the years 2000-plus. Many entries that strike me as defining I do not personally like. Some things not on the list I like quite a lot, but they belong on someone else's lists. I would rather listen to early Louis Armstrong, Ella Fitzgerald, or the Stones any day than Elliott Carter (and to Elliott Carter rather than Scriabin). "Serious" music I define as written-down music designed to be heard by nonparticipating—I almost said "passive," but that's wrong—audiences, and with the substance to warrant serious rehearing. Thus, for example, *Sweeney Todd*.

The question arises: by "defining," am I also implying a prophecy that the music on this list will still be played and respected into the next century and even beyond? I think I am. I must assume, of course, that the performing forces that occasioned this music will survive; in these days when not only symphony orchestras but whole national economies can fall off the map, that may be a foolhardy assumption. You gotta believe.

Music that embodies the strength to define its own era must also, I firmly believe, have the strength to outlast that era. There were string quartets, orchestras, and opera houses in 1799 and 1899, as they are in 1999; there's a chance, therefore, that something similar to them will be around in 2099, playing the new music of the day but also music created one, two, or three centuries before. There are other imponderables, of course, that sometimes create curious additions to any survivors' list. If I were compiling this kind of list in 1799, I probably wouldn't have included the name of Antonio Salieri, yet there he is on the charts today, for well-known reasons beyond his own making, with half a column of recordings in the last Schwann CD catalog (before that valuable publication shut down). In 1899 I wouldn't have dreamed of including the symphonies of Joachim Raff, or the piano concertos of Anton Rubinstein; yet, some current enthusiasts have exhumed these presumed-dead figures as well. I can't guarantee that someone, around 2050, won't make a movie about, say, George Rochberg or Nikolai Lopatnikoff, and then I will be reviled as a lousy prophet for not including those less-than-defining figures on my list. To make it look less listlike I've broken the chronology into twenty-five-year, twenty-five-item segments. That works out to be not as arbitrary as it sounds; 1925's *Wozzeck* and 1976's *Einstein on the Beach* are huge milestones, and 1950, plus or minus, works well as the nuptial year of music and technology. I've tried to surround each segment with some kind of essay on my own take on the music therein listed: not so much a history of the twentieth century, for which we don't have enough paper, but a memoir of my own evolving reactions to in the century's twilight years.

1901–25

1. Debussy: *Pelléas et Mélisande* (1902)
2. Satie: *Three Pieces in the Shape of a Pear* (1903)
3. Ives: *Central Park in the Dark* (1907)
4. Debussy: *La mer* (1905)
5. Scriabin: *Poem of Ecstasy* (1908)
6. Strauss: *Elektra* (1908)
7. Mahler: Symphony No. 9 (1910)

8. Stravinsky: *Petrushka* (1911)

9. Sibelius: Symphony No. 4 (1911)

10. Schoenberg: *Pierrot lunaire* (1912)

11. Stravinsky: *The Rite of Spring* (1913)

12. Cowell: *Advertisement* (for Piano) (1914)

13. Ives: Sonata No. 2 ("Concord") (1915)

14. Falla: *The Three-Cornered Hat* (1919)

15. Vaughan Williams: Symphony No. 2 ("London") (1920)

16. Janáček: *Katya Kabanova* (1921)

17. Varèse: *Amériques* (1921)

18. Prokofiev: Piano Concerto No. 3 (1921)

19. Hindemith: Kammermusik No. 1 (1922)

20. Gershwin: *Rhapsody in Blue* (1923)

21. Milhaud: *The Creation of the World* (1923)

22. Stravinsky: *Les noces* (1923)

23. Schoenberg: Suite for Piano (1923)

24. Copland: *Music for the Theater* (1925)

25. Berg: *Wozzeck* (1925)

No time in recorded history could match the sense of wonderment, the euphoria, the eager curiosity about the future that gripped the Western world right around 1900. The previous couple of decades had given the world the telephone, the light bulb, the phonograph, the automobile, and, a couple of years later, would give it the airplane; these were not merely improvements on things already in existence (as the compact disc might—just might—seem an improvement on the 78-rpm shellac disc, or the Airbus on the DC-3); they added up to an explosive expansion beyond what had previously been assumed the limits of human possibility. All the arts seemed to draw new energy from the spirit of innovation in the land; in the decade and a half from 1900 to the outbreak of World War I the air crackled with the shock of the new. Some of the newness may have been the logical consequence of the recent past; the whisperings and half-lights of Debussy's *Pelléas et Mélisande* clearly stemmed from the impulses that guided Claude Monet's brush at his lily pond; Gustav Mahler's last symphony and the first works of Arnold Schoenberg took the agonized harmonic frustrations of Wagner's *Tristan und Isolde* onto the concert stage. So, with more surface glitter and less inner substance, did Richard Strauss in his blood-drenched *Elektra*. Igor Stravinsky's first ballet scores were recognizably the work of Rimsky-Korsakov's star pupil. Yet the spirit of the times seemed to drive the new creators hard and fast. The merely two-year stylistic gap between Stravinsky's *Petrushka* and his *Rite of Spring* yawns wider than the twenty between Beethoven's "Eroica" and his Ninth. So do the two years between Mahler's Ninth Symphony and the *Pierrot lunaire* of his self-anointed apostle, Arnold Schoenberg.

Jump back a few decades—to 1880, say. The European bourgeoisie prospered; the great cities celebrated their grandiosity by building concert halls and opera houses. Virtuosos flourished—sopranos, pianists, conductors. The old masters—Beethoven, Haydn, and Bach in monstrously perverse reorchestrations—held their place; just the opening bars of Beethoven's Ninth Symphony, that supremely romantic gesture of bringing the music in gradually as if from a distant cloud, became the gambit for dozens of latter-day ripoffs, some successful. It was taken for granted, however, that by far the majority of the concert and operatic fare was to be music hot off the press. The audience eagerly awaited the latest Brahms symphony, the latest Verdi opera. Richard Wagner died in 1883, and the world awaited with bated breath the emergence of his successor, assuming beyond argument that there would be one.

Around 1900, however, the signs first appeared of a schism between "music" and "new music." Wagner had implanted some of the attitude, with his orotund pronouncements about "the music of the future." By 1900, too, Europe's great music publishing houses had caught up with the past, with complete performing editions of practically every major composer from Bach to Beethoven, and on through Schubert, Mendelssohn, Schumann, and Berlioz. Performers could, better than before, think in terms of a "repertory" of past masterpieces; audiences, too, developed a fondness for wallowing in the familiar. And so the world at large no longer awaited the next symphony by Mahler or the next string quartet by Debussy with the hunger for newness that had driven taste in, say, 1880. Newness had become newer, and therefore more fearsome, than in the good old days. The impact of *Pierrot lunaire* and *The Rite of Spring*—and the dozens of similar assaults on the musical status quo—drove the wedge.

Music's world expanded beyond its traditional French/German/Italian/ Slavic boundaries in these years. Finland's Jan Sibelius brought his country its first fame, with music basically rooted in the mainstream past but with at least one splendid work, the bleak, ascetic Fourth Symphony, that does indeed mirror the fog-shrouded bleakness of its native soil. Spain's Manuel de Falla wrote Spanish-tinged music that went past postcard prettiness in a dark, edgy, and wonderfully witty manner. England's Ralph Vaughan Williams, though defiantly anchored in his country's ancient musical styles, at least turned out a repertory of symphonies that did not sound fresh off the boat from Germany, as did those of his countryman Elgar. And the United States, whose handful of respectable nineteenth-century musicians also composed with heavy German accents, produced its first generation of indigenous crackpot/geniuses with the likes of good-ol'-boy Charlie Ives, Henry Cowell, Carl Ruggles, and the émigré Edgard Varèse, who proclaimed his Americanness with a wildly dissonant piece called *Amériques* that had the critics disputing whether it was more descriptive of a zoo or a boiler factory.

The war happened, and then jazz happened, and the timing was just right. Great wars always leave the creative world with the need for a fresh start from some zero point. In the post–World War II decade the musical world would flop around for a time in desperate search for fresh impetus, adopting and rejecting a variety of artistic possibilities; but in 1918 that impetus had come ready made, or so it seemed: a fresh, immensely vibrant language, laden with fascinating interconnections to other arts (cubism, for one), its horizons far out of sight. Like its music, its very name—jazz—was a hybrid of arguable origin. Its vitality was, however, beyond argument. Almost everybody was hooked at first; visiting New York, France's Darius Milhaud raided the shelves of Harlem record shops and returned home to create his *ballet nègre The Creation of the World* ; Germany's Paul Hindemith blended the kicky new rhythms into his Bach-inspired chamber concertos; Stravinsky tried his hand at a couple of ragtime pieces, both terrible. Paul Whiteman toured Europe with his big, symphonic jazz band and played George Gershwin's synthetic *Rhapsody in Blue* to awestruck crowds: lively stuff, even if neither jazz nor symphony. In Paris another young innovator, Aaron Copland, was urged by his teacher—the legendary Nadia Boulanger, godmother to a generation of American composers—to use music as a way to define himself and his world. He did so by including, in his delicious, lighthearted *Music for the Theater*, a generous admixture of the newfangled jazz.

Stravinsky's revolutionary orchestration in *The Rite of Spring* gave off all kinds of messages about new ways to make musical sounds. Ten years later, Stravinsky created *Les noces*, depicting a Russian folk wedding, with an orchestra consisting of four pianos and a huge battery of percussion; the American George Antheil, in cahoots with the cubist painter Fernand Léger, did some of the same in his *Ballet mécanique*, whose scoring included an airplane propeller. Before either of these, a San Francisco teenager named Henry Cowell astonished audiences with piano pieces that involved reaching inside the instrument to stroke the strings or whomping down on the keys with a fist or forearm to produce what he called "tone clusters." Later, Cowell would become mentor and role model to the most carefree and influential of the century's innovative spirits, the Los Angeles–born John Cage.

If Arnold Schoenberg had little taste for percussion ensembles or airplane propellers, he had his own visions of musical sounds hitherto unheard. Six months before Stravinsky's bombshell went off in Paris, Schoenberg's *Pierrot lunaire* had earned a comparably hostile—if less vociferous—reception in Berlin: music in which a solo voice keened, wailed, howled, and whispered poetry about a moonstruck madman, joined by a chamber-music ensemble enhancing the spooky atmosphere with music devoid of any sense of harmonic progression or key. Standing aloof from all the jazzy razzmatazz, Schoenberg sought to codify his wholesale revision of traditional musical values with his "method of composition employing all twelve tones," which he perennially explained as the logical extension of principles reaching back to Bach. His 1923 Suite for Piano, his first "pure" piece employing all twelve tones in strict serial order, did indeed link hands with Bachian models. But it was Schoenberg's disciple Alban Berg, in *Wozzeck*, his harrowing, immensely powerful operatic setting of Georg Büchner's play, who proved, even more fluently than his teacher, the expressive potential of the Schoenbergian style, moving in and out of twelve-tone writing and also in and out of the Mahlerian shadows, as the moods of the intensely moody story dictated. Just by themselves, *The Rite of Spring* and *Wozzeck* were enough to prove that the new century had not lost the ages-old power to produce masterpieces.

1926–50

26. Bartók: Quartet No. 4 (1928)

27. Walton: Viola Concerto (1931)

28. Weill: *Mahagonny* (1929)

29. Stravinsky: *Symphony of Psalms* (1930)

30. Villa-Lobos: *Bachianas Brasileiras* No. 1 (1930)

31. Crawford Seeger: String Quartet (1931)

32. Ravel: Piano Concerto (1931)

33. Webern: Concerto, Op. 24 (1934)

34. Thomson: *Four Saints in Three Acts* (1934)

35. Gershwin: *Porgy and Bess* (1935)

36. Berg: Violin Concerto (1935)

37. Schoenberg: Quartet No. 4 (1936)

38. McPhee: *Tabuh-Tabuhan* (1936)

39. Orff: *Carmina Burana* (1936)

40. Harris: Symphony No. 3 (1937)

41. Shostakovich: Symphony No. 5 (1937)

42. Prokofiev: *Alexander Nevsky* (1939)

43. Cage: Second Construction (1940)

44. Bernstein: *On the Town* (1943)

45. Britten: Serenade for Tenor, Horn and Strings (1943)

46. Messiaen: *Quartet for the End of Time* (1944)

47. Copland: *Appalachian Spring* (1944)

48. Bartók: *Concerto for Orchestra* (1944)

49. Barber: *Knoxville, Summer of 1915* (1947)

50. Sessions: Symphony No. 2 (1948)

In attempting to force any aspect of artistic history into the listmakers' Procrustean bed, you inevitably end up with a dualism, "then" versus "now." The musical "then" is a vast, safe area of surefire masterpieces, beloved by audiences and by concert managements as well: two centuries, give or take, bounded at the far and near ends respectively by, say, Bach's "Brandenburg" Concertos and Richard Strauss's *Till Eulenspiegel's Merry Pranks*. You wouldn't mistake one for the other, yet there are aspects they share: they are both entertainments composed for performing forces that are required to exhibit a certain amount of solo virtuosity; their harmonies obey the intrinsic notion that listeners like the security of the music being in a given key; their rhythms can, if you're so inclined, set your toes to tapping in regular patterns of twos, threes, or fours. (There had been music before Bach, of course, and one of the great events of recent decades has been its accession to popularity in something close to its original sounds.) Over the 200 or so years of music's "then," the works that best exemplify the ideals of those years were developed in a certain few countries of central Europe—France, Germany, Austria-Hungary, and Italy—plus an occasional outsider from England, Spain, or the Slavic lands who, most likely, had studied music within the inner circle.

The crumbling of that tradition that began right after World War I— the invasion of that inner circle by aliens from (horror!) the United States, by alien styles (jazz, Asian gamelan, Appalachian folksong) and sounds (percussion ensembles, junkyard salvage, silence)—brought about a vast expansion of the means by which a composer might achieve uniqueness of musical language. That expansion, in turn, meant that the differences among the works composed during music's "now" tend to be far wider than in any previous century of even two centuries. Not all the aliens, of course, carried the seeds of revolt. Britain's William Walton and Benjamin Britten and America's Samuel Barber found plenty of new things to say within the old conservative language. One of the first Americans to respond sympathetically to Arnold Schoenberg's principles, the still underappreciated Ruth Crawford Seeger (stepmother of folksinger Pete), blended the atonal manner into her own powerful outlooks in her vibrant, intense String Quartet, music that has only now, sixty-seven years later, been accorded worldwide masterpiece status. Only Stravinsky, among music's towering role models then and now, never handed down a legacy for others to follow.

With the vast expansion of sources and resources available to musicians practically from the start of this century, the cutting edge of new music in this century remains sharp, even painful, far longer than before. People still flee the concert hall during Igor Stravinsky's *Rite of Spring* (of 1913!) and probably always will. Béla Bartók's Fourth String Quartet, seventy years old, still strikes me, approximately the same age, as a very "daring," very "modern" work, with the needle-sharp pizzicatos of its scherzo and the shiver-inducing nocturnal sounds of its slow movement. So does much other music as it approaches respectable dotage: Crawford Seeger's Quartet (1931) and Schoenberg's Fourth (1936), with their slow movements that seem suspended in outer space while holding us spellbound here on Earth. So does the searing beauty in the 1935 Violin Concerto of Alban Berg, his last completed work, which—as in his *Wozzeck* of a decade before—explores the "romantic" potential in the twelve-note serial technique. And so, from a decade later, does the interplay of deep mystery and sublime wit in Bartók's *Concerto for Orchestra*—the most recent large-scale work on this list to achieve permanent repertory status—music by a composer desperately ill and impoverished, but driven by that indefinable force that makes music happen against all odds. Compare the situation of a century ago. Beethoven's Ninth Symphony may have cast its influence throughout the nineteenth century; just its cloudy opening with its tonality undefined became the gambit of choice for dozens of composers. Yet by 1895, age seventy, this most pioneering of classical symphonies had assumed the mantle of respectable old age, while the above-mentioned works from early in this century still jar us with their newness.

From my 1999 vantage point, the music of this second quarter is astounding above all for its mix. Jazz continues its inroads into the "classical" world, thus speeding the crumbling of the wall between "serious" and "popular" that the nineteenth-century bourgeoisie had erected and labored to maintain. Maurice Ravel's fascination with blues harmonies shines forth in his elegant Piano Concerto. In Berlin Kurt Weill and the poet Bert Brecht stirred their preachments into a pot already a-boil with jazz, ragtime, and atonality, and produced the sizzling agitprop opera *The Rise and Fall of the City of Mahagonny*. Four years later Virgil Thomson and the sibylline Gertrude Stein wove their *Four Saints in Three Acts* out of a much politer jazz plus hits from a Baptist Sunday-school hymnal. In his 1935 *Porgy and Bess* George Gershwin's attempt to meld a vivid blues style into a grand-opera format was uneasily received at first but grew to masterpiece stature only slowly. And eight years later, the arrogant, jazzy rhythms of Leonard Bernstein's *On the Town* signaled a huge forward step in literary and musical quality for the Broadway show, a breaking down of the wall of snobbery between musical theater and opera.

The American Colin McPhee traveled to Bali and came home to compose music inspired by the rhythmic patterns of the Indonesian gamelan. Brazil's Heitor Villa-Lobos produced amusing amalgams of his native folk rhythms and the austere outlines of Bach. Closer to home, Roy Harris proclaimed his symphonies illustrative of the "hard fastness" of the prairie soul; Aaron Copland succeeded somewhat better, with his own fashionings of authentic or contrived "American" tunes in his cowboy ballets *Billy the Kid* and *Rodeo* and the eloquent *Appalachian Spring*.

All this happened within the context of an even greater upheaval, one that probably helped shape some of these other changes: the great communications explosion and its impact on the availability of music. By 1930 radio listeners coast to coast could hear live broadcasts by the New

York Philharmonic and the Metropolitan Opera; by 1950 they could also watch them on television. In 1926 the process of recording was greatly advanced by the development of electronic technology to supplant the acoustic horn; in 1948 the long-playing record made it possible to survey the realm of master- and not-so-masterful-pieces in remarkable likenesses of the original performances. Consumerism's exalted catchphrase, "high fidelity," which had first appeared in record advertising in the acoustic-horn, scratchy-disk days of 1920, was by 1950 the great domestic obsession (and remains so today). The spread of broadcasting also established music as an unparalleled political resource. In Adolf Hitler's Germany Carl Orff turned medieval German songs into musical poster art to help celebrate his nation's past; Joseph Stalin's Soviet Union made good use of its composers—the great Sergei Prokofiev and Dmitri Shostakovich among them—to spread the Communist word, and came down hard on them when they strayed in the direction of originality.

In previous centuries, the construction of the first public concert halls and grand-opera houses, offering accessibility to an ever broadening social spectrum of consumer, had greatly influenced the development of grander, noisier, and more flamboyant music. In our own century, the infinitely greater expansion of access through recordings and broadcasts seems to be having the same effect, infinitely magnified. The results are still being measured.

1951–75

51. Stravinsky: *The Rake's Progress* (1951)
52. Carter: Quartet No. 1 (1951)
53. Cage: *4'33"* (1952)
54. Boulez: *Le marteau sans maître* (1954)
55. Britten: *The Turn of the Screw* (1954)
56. Stockhausen: *Gesang der Jünglinge* (1956)
57. Stravinsky: *Agon* (1957)
58. Copland: Fantasy (Piano) (1957)

59. Henze: *Kammermusik* (1958)

60. Shostakovich: Quartet No. 8 (1960)

61. Penderecki: *Threnody for the Victims of Hiroshima* (1960)

62. Riley: *In C* (1964)

63. Babbitt: *Philomel* (1964)

64. Xenakis: *Eonta* (1964)

65. Ligeti: Requiem (1965)

66. Partch: *Delusion of the Fury* (1966)

67. Reich: *Come Out* (1966)

68. Subotnick: *Silver Apples of the Moon* (1966)

69. Schnittke: Violin Concerto No. 2 (1966)

70. Nancarrow: Studies for Player Piano (1968)

71. Stockhausen: *Kurzwellen* (1968)

72. Berio: *Sinfonia* (1969)

73. Crumb: *Ancient Voices of Children* (1970)

74. Lutosławski: Symphony No. 3 (1973)

75. Harrison: Suite for Violin and American Gamelan (1973)

To John Cage, composing music meant redefining music. One of his first teachers, Arnold Schoenberg at UCLA, tried to stanch his creative juices by telling him that he was more an inventor than a composer; Cage took it as a compliment. He invented the notion of creating music by pounding on resonant junkyard objects, by "preparing" a piano (i.e., imposing bits of hardware among the strings) to alter its tone quality, of allowing four minutes and thirty-three seconds' worth of the ambient room noise around a silent performer seated at a piano to stand for the entirety of a titled (and even published) piece. In 1951 Cage established the Project for Magnetic Tape in New York, encouraging composers to create music out of taped sounds collected the world over. Magnetic tape had been invented in Germany in the 1930s. By the 1950s, armed with electronic sound-producing and sound-processing equipment—and, not many years later, reinforced with the ancillary marvels of computer technology—a composer could state with justification that the previous two millennia of music represented only the base of the mountain of possibilities. Cage's project was more a gathering place than a laboratory, but the technology for the latest (of many) musical revolutions was already in place, or soon would be: in Cologne and Paris and at Stanford University, MIT, and Columbia University.

Actually, there had been some attempt to redefine the very sound of music long before Cage. As early as 1914 the "Futurist" poet/painter/composer Luigi Russolo had built huge room-filling machines to produce an array of harsh, mechanized cacophony that he and his Italian cohorts had proclaimed "the music of the future"; unfortunately (you might say), Russolo's machines and most of his musical sketches were destroyed during World War II. After that war, several composers in France—Pierre Henri, Henri Schaeffer, and, for a time, the young Pierre Boulez—had used the recently invented tape recorders to process natural sounds, overlaid upon themselves or otherwise transformed into the designs of what came to be called *musique concrète*. There experiments would soon be supplanted, however, by the broader potential in the range of sounds produced by electronic means and processed by computer.

Karlheinz Stockhausen, one of music's most ardent redefiners, used the vast electronic mainframe facilities of West German Radio at Cologne to produce his *Gesang der Jünglinge*, a work of symphonic proportions constructed entirely out of synthesized sounds plus the processed voice of a boy soprano. The Hungarian expatriate György Ligeti worked at Cologne for a time and then succeeded in duplicating some of tape music's marvelously atmospheric sounds with live performers. Some of the ethereal swooshing in Ligeti's spellbinding Requiem found their way into Stanley Kubrick's *2001: A Space Odyssey*, where they underscored the spaceship's journey to Jupiter through psychedelic space. In California young composers—among them Morton Subotnick, Pauline Oliveros, and Terry Riley—worked at the San Francisco Tape Music Center, blending poetry, visual art, and electronically produced sounds into a unique multimedia art. Their guru was the Michigan-born Robert Erickson, whose own music often included natural sounds (waves pounding the coast, a brooklet in the Sierra Nevada) blended with instruments.

A building-filling electronic installation, set up in New York and funded by Columbia, Princeton, and the Bell Laboratories, attracted hordes of composers young and old, including the venerable twelve-note evangelist Milton Babbitt, whose immensely appealing *Philomel* used synthesized sounds to describe the maiden of legend transformed into a nightingale. Not many years later, Subotnick used a synthesizer designed by Donald Buchla, not any larger than a dining-room tabletop, to compose his *Silver Apples of the Moon*. The electronic facilities shrank in size (and in price) as their versatility expanded. Subotnick would soon move on to the California Institute of the Arts (founded with money from the estate of Walt Disney) and develop one of the pioneer college-run electronic-music curricula.

Whether admittedly inspired by John Cage's libertarian proclamations or off on their own, composers in these years seemed hell-bent on redefining music as something it never had been. Freedom rang; to La Monte Young, a proper musical experience might consist of watching a violin burn in an East Village loft or enduring a single tone sustained for two weeks. Stockhausen, not long after the implicit rigidity of his electronic pieces, turned 180 degrees to invoke principles of chance in his "happenings," quasi-theatrical events to bear out the Cageian dictum that "music is whatever we say it is"; his *Kurzwellen* had live musicians improvising on the spot to whatever happened to be emerging from a shortwave radio at the time of performance. In San Francisco Terry Riley dreamed up a trance-inducing piece called *In C*, in which any number of performers played a series of short fragments at any speed and at any length; a performance might last twenty minutes or three hours. Steve Reich concocted an extended piece in which a short spoken phrase, "come out to show them," was repeated on multitrack tape with the tracks gradually oozing out of phase to create a huge onslaught of sound. A new word, minimalism (borrowed, like so much of music's vocabulary, from the visual arts), stood for their kind of music: maximum impact created out of a minimum of material, repeating and gradually, even imperceptibly, changing.

Wherever you tuned in, there were new sounds. The Greek-born Iannis Xenakis, renowned both as a composer and as a disciple of the great architect Le Corbusier, devised music that did, indeed, seem in its undulations to suggest physical structures—proving Goethe's famous dictum that architecture is frozen music. Lou Harrison—like Cage a one-time Schoenberg student—flooded his music with the bright jangle of the Indonesian gamelan. Conlon Nancarrow, an American expatriate working in Mexico, composed music for player piano, punching out the paper rolls by hand and thus creating rhythmic complexities beyond the reach of any "normal" pianist. George Crumb's haunting *Ancient Voices of Children* (based on Federico Garcia Lorca's poetry) used small tuned stones as part of its "orchestra." Crumb's *Black Angels*, written in 1970 as a Vietnam protest, subjected a string quartet to violent overamplification—grinding, gnashing, intensely disturbing—to send its outcry skyward. (The young David Harrington, sitting out the draft in Canada, was inspired by this music to form a string quartet dedicated entirely to playing and commissioning new music. That quartet, the Kronos, has at this writing brought something like 400 works into existence, performing for the most part before turnaway crowds.) The self-taught hobo-turned-composer Harry Partch devised fantastic, colorful pieces that employed scales of forty-three tones (instead of the "normal" twelve), and built his own fantastic, colorful instruments to play them. Luciano Berio's exhilarating *Sinfonia* included one movement in which a vocal ensemble (originally the Swingle Singers, whose early fame grew out of their recordings of Bach declaimed as scat) recited selections from various activist writings while the orchestra performed a collage compiled from familiar symphonic works of the past.

It was a time, too, of striking contradictions. John Cage and his disciples proclaimed the notion of "anything goes." The element of randomness, of "chance" motivated others as well, notably Poland's Witold Lutosławski, whose Second and Third Symphonies contained episodes that freed the players in certain passages to improvise (within, of course, a stipulated time frame). In sharp contrast, the young Frenchman Pierre Boulez reexamined the Schoenbergian principles of strict twelve-note organization and discovered that Schoenberg's disciple Anton Webern had taken the notion of strict serial organization into matters of organized tone color and rhythm as well as the notes. Boulez earned his early fame with *Le marteau sans maître*: poetry by René Char intoned by a soprano with a chamber ensemble (a conscious tribute to Schoenberg's seminal *Pierrot lunaire*), remarkable also for the way that recurrences and structural details in both words and music are rigidly worked out as a kind of audible mathematics. Boulez would go on to found his famous Parisian Institute for Acoustic/Musical Research and Coordination (IRCAM), a hotbed for experimentation in the ways the computer, the live musician, and the electronically generated sound might join in this whole redefinition process.

Some, of course, found new things to say with traditional forces. Benjamin Britten's powerful if small-scale operas, including a harrowing setting of Henry James's *Turn of the Screw*, sustained faith in the supremacy of the lyric stage. Deeply distressed by his first view of war-ravaged Dresden, Shostakovich—for whom the death of Joseph Stalin was an act of liberation—produced in his Eighth String Quartet a transfixing personal statement. Its mood was echoed, surely not entirely by coincidence, in the glistening, convoluted writing for full string orchestra in Krzysztof Penderecki's wrenching *Threnody for the Victims of Hiroshima*, composed in the same year. Igor Stravinsky, who for most of his life had stood as a kind of antithesis to Schoenberg's atonality, began after Schoenberg's death to incorporated some of that methodology into his own work, notably the ballet *Agon*, arguably his last masterpiece. Even Aaron Copland, his fame secured by his "cowboy" ballets, tried his hand at a more abstract style in his powerful, edgy Piano Fantasy and also in his *Connotations*, composed in 1962 for the opening offerings at Philharmonic Hall, the first component of New York's Lincoln Center. That music, at the time, drew far more critical admiration than the building itself.

1976–2000

76. Glass/Wilson: *Einstein on the Beach* (1976)

77. Reich: *Music for Eighteen Musicians* (1976)

78. Górecki: Symphony No. 3 (1976)

79. Kurtag: *Messages of the Late Miss R. V. Troussova* (1976)

80. Erickson: *Night Music* (1978)

81. Sondheim: *Sweeney Todd* (1979)

82. Ung: *Khse Buon* (Solo Cello) (1980)

83. Gubaidulina: *Offertorium* (1980)

84. Riley: *Cadenza on the Night Plain* (1981)

85. Harbison: *Mirabai Songs* (1982)

86. Messiaen: *St. Francis* (1983)

87. Carter: *Triple Duo* (1983)

88. Pärt: *Fratres* (1980, revised 1983)

89. Takemitsu: *riverrun* (1984)

90. Feldman: *For Philip Guston* (1984)

91. Birtwistle: *Secret Theater* (1984)

92. Ligeti: Etudes (1985)

93. Lindberg: *Kraft* (1985)

94. Schnittke: Viola Concerto (1985)

95. Adams: *Nixon in China* (1987)

96. Cage: *Fourteen* (1990)

97. Kancheli: *Midday Prayers* (1991)

98. Knussen: Horn Concerto (1994)

99. Tan: *Ghost Opera* (1994)

100. Salonen: *LA Variations* (1997)

Now, at century's end, a multitude of strands become visible; the most obvious thing to be said about music in the last 100 years is that there isn't just one thing to be said.

The sonata tradition continues, grown dense with newly devised structural complexity and abstract inner messages from America's Roger

Sessions and Elliott Carter and Britain's Harrison Birtwistle and Oliver Knussen (who of all this group at least holds onto a sense of humor). German opera pretty much died out after Richard Strauss, but Olivier Messiaen's spacious (if ponderous) 1983 *St. Francis* couldn't have been written if Wagner's *Parsifal* hadn't paved its way. Comic opera has spawned a populous and populist brood, Broadway theater written purely for money but also an occasional stage piece—Stephen Sondheim's works culminating in his *Sweeney Todd*, Leonard Bernstein from *On the Town* to *West Side Story*—that suggests that artistic quality and box-office success can sometimes coexist. The collaboration of the filmmaker Sergei Eisenstein and the composer Sergei Prokofiev, in their *Alexander Nevsky* and *Ivan the Terrible*, might have presaged a possible future for the epic-nationalist style that Mussorgsky's *Boris Godunov* had spawned eighty years before, but this has not yet happened. When Hitler's proscription drove Germany's leading composers to seek refuge in other countries, some came West with hopes of creating a new kind of musical drama—modeled, perhaps, after Wagner's dream of a "total artwork" – hand in hand with the film industry. The composers who succeeded best, however, were the ones who could scale their ambitions down to fit the straitjacket of the Hollywood soundtrack.

The traditions held fast, but the impact of *Einstein on the Beach* was its complete disassociation from any kind of musical past. Philip Glass had studied with Nadia Boulanger in Paris; more to the point, he had traveled extensively through the music of other worlds—India, North Africa, Central Asia—and absorbed the ways of making music out of stillness and stasis instead of sonata forms and twelve-tone rows. The minimalist works of Terry Riley and La Monte Young were also part of the mix. With the poet/director/designer Robert Wilson, Glass evolved an allegory about the space age and the atomic threat, with the iconic figure of Albert Einstein (playing the violin but not speaking) as the generative force. Dance, chant (sometimes just strings of numbers repeated, repeated) and lighting effects blended into an uninterrupted five-hour musical trance.

Unlike Stravinsky's *Rite of Spring* of sixty-three years before, *Einstein* hasn't exactly become a repertory item; its physical proportions are too daunting. Like the *Rite*, however, it looms large among the century's defining works. Like the *Rite*, too, it came out of nowhere.

In its pure state (with Riley's *In C* as its textbook paradigm) minimalism didn't last very long. Steve Reich, who had once played in the Philip Glass Ensemble, created one other masterpiece in the style, the hourlong *Music for Eighteen Musicians*. John Adams's early *Shaker Loops* and his stunning piano piece *Phrygian Gates* also belong on that list. Glass found it profitable to remain anchored in doctrinaire minimalism, but both Reich and Adams moved on: Reich most recently to multimedia dramatic works incorporating music and video; Adams, via the astounding "newsreel" opera *Nixon in China*, sometimes awash in its own brilliance, to a large legacy of orchestral works as successful and often played as anyone's new serious music these days.

The musical buffet is well stocked at century's end. Over here there is the curious mix of the so-called holy minimalists, Estonia's Arvo Pärt and Poland's Henryk Górecki, with music that looks far back into history and tries—often with stunning effect—to reconcile the pretonal harmonies of the Middle Ages with a contemporary awareness, with both the eleven-minute *Fratres* of Pärt and the nearly hourlong Third Symphony of Górecki spinning their webs of enchantment by obsessive reiteration of austere but ultimately hypnotic ancient-sounding harmonies. Over there is the growing influence of the Pacific Rim, with China's Tan Dun and Chen Yi, Cambodia's Chinary Ung, and Japan's Toru Takemitsu casting their shadows over their eager American admirers Lou Harrison and Terry Riley. Among us also, the smiling countenance of John Cage encourages all comers to continue to dare, to question; his old friend and disciple Morton Feldman hands off his four- and six-hour concoctions of few notes and many silences and rewards our patience. An extraordinary generation of Russians—Alfred Schnittke, Sofia Gubaidulina, and the Georgian Giya Kancheli—bursting out of captivity after the end of Soviet artistic repression, turns out symphonies, quartets, and operas that cram these venerable forms with music of extraordinary vitality that, once again, sounds like nothing else in this wide musical world.

I was attracted to California by the new-music scene here: the electronic music at CalArts and Stanford; the mix of acoustic instrumental virtuosity and natural sounds at the University of California, San Diego as taught by Robert Erickson (whose *Night Music* is the only work on my "100" list currently unavailable on disc); the Monday Evening Concerts at the County Museum, with their tradition reaching back to 1939; Ojai, with its unlikely mix of Pierre Boulez's music in a rural setting; the Los Angeles Philharmonic's ongoing service to new music, more ardent than the work of any other American orchestra I know, via the Green Umbrella concerts and similar projects. With the music patrons Betty Freeman and Judith Rosen I have helped produce in-home concerts of new music, which got me to shake hands with György Ligeti, John Cage, Elliott Carter, Lou Harrison, Morty Feldman...you name 'em.

That was actually my second California incarnation. In the first, I studied music at the University of California, Berkeley during the days of Roger Sessions and Ernest Bloch, with Darius Milhaud a few miles away at Mills College. I helped start KPFA, the first-ever venture into public radio. We put Harry Partch's music on the air, and when the rapturous phone calls came in after a live studio performance of Bartók's Sonata for Two Pianos and Percussion (music still terra incognita in 1949), we simply had the players repeat the performance on the spot.

A few other memories: Shaking hands with Bartók in Boston after the world premiere of his *Concerto for Orchestra*. My first hearing of Mahler's Ninth, conducted by Bruno Walter (December, 1945) in Carnegie Hall (and a revelatory later performance conducted by Carlo Maria Giulini). Pushing my car with its dead fuel pump into an illegal parking space in order to get to the Metropolitan Opera House for the premiere of *Einstein on the Beach* (and finding it neither towed nor ticketed five hours later). Discovering for the first time the music of Schnittke and Gubaidulina, on tape in a Soviet information office in Boston. My first hearing of Bob Erickson's *Night Music*, on a tape in his office. Sitting for four hours on a chair carved out of stone at Los Angeles's Ace Gallery for Morty Feldman's *For Philip Guston* and remembering not having moved a muscle. The ovation after Esa-Pekka Salonen's *LA Variations* at the Music Center.

If there were room for No. 101 to start the new list, it would surely be some brand-new work by the immensely talented young Brit Thomas Adès, just out of his twenties, whose brand-new opera on Shakespeare's *Tempest* revives my hopes for music's future as vividly as anything the new century has yet brought forth. Onward!

[December 1999]

PERSONAL SEDUCTIONS

Then there are those times when, on driving home from Music Center, Bowl, or college music hall, the matter recently heard comes around and hits me once again. An old woman that I spoke to at a kiddie opera haunted my memory for days. A flourish at the end of a slow movement of a Mozart sonata for two pianos so inflamed my memory that for an entire summer I drove with that music—nothing else—on my car stereo. A friend played me a particular recording of the Brahms Violin Concerto, against my protest, and laid me out flat on the floor. A spider kept me company at an outdoor concert; I remember the web she wove, but not the music. These are the things that make my job—no, my *life*—worthwhile.

The Care and Feeding of Warhorses

The bulls ran at Pamplona last week, and the warhorses ran at the Cahuenga Pass. The choice, therefore, was between being gored or bored.

Warhorses were bred into existence in about the mid-nineteenth century, when concert managements came up with the idea that just because a composer was dead didn't mean that his music couldn't be played. Felix Mendelssohn had put J. S. Bach's music back on the map; the young Wagner made a name by conducting the symphonies of Beethoven. Instead of serving as showcases for the latest trends in composition—and, thus, placing audiences in the hazardous position of having to face unfamiliar and provocative ideas week after week—orchestras began to woo listeners with the promise of a comforting wallow in the familiar. The orchestral hall became the diadem of a city's social life, where large audiences could tap their toes to music they already knew. Free from the fear of attack from some symphonic revolutionary bent on adding extra notes to the harmonic system or extra instruments to the orchestra on stage, titillated by the antics of the supernally endowed solo violinist or the corybantic gesticulations of the conductor, the musical bourgeoisie suddenly discovered that they no longer had to bring their brains to the concert, that they could relax and enjoy the virtuosic star turns in the company of the same old musical friends who had serenaded them the week before. I have a pet theory, that audiences given to excessive use of the standing ovation or the yelling of "bravo," as here, do so out of relief: despite their worst fears (stoked by dire warnings from some recently departed reactionary local critic) they've gotten through a whole symphony or concerto without once having had to think.

The usual stampede of warhorses fills the program offerings on the symphony nights (Tuesdays and Thursdays, except for this weekend's Beethoven Ninth performances on Friday and Saturday) at the Hollywood Bowl: Tchaikovsky, Brahms, Sibelius, Rachmaninoff—heavy on the carbohydrates, easy on the spice. The rewards for the adventure seekers are, as usual, meager: a curtain raiser by John Adams one night, the Berlioz *Damnation of Faust* another, a fair sampling of Mozart but not a note of Haydn, Handel, Bach, or Vivaldi. There's lots of Brahms for his anniversary year, but only one measly Schubert overture for his. The first week's offerings included the Brahms Violin Concerto on Tuesday and the Grieg Piano Concerto and Sibelius's First Symphony on Thursday—all conducted by Esa-Pekka Salonen, a considerable departure from his programming at the Music Center, or from his concerts last summer at the Bowl where, at least, he gave us two Stravinsky symphonies plus the *Rite*.

Don't misunderstand me; I am not trying to suggest that familiar music is necessarily bad music, and that every acknowledged warhorse should be dispatched forthwith to the glue factory. I also don't mean to imply that I have a lousy time at the Bowl, because I usually don't. But warhorses need special care; they thrive on an ongoing alternation of neglect and rediscovery, spread over long time lapses. The Brahms Violin Concerto, warhorse or no, is some kind of great piece. Its intricacies are remarkable: the way, say, that a dinky little countermelody buried down in the bassoons emerges later on as a full-fledged tune. A superior performance, with soloist and conductor in exalted rapport with the inner workings of the music, can really make its point, especially if we haven't also heard the work the day before. In New York recently a friend played me a performance of this music that held me spellbound: Jascha Heifetz and Arturo Toscanini on a New York Philharmonic broadcast from February 1935 so full of ecstasy (including Bruno Labate's oboe solo in the slow movement) and so beautifully coordinated that I had to swallow—for the moment, anyhow—everything I'd ever thought or written about Brahms, Heifetz, and Toscanini. Perhaps that spoiled me for last week's performance, which I found perfunctory on the part of Salonen, superficial by the soloist, Maxim Vengerov, who played it as Glazunov and who was also badly overmiked. (The Heifetz/Toscanini, by the way, is part of a ten-disc set of New York Philharmonic broadcasts to be released by the orchestra, their sound remarkably restored, going all the way back to 1922.)

The Grieg concerto is a lesser work, but it has its moments, too, or can. Unfortunately, it has become a concerto to be tossed off by performers on their way up; you have to go back to the old Dinu Lipatti recording (on EMI Classics) to discover that the piece really has its strengths and a fund of real eloquence. Laura Mikkola tossed it off, her young fingers clattering graciously around all those notes but with nary a hint of what they were supposed to be telling us and with, once again, no prodigies of support from Salonen and the orchestra.

At the end came the Sibelius First, truly terrible music, one warhorse I find irredeemable beyond the ministrations of steroids or conductor; it survives only through Sibelius's later fame. I am offended, for starters, by the sheer ugliness of the scoring—not the clever opening, where Michele Zukovsky's solo clarinet sounded as if from another planet, but the clumsy patches afterward, culminating in the socko climax with the final Big Tune buried in a thick orchestral morass. The melodic material is second-rate, and the few promising melodic ideas—the recurrent cadence in the slow movement, for one—shatter whenever Sibelius tries to develop them. I don't get much from Sibelius in general—except for the sparse, muttering Fourth Symphony, remarkable music that, therefore, will probably never make it to the Bowl—but the First Symphony is beyond salvation. It wouldn't surprise me if even Salonen agrees; his conducting of it the other night was the work of a man with his mind somewhere else.

[July 1997]

Mass Hypnosis, Even at the Bowl

At the season's final classical concert at the Hollywood Bowl last month, Yo-Yo Ma was the marvelous soloist in John Tavener's forty-eight-minute *The Protecting Veil* with Jeffrey Kahane and his Los Angeles Chamber Orchestra; at the end the crowd of just under 10,000 held its silence for a full minute as the last quiet sounds mingled with the cool evening air—an event possibly describable as hypnotic. The next night, alone, I allowed myself to be hypnotized again at even greater length, by the new ECM recording of Arvo Pärt's *Kanon Pokajanen.* The two works sang the same language: Tavener's, with a solo cello weaving its incantatory, sinuous, nonstop melody in and out of the string orchestra's enveloping haze; Pärt's, with its unaccompanied chorus spinning immensely long vocal lines of penitence and exaltation, expanding from time to time into harmonies of almost palpable lushness, then falling back into an ages-old-sounding single strand like a small light in a huge, dark room.

This is what the phrase spinners have dubbed "holy minimalism," and the tag is not far off the mark. It has nothing to do with the archetypal minimalism of Steve Reich or Philip Glass, their throbbing, repetitive patterns oozing almost imperceptibly from one shape to the next. I hear this music as "minimal" only in the sense that so much emotional power can grow out of such modest resources. The breakthrough work, in terms of surging public acclaim, was Henryk Górecki's Third Symphony; it rode to the charts a few years ago via the proselytizing efforts of crossover

deejays here and abroad, even though the recording that put it there—
David Zinman and the Baltimore Symphony on Nonesuch, with Dawn
Upshaw's angelic singing—differed markedly from two previous versions
and also from the extraordinary performance Górecki himself conducted
last year at USC.

The Protecting Veil, its title derived from a millennium-old Eastern
Orthodox legend about the Mother of God casting down her veil to
protect the Greeks from the invading Saracens, is too eloquent on its
own to be thought of as a ripoff on the Górecki. Let's just say that it rises
effortlessly from the older work. Tavener's hand—here, and in much of
his considerable output—is guided by his religious involvement. I resisted
the *Veil* on first hearings; despite its prevailingly thin textures it demands
full attention. (It seems to be getting it; Yo-Yo Ma's new Sony recording,
again with Zinman and Baltimore, is already the third.) Whoever in the
Bowl management decided to accompany the performance with changing
colored lights in the shell surrounding the performance—climaxing in a
barfworthy hot magenta at the music's ecstatic climax—should be brought
up on charges of heresy.

Arvo Pärt's eighty-three-minute ecstasy is a setting for unaccompanied
choir of a Greek/Russian Orthodox morning service; its text, teeming with accents of repentance and atonement, even at times of abject
groveling, might play well these days at the White House. If you know
the great works in the Pärt legacy—the early and extraordinary *Fratres*,
whose harmonic pulsations come at you like the summoning of distant
bells; *Passio*, recounting the mysteries of the Passion through a pall of
darkness; the glorious, brief, sun-drenched *Magnificat*—you should have
mastered by now the task of relaxing in the face of his music's daunting
demands. *Kanon Pokajanen's* time scale is daunting, but its sounds are
gorgeous. The ongoing chanted melodic line is the unifying force; that
line, at times unadorned and austere, is then bathed at other times in the
blinding light of rich, lush harmonies of indescribable beauty. Now and
then the basses in the chorus hold a single low note at what seems like

excruciating length, an effect familiar in some of the Russian liturgical pieces by Tchaikovsky and Rachmaninoff, or in distant memories of the singing of the old Don Cossack Choir.

Some of the profound impact of the work, as heard on this new two-disc set, comes from the performance itself and the way it has been recorded. The singers are Tönu Kalljuste's Estonian Philharmonic Chamber Choir, who sang at the Irvine Barclay Theater last year in a concert I will not soon forget. The recording was made at the Niguliste Church in Tallinn, which looks from photographs to be a fairly small, unadorned structure; the singing is enveloped in an aura of resonance that, once again, suggests distant bells. (The work was actually composed to celebrate the 750th anniversary of the huge cathedral at Cologne, where it would probably sound even more resonant but not nearly as well defined.) I cannot in honesty propose this music as the latest adjunct to the easy-listening shelf. There is a quiet, subtle sense of vastness in the best of this music, and it seems to reach a great many people of all ages these days—in whose ranks I gladly include myself. Both the music and its realization on these discs make for an extraordinary experience.

The indoor concert season began not in one of our major masonry edifices but in the intimate, welcoming space of Pasadena's Neighborhood Church, where Vicki Ray inaugurated the fifth season of PianoSpheres with music making no less hypnotic than any of the above. The house was full, as it deserved to be; this series—five yearly concerts by five pianists, a consortium devoted to innovation and adventure in music mostly but not entirely new—has become a resource valuable and enchanting.

The program consisted of Morton Feldman's *For Bunita Marcus*, ninety minutes nonstop of vintage, exquisite music oozing—slowly, and on the edge of silence—around the periphery of some nameless vastness. For this performance the video artist Clay Chaplin devised a real-time visual counterpoint, projected images and abstractions of Vicki's hands in action, moving in and out of focus, with words of John Cage, fragments from his

1959 *Lecture on Something*, on the screen, woven through the images. Once again, as with the Tavener piece at the Bowl, the participatory silence around the performance became a part of it; I've seldom known ninety minutes to go by so quickly.

[September 1998]

The Accordion and the Spider

A couple of Saturdays ago several of us, in a corner of the performance space at the Schindler House in West Hollywood, watched as a small spider did what spiders do best. She had anchored her new web between two light bulbs on an overhead cable. From there she swung down on a strand of web, curving her trajectory to clear the heads of people in the front row, and then made her way back up on another strand, then down again, then up. All the while, the soft, silky moans of Pauline Oliveros's accordion filled the space with sound, gently guiding the crowd toward an experience of what she calls "deep listening." Somehow the bond took shape, between the intricate design imposed onto the surrounding air by the spider and her web and by the sounds of Pauline's music. Later that evening came another kind of bonding, no less satisfying: Pauline and the shakuhachi player Philip Gelb drawing each other out during over a half hour of serene improvised "conversation," full of deep if wordless meanings. By then the spider was lost in darkness, but you could still feel her presence if you wanted to.

Deep listening: in Pauline's world it suggests that charting the course of a classical symphonic movement or a romantic virtuoso exercise, however lavish their rewards, is still the base of the mountain. Up on the slopes are the infinitesimal sounds of spiders at their weaving, the rustlings and breathings in the room around John Cage's famous "silent" piece, the slow drone of Pauline's accordion, tuned to harmonies that break clear of our well-tempered scale. Her instrument engulfs her body as it engulfs our senses; the only picture I can summon up comparable to watching her playing is the memory of Segovia wrapped around his guitar; he, too, could so transport an enthralled audience to the brink of silence, even in the 3000-seat expanse of Carnegie Hall, as to command a kind of deep listening. Friends who have been there tell me that listening to music in India, where families with small children partake of the experience without abandoning their own sounds and rhythms—so that the world itself creates a part of the experience—also demands a way of listening far different from the artificial attentiveness we sometimes have to manufacture at the Dorothy Chandler Pavilion. (Please do not, however, take this as extending a welcome to cell phones as a component to the process of listening deeply at the Philharmonic.)

The Schindler House itself, with its marvelous flow from indoor to outdoor space, generates its own kind of music and always has; it currently houses the MAK Center for Art and Architecture. In April 1935 the very young John Cage and his mentor, Henry Cowell, presented some Japanese visitors in a concert of *gagaku*—at that time a most exotic and unfamiliar art—at the house; the venture earned a net profit of $13. Three years later Rudolf Schindler designed a small performance studio on the roof of Peter Yates's home at 1735 Micheltorena Street in Silverlake, where Yates—a self-taught aficionado whose adoration of the compositional process shines a bright light in the annals of music consumership—invited musicians to perform new music for select audiences. His concerts, then known as Evenings on the Roof and later renamed the Monday Evening Concerts, still go on (at LACMA) and still challenge. The studio also still exists, and there will be music there—new, of course—this very weekend: two concerts under MAK Center auspices on Saturday, August 18.

[July 2001]

Past Presence

Mnemosyne is the goddess of memory, the mother (by Zeus) of the nine Muses, and the title of a magical two-disc release on ECM that might persuade you to discard all your other CDs and stay with this album alone. The performers are the four Brits of the Hilliard Ensemble plus the saxophonist Jan Gabarek—those wonderful people who brought you *Officium* a few years ago, now back with more of the same and equally wondrous. The repertory this time is broader than on the previous disc, a haunting mix of ancient liturgy—Greek ritual, Hildegard von Bingen, Thomas Tallis—and music from folk sources as diverse as Estonian and Iroquois. Some manic genius has arranged the order of these pieces, which last anywhere from two minutes to eleven, so that totally unalike musics juxtaposed can seem to arise from a single unifying impulse. The abiding sense is not so much what you're listening to but how you're listening—with your ears, with your gut, and with everything in between.

Am I making complete sense? Probably not; I just played the set again, and so I'm writing under hypnosis. Just a few seconds into the first disc and you could already be hooked. A distant, throbbing harmony among the four voices resounds among the stones and pillars of an ancient monastery (Austria's Propstei St. Gerold), whose ambience the sound engineers have miraculously captured. Then, like a shaft of sunlight through a high window, Gabarek's alto sax proclaims an ecstatic discant, and this is answered in turn in a solo line by the ensemble's countertenor,

David James. The music is a fragment from a Peruvian folksong, obviously created on a mountaintop although the program note doesn't say so. (The booklet—handsome, in the usual ECM manner—delivers a higher level of relevant information, in the form of stills of seascapes and vast distances from Ingmar Bergman's *The Seventh Seal*.) Much of the music consists of mere fragments from larger works, chosen and improvised on the spot: five guys miraculously in tune with one another, journeying through a timeless treasury amassed out of many musics, ending up not so much merely shaking the dust from the music as entering into enlightened conversation with it.

I cannot, of course, proclaim, that the one-of-a-kind performance art on these discs tears the veil of time from these ancient repertories; you still need the Tallis Scholars and Anonymous 4, along with the Hilliard's many other discs, for the straight historical skinny on Hildegard and her pals. *Mnemosyne* is all about a latter-day state of mind toward an important part of our musical past, the state of mind that guided the hands of Hieronymous Bosch and the makers of those marginal grotesques in ancient prayer books, perhaps even the state of mind that brought the picket lines to the Brooklyn Museum last month: the timeless power of ancient art to generate new art.

Some other music performed recently hereabouts also relates to this "timeless power." Two of the four works at the County Museum on the Monday Evening Concert by Xtet, that splendid group—IX regulars or XIII with guests—of local freelancers, turned out to be attractive new paraphrases of very old music: Eve Beglarian's *Machaut in the Machine Age* twisted a few new contrapuntal lines through the gnarled texture of a fourteenth-century chanson, a congenial trifle; Stephen Hartke's *Wulfstan at the Millennium*, a work of greater length and substance, used the outlines of liturgical pieces by the Anglo-Saxon cleric Wulfstan of just about a millennium ago as frames for new music that somehow manages to stay interestingly close to its ancient inspiration—in, for example, the antiphonal back-and-forth answerings in several sections. A lovely concert all told, it also included a wonderful work from the recent past too seldom revived: Vicki Ray as soloist in Manuel de Falla's crisp, jaunty Harpsichord Concerto, with its slow movement that, secular in intent, nevertheless showed the hand of God.

Morten Lauridsen's *Lux Aeterna* began the Master Chorale's concert at the Music Center and rendered the ensuing Brahms Requiem redundant. Lauridsen, who teaches at the University of Southern California, is the musical counterpart to what you would call in today's lingo a compassionate conservative. His best music, most of it choral, holds no more terrors than that great clod of Brahmsian turgidity and makes its points with far greater ease. Out front, it goes down smoothly; it's also probably fun to sing—as the Brahms, I know from experience, is not. Much of the vital organism in Lauridsen's twenty-five-or-so-minute piece is grafted onto old roots: bygone harmonic modes, an occasional cantus firmus of Gregorian origin, long passages in that archaic harmonic style known as fauxbourdon, which always makes you think of spires and domes and eternal light through stained glass. Its performance demands are modest, which serves the purpose of Paul Salamunovich's pretty-good chorus and his only-fair pickup orchestra, for which it was composed.

If the Hilliard's and Lauridsen's music evokes models from a millennium or so ago, those are the new kids on the block compared to the amazements concocted by Harry Partch—who came to the conclusion early on that music had taken a wrong turn around 1000 A.D., and that the only salvation lay in restoring the elaborate but eminently logical principles preached and practiced by the ancient Greeks. It mattered not, of course, that these principles have survived only as speculation; what mattered far more was that Partch went on to invent what he imagined as an evocation of the old ways—including a scale with a possible forty-three tones as opposed to the familiar twelve—built his glorious instruments (out of glass, bamboo, tuned stones and assorted found objects) to perform his imaginings, and put them to work in music wacko perhaps but also irresistible beyond belief. His stupendous stage work *Delusion of the Fury* was first performed at UCLA in 1969 under the patronage of Betty Freeman and recorded at the time by Columbia Records. Now that recording, unavailable for years, has been reissued on the Minnesota-based Innova label as part of its ongoing series of Partch discs, books, and videos. Hallelujah!

Partch concocted his *Delusion* out of a couple of folk legends, acted out onstage by dancers with occasional chanting, with his fantastic "orchestra" led by his longtime associate Danlee Mitchell. The sounds range from sozzled gamelan to boiler factory to the swoopings of great predatory birds; what holds the work together is its exuberant rhythmic sweep. If the music of *Mnemosyne* transports you into a happy trance, Partch makes you want to fly. Both recordings, it seems to me, are essential.

[October 1999]

Brundibár: The Spirit Survives

Little Joe's mother is sick, but there's no money for milk. Joe and his friend Annette go to the village square to sing for money, but that annoys Brundibár, the town minstrel. He drowns them out with a loud song. With the help of the Cat, the Bird, and the Dog, Joe and Annette muster the village children, who defeat the minstrel and cure the mother. Curtain.

That's not much, as opera plots go, but the story of *Brundibár* itself, which I saw performed by a bunch of exuberant kids at Santa Monica's Miles Memorial Playhouse a couple of Fridays ago, is better yet. Its composer, Hans Krása, created the short opera in Prague in 1938 for the children of a Jewish orphanage. Came the Nazi takeover, and the establishment of the concentration camp at Terezín (Theresienstadt) as a showcase to prove to the outside world that Hitler's thugs did, indeed, care for the arts. Krása led fifty-five performances of *Brundibár* at Terezín, including one before a visiting Red Cross commission and one that was filmed and circulated in a documentary about those lovely, art-loving Nazis. Soon thereafter, Krása was dragged off to the gas ovens at Auschwitz. In addition to the opera, his name survives in a small repertory of chamber and vocal works, some of them composed during his years of imprisonment.

Brundibár arrived here garlanded in publicity, but it turns out to be a slight work, its harmonies nicely spiced with a touch of Weill and Hindemith, its tunes obviously the work of a man who knew how to make young singers and their audiences feel good—which this ensemble certainly did in Eli Villanueva's staging and Daniel Faltus's musical direction. This was the latest production of Opera Camp, a project now three years old, a partnership of the Los Angeles Opera and the Madison Project of Santa Monica College, with additional collaboration this time from the Museum of Tolerance and Santa Monica's Miles Memorial Playhouse. The value of such a project should be obvious every time you face another snoozing, doddering operatic audience at the Music Center.

One further aspect of this particular event moved me deeply: next to me at the Miles Playhouse sat a lady by the name of Ela Weissberger, smiling and giving off waves of pride. It turned out that she had been the Cat in the 1944 performances of *Brundibár* at Terezín (including the one on film). Imagine! Imagine the memories this glorious old person can wear like a bright medallion! Mrs. Weissberger emigrated to the United States shortly after World War II and now lives in my old stomping ground, New York's Rockland County. (The Nazi-made film of Terezín's children, including a scene from *Brundibár* with Ela Weissberger, has been incorporated into *Prisoner of Paradise*, Malcolm Clarke and Stuart Sender's new documentary on the treacherous charms of Terezín.)

So there we were, this authentic piece of history and my humble self, side-by-side, schmoozing about the 76 House and the Community Market and Mr. Hitler. Tell me I don't have the world's best job!

[December 2003]

Salvation through K. 448

This was the summer that I fell in love with K. 448. Several years ago some intellect-measuring scientists at one or another of the Ivy League schools announced that prolonged listening to the slow movement of K. 448 tended to raise the I.Q. of the students in a test group. I wondered at the time about the wisdom of isolating a single movement (out of the three); that's the kind of thing radio stations do as part of their dumbing-down process. I have spent a great portion of my summer with K. 448 in its entirety; whether that has left me three times as smart, or only a third, is for someone else to decide.

K. 448 is Mozart's Sonata in D for Two Pianos. I don't remember exactly why I started listening to it at the beginning of the summer. Perhaps it was because Philips had just reissued the marvelous performances, from its complete Mozart edition, of all of Mozart's piano-duet and two-piano music, two discs for the price of one. More likely, it was because at the moment of rediscovery I was in particular need of a friendly, conversa- tional voice. "Be my friend," ordered K. 448 in its irresistible opening summons. "And here's why you should," as the music rolled on, its lyrical exultation punctuated with distant flashes.

The miracle of Mozart—one of many, at least—lies in the flexibility with which his music both fits and violates the ethic of its time. In the age of classical rediscovery, sparked by Winckelmann's famous treatise on the Parthenon (a best seller in its day—imagine!), composers worked hard at creating clear, balanced musical structures: so much of this, so much of that for contrast, so much of this again to round things off. It's easy to align K. 448 with this simple, logical outline. What moves it into the stratosphere is the richness of its coloration. A theme plays itself out and, in accordance with the unwritten rules of late-eighteenth-century structure, heads along a more or less straight line toward an immediately recognizable second theme. So with K. 448; its easily identifiable opening theme, a kind of transit, a clearly defined second theme, some cadences that bring this part of the first movement to a close.

But the music itself . . . how glorious! The themes are all conversations, the one voice answering the other, the harmony constantly sideslipping from major to minor and constantly amazing us by so doing. Midway in the first movement, Mozart picks out a small fragment—nothing more than five notes—from one of the tunes he's already beguiled us with, and sends it off on its own on a journey. Without the words of an opera, and with nothing more than a pair of pianists, he builds the tensions and releases them—and, therefore, us—at exactly the right moment. Without raising its voice or banging on drums, K. 448 becomes our friend for life.

The wonder continues. The slow movement starts up in thin air: a faint summons, unharmonized for the first couple of seconds, then building out to a gorgeous patchwork of tunes, a conversation on many topics. I love the way Mozart will state a short tune and then repeat it with a few more notes at the end so that the music seems to build, to go somewhere. (If you want to know how Mozart's music towered above the merely correct hackwork of a Salieri or a Boccherini, much of the answer lies in this wonderful ability to create a sense of propulsion—even, as in this case, at a relaxed, genial tempo.) Ingrid Haebler and Ludwig Hoffmann capture this geniality on the Philips recording, better than in any of the competing versions I've heard.

At the end of the slow movement there is a further miracle, tiny but unforgettable. The music draws to its close, and about four measures from the end the first pianist spins a bit of stardust, a tiny, quiet filigree. A similar thing happens at the end of the great act 3 sextet in *Figaro*, as

Susanna, reassured that Figaro still loves her, spins the same sort of radiant benediction, and we know that we're in a better world. Those two measures of K. 448 are heaven sent. Then I go back and hear the slow movement again, and after the amusing roughhouse in the finale, I arrive at the end, restored.

Dear God, I truly love this music.

[September 1997]